Financial Derivatives

Second Edition

Robert W. Kolb

University of Miami

First published 1996

Blackwell Publishers, Inc.
238 Main Street
Cambridge, Massachusetts 02142
USA

Blackwell Publisher, Ltd.
108 Cowley Road
Oxford OX4 1JF
UK

Library of Congress Cataloging-in-Publication Data

Kolb, Robert W.
    Financial derivatives / Robert W. Kolb. – 2nd ed.
       p.   cm.
    Includes bibliographical references and index.
    ISBN 1-55786-930-8 (pbk.)
    1. Derivative securities.   2. Financial Engineering.   I. Title.
HG6024.A3K648   1996
332.6–dc20   95-51323
                                        CIP

British Library Cataloguing in Publication Data
A CIP catalogue record for this book is available from the British Library.

Composition by Megan H. Zuckerman

Printed in the USA by Book Crafters

This book is printed on acid-free paper

TABLE OF CONTENTS

Dedication

To my splendid Lori,
an original who is anything but derivative.

PREFACE

Financial Derivatives introduces the broad range of markets for financial derivatives. A **financial derivative** is a financial instrument based upon another more elementary financial instrument. The value of the financial derivative depends upon, or derives from, the more basic instrument. Usually, the base instrument is a cash market financial instrument, such as a bond or a share of stock.

Introductory in nature, this book is designed to supplement a wide range of college and university finance and economics classes. Every effort has been made to reduce the mathematical demands placed upon the student, while still developing a broad understanding of trading, pricing, and risk management applications of financial derivatives.

The text has two principal goals. First, the book offers a broad overview of the different types of financial derivatives (futures, options, options on futures, and swaps), while focusing on the principles that determine market prices. These instruments are the basic building blocks of all more complicated risk management positions. Second, the text presents financial derivatives as tools for risk management, not as instruments of speculation. While financial derivatives are unsurpassed as tools for speculation, the book emphasizes the application of financial derivatives as risk management tools in a corporate setting. This approach is consistent with today's emergence of financial institutions and corporations as dominant forces in markets for financial derivatives.

Chapter 1, *Introduction*, surveys the major types of financial derivatives and their basic applications. The chapter discusses three types of financial derivatives – futures, options, and swaps. It then considers **financial engineering** – the application of financial derivatives to manage risk. The chapter concludes with a discussion of the markets for financial derivatives and brief comments on the social function of financial derivatives.

Chapter 2, *Futures*, explores the futures markets in the United States and the contracts traded on them. Futures markets have a reputation for being incredibly risky. To a large extent, this reputation is justified, but futures contracts may also be used to manage many different kinds of risks. The chapter begins by explaining how a futures exchange is organized and how it helps to promote liquidity to attract greater trading volume. Chapter 2 focuses on the principles of futures pricing and some of the most important applications of futures for risk management.

The second basic type of financial derivative, the option contract, is the subject of Chapter 3, *Options*. Options markets are very diverse and have their own particular jargon. As a consequence, understanding options requires a grasp of the institutional details and terminology employed in the market. Chapter 3 begins with a discussion of the institutional background of options markets, including the kinds of contracts traded and the price quotations for various options. However, the chapter focuses principally on the valuation of options. For a potential speculator in options, these pricing relationships are of the greatest importance, as they are for a trader who wants to use options to manage risk.

Compared to futures or options, swap contracts are a recent innovation. A **swap** is an agreement between two or more parties, called **counterparties**, to exchange sets of cash flows over a period in the future. For example, Party A might agree to pay a fixed rate of interest on $1 million each year for five years to Party B. In return, Party B might pay a floating rate of interest on $1 million each year for five years. The cash flows that the counterparties make are generally tied to the value of debt instruments or to the value of foreign currencies, giving rise to two basic kinds of swaps: **interest rate swaps** and **currency swaps**. Chapter 4, *The Swap Market*, provides a basic introduction to the swap market, a market that has grown incredibly over the last decade. Today, the swap market has begun to dwarf other derivatives markets, as well as securities markets, including the stock and bond markets.

Chapter 5, *Synthesizing and Transforming Securities*, has been completely rewritten for this edition. The chapter shows how forwards, futures, options, and swaps are building blocks that can be combined to create new securities. Thus, the chapter stresses the concepts of put-call parity and shows how to analyze one security as a portfolio of other simpler securities.

Faced with the phenomenal growth of derivatives markets and the usefulness of financial derivatives in managing risk, an entirely new area of finance specialists is emerging. Chapter 6, *Risk Management and Financial Engineering*, shows how financial engineers use derivatives to manage risk. This is a new chapter, added for this edition, to reflect the maturation of financial engineering as a financial specialty. By combining financial derivatives and linking them to securities, the financial engineer can create new instruments that have highly specialized and desirable risk and return characteristics. While the financial engineer cannot create instruments that violate the well-established trade-offs between risk and return, it is possible to develop positions with risk and return profiles that fit a specific situation almost exactly.

As always, in creating a book of this type, an author incurs many debts. All of the material in the text has been tested in the classroom and revised in light of that teaching experience. For their patience with different versions of the text, I want to thank my students at the University of Miami. Shantaram Hegde of the University of Connecticut read the entire text of the first edition and made many useful suggestions. I would like to thank Megan Zuckerman for her book composition and cover design, Shirley Kessel for preparing the index, Gnomi Gouldin for her editorial efforts, Mary Beckwith for developmental editing, and Jan Leahy for managing the production process. For their work on the previous edition, I would like to thank Andrea Coens, and Sandy Schroeder. I would also like to thank the many professors who made suggestions for improving this new edition.

– Robert W. Kolb
University of Miami

■ Chapter 1 ——————

Introduction

A **financial derivative** is a financial instrument that is based upon another more elementary financial instrument, and the value of the financial derivative depends upon the more basic instrument. Usually, the base instrument is a cash market financial instrument, such as a bond or a share of stock. For example, a stock option gives its owner the right to buy or sell the shares of stock that underlie the stock option. In this sense, the stock option is based upon a share of stock. Because the stock option cannot exist without the underlying stock, the stock option is derived from the stock itself. Because the stock is a financial instrument, the stock option is a *financial* derivative.

This chapter briefly discusses the major types of financial derivatives and explains the basic applications of the different types of derivatives. In succeeding sections, this chapter discusses three types of financial derivatives – futures, options, and swaps. We then turn to a brief consideration of **financial engineering** – the application of financial derivatives to manage risk. The chapter concludes with a discussion of the markets for financial derivatives and brief comments on the social function of financial derivatives.

1

FUTURES

Futures markets arose in the mid-1800s in Chicago. A futures contract is a type of **forward contract** – an agreement reached at one point in time calling for the delivery of some commodity at a specified later date at a price established at the time of contracting. For example, an agreement made today to deliver 1 ton of sugar a year from today at a price of $.59 per lb., with the payment to be made upon delivery, is a typical kind of forward contract. A **futures contract** is a forward contract traded on an organized exchange with contract terms clearly specified by the rules of the exchange.

Futures markets began with grains, such as corn, oats, and wheat, as the underlying good. **Financial futures** are futures contracts based upon financial instruments. Today, financial futures based on currencies, debt instruments, and financial indexes trade actively. **Foreign currency futures** are futures contracts calling for the delivery of a specific amount of a foreign currency at a specified future date in return for a given payment of U.S. dollars. **Interest rate futures** take a debt instrument, such as a Treasury bill (T-bill) or Treasury bond (T-bond), as their underlying good. With these kinds of contracts, the trader must deliver a certain kind of debt instrument to fulfill the contract. In addition, financial futures trade based on financial indexes. For these kinds of financial futures, there is no delivery, but traders complete their obligations by making cash payments based on changes in the value of the index. **Stock index futures** are futures contracts that are based on the value of an underlying stock index, such as the S&P 500 index. For these futures, the gains and losses are determined by movements in the index. Rather than attempt to deliver a basket of the 500 stocks in the index, traders settle their accounts by making cash payments that are consistent with movements in the index. Table 1.1 lists the major futures exchanges and the types of financial futures that they trade.[1] Financial futures were introduced only in the early 1970s. The first financial futures contracts were for foreign exchange, with interest rate futures beginning to trade in the mid-1970s, followed by stock index futures in the early 1980s.

FORWARDS VERSUS FUTURES

To understand the basic ideas underlying the concept of a financial derivative, and futures in particular, we consider the obliga-

■ Table 1.1

FUTURES EXCHANGES AND THE FINANCIAL FUTURES
CONTRACTS THEY TRADE

Futures Markets in the United States	FX	IRF	Index
Chicago Board of Trade (CBOT)		✖	✖
Chicago Mercantile Exchange (CME)	✖	✖	✖
Coffee, Sugar and Cocoa Exchange (New York)			✖
Kansas City Board of Trade (KCBT)			✖
Mid-America Commodity Exchange (Chicago)	✖	✖	
New York Cotton Exchange, Inc.	✖		✖
New York Futures Exchange (NYFE)			✖

Note: FX indicates foreign exchange, IRF indicates interest rate futures, and Index indicates any of a variety of indexes, including stock indexes, interest rate indexes, and physical commodity indexes.

Source: *The Wall Street Journal, Futures Magazine, Intermarket Magazine*, various issues, and *Chicago Mercantile Exchange*, Annual Report, various editions.

tions and privileges involved in forward and futures contracting. In a typical forward contract, calling for the delivery of a commodity at a future time for a payment to be made upon delivery, two parties come together and agree to terms that they believe to be mutually beneficial. Although very desirable for both parties, this kind of contract has a number of characteristics that may be drawbacks, and these can be illustrated by using our example of the forward contract for the delivery of 1 ton of sugar in a year.

In the forward contract for sugar, both parties must trust each other to complete the contract as promised. The contract price was $.59 per lb., and that is the amount promised to be paid upon delivery of the sugar in one year. At the time of delivery, the price of sugar is quite likely to be different from $.59. Let us assume that the price of sugar at the time of delivery is $.69. This is the cash price or **spot price** – the price for immediate delivery of a good. In this event, the seller is obligated to deliver the ton of sugar and receive only $.59 per lb. for it. In the open market, however, the sugar could be sold for $.69 per lb. Obviously, the seller will be tempted to default on the forward contract obligation and sell the ton of sugar in the open market at the spot price of $.69 per lb., giving rise to credit risk. The strong incentives to default on the contract are known in advance to both parties. Consequently, this kind of forward contract can reasonably take place only between two parties that know and trust each other to honor their commitments. But, if we restrict ourselves to doing business only with people we trust, there is likely to be very little commerce at all.

A second problem with this kind of forward contract is the difficulty of finding a trading partner. One party may wish to sell a ton of sugar for delivery in one year, but it might be difficult to find someone willing to contract now for the delivery of sugar one year from now. Not only must the timing be the same for both parties, but both parties must want to exchange the same amount of the good. These conditions can be quite restrictive and leave many potential traders unable to consummate their desired trades. Thus, without an organized exchange, there can be a lack of liquidity in a derivatives market.

A third and related problem with this kind of forward contract is the difficulty in fulfilling an obligation without actually completing delivery. In the example of the sugar contract, imagine that one party to the transaction decides after six months that it is undesirable to complete the contract by delivery. This trader has only two ways to fulfill such an obligation. The first is to make delivery as originally agreed. The second is to ask the trading partner to settle the contract now, by early delivery or the payment of cash, for example. This could be difficult to arrange unless the trading partner is willing to cooperate. As we will see in Chapters 2 and 3, the existence of organized exchanges makes it easy for traders to complete their obligations without actually making or taking delivery.

Because of credit risk, the difficulty of finding a trading partner, heterogeneity of contract terms, and the need for a flexible means of settling the contract, forward markets have always been restricted in size and scope.[2] Futures markets have emerged to provide an institutional framework that copes with these deficiencies of forward contracts. The organized futures exchange standardizes contract terms and guarantees performance on the contracts to both trading partners. As we will see in Chapter 2, an organized exchange also provides a simple mechanism that allows traders to complete their obligation at any time.

OPTIONS

As the name implies, an **option** is the right to buy or sell, for a limited time, a particular good at a specified price. Such options have obvious value. For example, if IBM is selling at $120 and an investor has the option to buy a share at $100, this option must be worth at least $20, the difference between the price at which you can buy IBM ($100) and the price at which you could sell it in the open market ($120).

Prior to 1973, options of various kinds were traded over-the-counter. An **over-the-counter market** (OTC) is a market without a centralized exchange or trading floor. In 1973, the Chicago Board Options Exchange (CBOE) began trading options on individual stocks. Since that time, the options market has experienced rapid growth, with the creation of new exchanges and many different kinds of new option contracts. These exchanges trade options on goods ranging from individual stocks and bonds, to foreign currencies, to stock indexes, to options on futures contracts.

There are two major classes of options, call options and put options. Ownership of a **call option** gives the owner the right to buy a particular good at a certain price, with that right lasting until a particular date. Ownership of a **put option** gives the owner the right to sell a particular good at a specified price, with that right lasting until a particular date. For every option, there is both a buyer and a seller. In the case of a call option, the seller receives a payment from the buyer and gives the buyer the option of buying a particular good from the seller at a certain price, with that right lasting until a particular date. Similarly, the seller of a put option receives a payment from the buyer. The buyer then has the right to sell a particular good to the seller at a certain price for a specified period of time.

In all cases, ownership of an option involves the right, but not the obligation, to make a certain transaction. The owner of a call option may, for example, buy the good at the contracted price during the life of the option, but there is no obligation to do so. Likewise, the owner of a put option may sell the good under the terms of the option contract, but there is no obligation to do so. Selling an option does commit the seller to specific obligations. The seller of a call option receives a payment from the buyer, and in exchange for this payment, the seller of the call option (or simply, the call) must be ready to sell the given good to the owner of the call, if the owner of the call wishes. The discretion to engage in further transactions always lies with the owner or buyer of an option. Option sellers have no such discretion. They have obligated themselves to perform in certain ways if the owners of the options so desire.

As Table 1.2 shows, there are quite a few options exchanges in the United States, trading a variety of goods. This list can be expected to expand in the future. The present is a time of expansion and

■ **Table 1.2**

U.S. OPTIONS EXCHANGES AND GOODS TRADED

Chicago Board Options Exchange

Individual Stocks
Long-Term Options on Individual Stocks
Stock Indexes
Interest Rates

American Exchange

Individual Stocks
Long-Term Options on Individual Stocks
Stock Indexes

Philadelphia Exchange

Individual Stocks
Long-Term Options on Individual Stocks
Stock Indexes
Foreign Currency
Precious Metals Index

Pacific Exchange

Individual Stocks
Long-Term Options on Individual Stocks
Stock Indexes

New York Stock Exchange

Individual Stocks
Long-Term Options on Individual Stocks
Stock Indexes

Note: This listing does not include options on futures contracts.

experimentation in the options market, and there will be a continuing process of maturation.

In many respects, options exchanges and futures exchanges are organized similarly. In the options market, as in the futures market, there is a seller for every buyer, and both markets allow offsetting trades. To buy an option, a trader simply needs to have an account with a brokerage firm holding a membership on the options exchange. The trade can be executed through the broker with the same ease as executing a trade to buy a stock. The buyer of an option will pay for the option at the time of the trade, so there is no more worry about cash flows associated with the purchase. For the seller of an option, the matter is somewhat more complicated. In selling a call option, the seller is agreeing to deliver the stock for a set price if the owner of the call so chooses. This means that the seller may need large financial resources to fulfill his or her obligations. The broker is representing the trader to the exchange and is, therefore, obligated to be sure that the trader has the necessary financial resources to fulfill all obligations. For the seller, the full extent of these obligations is not known when the option is sold. Accordingly, the broker needs financial guarantees from option writers. In the case of a call, the writer of an option may already own the shares of stock and deposit these with the broker. Writing call options against stock that the writer owns is called writing a covered call. This gives the broker complete protection, because the shares that are obligated for delivery are in the possession of the broker. The writer of a call who does not own the underlying stocks has written a naked option, in this case a naked call. In such cases, the broker may require substantial deposits of cash or securities to ensure that the trader has the financial resources necessary to fulfill all obligations.

The Option Clearing Corporation (OCC) oversees the conduct of the market and assists in making an orderly market. As in the futures market, the buyer and seller of an option have no obligations to a specific individual but are obligated to the OCC. Later, if an option is exercised, the OCC matches buyers and sellers and oversees the completion of the exercise process, including the delivery of funds and securities.

This management of the exercise process and the standardization of contract terms are the largest contributions of the OCC. Standardized contract terms have made it possible for traders to focus on their trading strategies without having to learn the intricacies of many different option contracts.

SWAPS

A **swap** is an agreement between two or more parties to exchange sets of cash flows over a period in the future. For example, Party A might agree to pay a fixed rate of interest on $1 million each year for five years to Party B. In return, Party B might pay a floating rate of interest on $1 million each year for five years. The parties that agree to the swap are known as **counterparties**. The cash flows that the counterparties make are generally tied to the value of debt instruments or to the value of foreign currencies. Therefore, the two basic kinds of swaps are **interest rate swaps** and **currency swaps**.

A significant industry has arisen to facilitate swap transactions. This section considers the role of **swap facilitators** – economic agents who help counterparties identify each other and consummate swap transactions. Swap facilitators, who are either brokers or dealers, may function as agents that identify and bring prospective counterparties into contact with each other. Alternatively, swap dealers may actually transact for their own accounts to help complete the swap.

By taking part in swap transactions, swap dealers expose themselves to financial risk. This risk can be serious, because it is exactly the risk that the swap counterparties are trying to avoid. Therefore, the swap dealer has two key problems. First, the swap dealer must price the swap to provide a reward for his or her services in bearing risk. Second, the swap dealer essentially has a portfolio of swaps that results from his numerous transactions in the swaps market. Therefore, the swap dealer has the problem of managing a portfolio of swaps. Chapter 4 explores how swap dealers price their swap transactions and manage the risk inherent in their swap portfolios.

The origins of the swaps market can be traced to the late 1970s, when currency traders developed currency swaps as a technique to evade British controls on the movement of foreign currency. The first interest rate swap occurred in 1981 in an agreement between IBM and the World Bank. Since that time, the market has grown rapidly. Table 1.3 shows the amount of swaps outstanding at year-end for 1987–1993. By the end of 1993, interest rate and

■ **Table 1.3** ───────────────────────────

VALUE OF OUTSTANDING INTEREST RATE AND CURRENCY SWAPS
($ Billions of Notional Principal)

Year	Total Swaps Outstanding
1987	$ 682.9
1988	1,010.2
1989	1,539.3
1990	2,311.5
1991	3,065.1
1992	3,851.0
1993	6,177.0

Source: International Swaps and Derivatives Association.

currency swaps with $6.17 trillion in underlying value were out-standing. About 80 percent of the swaps are interest rate swaps and the remaining 20 percent are currency swaps. Of these swaps, about 50 percent involved the U.S. dollar.

Table 1.4 presents information about the initiation of swaps by semi annual periods and sustains the impression of phenomenal growth. For example, interest rate swaps grew at a compounded annual rate of 51 percent over the 1987–1994 period, and currency swaps grew at a 23 percent rate over the same period. In short, the growth of the swaps market has been the most rapid for any financial product in history. With over $6 trillion in outstanding principal, the figures in the swaps market exceed the U.S. federal debt and the swaps market is growing even faster than federal debt.

Chapter 4 provides a basic introduction to the swaps market. As we will see, the swaps market is growing so rapidly because it provides firms that face financial risks with a flexible way to manage that risk. We will explore the risk management motivation that has led to this phenomenal growth in some detail.

FINANCIAL ENGINEERING

One of the most important uses of financial derivatives is risk management. Some types of risk are simple to manage with financial

■ **Table 1.4** ───────────────────

SWAPS INITIATED BY SEMI-ANNUAL PERIODS
($ Billions of Principal)

Semi annual Period	Total Interest Rate Swaps	Total Currency Swaps
1987:1	$181.5	$43.5
1987:2	206.3	42.3
1988:1	250.5	60.3
1988:2	317.6	62.3
1989:1	389.2	77.6
1989:2	444.4	92.0
1990:1	561.5	94.6
1990:2	667.8	118.1
1991:1	762.1	161.3
1991:2	859.7	167.1
1992:1	1,318.3	156.1
1992:2	1,504.3	145.8
1993:1	1,938.4	156.8
1993:2	2,166.2	138.4
1994:1	3,182.9	181.0

Source: International Swaps and Derivatives Association.

derivatives, but others require custom solutions. **Financial engineering** generally refers to the creation of custom solutions to complex risk management problems. The financial engineer might use a combination of futures, options, and swaps to tailor a solution to a specific risk management problem. In this section, we show a simple example of how to manage risks with financial derivatives. We then consider some of the complexities that may call for a custom solution by a financial engineer.

A RISK MANAGEMENT EXAMPLE

Assume that a pension fund expects to receive $1 million in three months to invest in stocks. If the fund manager waits until the money is in hand, the fund will have to pay whatever prices prevail for the stocks at that time. This exposes the fund to risk because of the uncertainty of the value of stocks three months from now. By contrast, the fund manager could use financial derivatives to manage that risk. The manager could buy stock index futures calling for delivery in three months. If the manager buys stock index futures today, the futures transaction acts as a substitute for the cash purchase of stocks and immediately establishes the effective price that the fund will pay for the stocks it will actually purchase in three months. Let us say that the stock index futures trades for 100.00 index units, each unit being worth $1, and the fund manager commits to purchase 10,000 units. The manager now has a $1 million position in stock index futures. (This futures commitment does not involve an actual cash purchase. As Chapter 2 explains in detail, purchasing a futures contract commits the buyer to a future exchange of cash for the underlying good.)

Three months later, let us assume that the index stands at 105.00, so the fund manager has a futures position worth $1,050,000 and a futures trading profit of $50,000. The manager can close this position and reap the $50,000 profit. At this time, the pension fund receives the anticipated $1 million for investment. Because the index has risen 5 percent, the stocks the manager hoped to buy for $1 million now cost $1.05 million. By combining the $50,000 futures profit with the $1 million the fund receives for investment, the fund manager can still buy the stocks as planned. A manager who had not entered the futures market would not have been able to buy all of the shares that were anticipated because, despite the $1 million in new investable funds, the stocks would have risen in value to $1.05 million. By trading the futures contracts, the manager successfully reduced the risk associated with the planned purchase of shares, and the fund is able to buy the shares as it had hoped.

In this example of the pension fund, the stock market rose by 5 percent and the fund generated a futures market profit of $50,000 that offset this rise in the cost of stocks. However, the market could have just as easily fallen by 5 percent over this three-month period. If the stock index fell from 100.00 to 95.00, the fund's futures position would have generated a $50,000 loss. (The fund manager bought a $1 million position at an index value of 100.00, so a drop in the index to 95.00 means that the manager's position is worth only $950,000, for a $50,000 loss.) In this case, the manager receives the same $1 million for investment. The stocks the manager planned to buy now cost only $950,000 instead of the anticipated $1,000,000. Therefore, the manager pays $950,000 for the stocks and uses the remaining $50,000 to cover the losses in the futures market. With a drop in futures prices, the pension fund would have been better off to have stayed out of the futures market. Had it not traded futures, the fund could have bought the desired shares for $950,000 and still had $50,000 in cash.

By trading stock index futures in the way just described, the pension fund manager effectively establishes a price for the shares of $1 million. If the stock market rises, we saw that the pension fund reaps a futures profit and the stocks cost more than was anticipated. In this case, the gain on the futures offsets the increase in the cost of the shares, and the pension fund still pays out the $1 million it receives in new funds plus its futures market gains in order to acquire the shares. If the stock market falls, the pension fund suffers a loss in the futures market and the stocks cost less than was anticipated. In the case of a falling market, the loss on the futures is offset by the decrease in the cost of the shares. The pension fund still pays out the full $1 million it receives to acquire the shares and pay its loss in the futures market. Thus, the pension fund has used the futures market to secure an effective price of $1 million for the shares. Once it enters the futures transaction, the pension fund knows that it will be able to buy the shares that it wants in three months when it receives the $1 million and that it will have no funds left over. Thus, the pension fund has used the futures market to reduce the risk associated with fluctuations in stock prices.

The example of the pension fund illustrates the usefulness of financial derivatives as a risk management tool. At the time the fund entered the market, it could not know whether stock prices would rise or fall. If the fund buys futures as just described and the stock market rises, the fund benefits by being in the futures market. However, if the fund buys futures and the stock market falls, the fund suffers by being in the futures market. By trading futures, the fund was effectively ensuring that it would pay $1 million for the stocks it wished to purchase. This decision reduced risk. The decision protected against rising prices, but it sacrificed the chance to profit from falling stock prices.

COMPLEXITIES IN RISK MANAGEMENT

In our example of the pension fund, the risk management problem faced by the pension fund manager was quite simple. A single futures derivative served to provide a virtually complete solution to manage the risk of an anticipated purchase of stock. Risk management problems are often much more complex. This section introduces some of the complexities that frequently arise.

Exchange-traded futures and options typically have fairly brief horizons. Financial futures trade for maturity dates up to four years into the future. Exchange-traded stock options usually expire within one year. Financial risk faced by firms often has a much longer horizon. For example, a firm that issues a bond with a fixed rate of interest may be undertaking a commitment as long as 30 years. The longer the horizon, the less satisfactory are exchange-traded derivatives as risk management tools.

As we will see in more detail in Chapters 2 and 3 on futures and options, exchanges trade derivatives based on a limited array of instruments. Firms often face financial risks that are only partially correlated with the instruments that underlie financial futures or exchange-traded options. Faced with such a situation, trading a single financial derivative offers a poor solution to the risk management problem, and even a combination of exchange-traded instruments may not be satisfactory as well. For example, a U.S. auto firm might consider building a plant in Germany and financing it in German marks over the 10 years it will require to build the plant. Such a transaction involves long-term interest rate risk and foreign exchange risk. It would be difficult to manage this risk with exchange-traded instruments alone.

Exchanges trade financial derivatives that are based on well-known and fairly simple single instruments. Many times, however, firms encounter financial risks that have complex payoff distributions over an extended period. For example, a firm might issue a callable convertible bond. Such an instrument can be retired upon demand by the issuer under the terms of the bond covenant. However, the same bond can be converted into stock at the discretion of the bondholder under other terms of the bond covenant. Such a complex security involves complex risks for both the issuer and the purchaser. To fully comprehend the various risks associated with such an instrument may require the services of a financial engineer. Managing the risks associated with the bond would likely require an assortment of exchange-traded financial derivatives and one or more swap agreements as well.

THE FINANCIAL ENGINEER AND RISK MANAGEMENT

Not all financial risk is bad, and not all financial risk should be avoided. However, prudence requires that investors understand the risks to which they are exposed and manage those risks wisely. Investing in financial instruments, borrowing, and raising funds through stock offerings all involve financial risk. When the amounts at risk are small and when the instruments employed are simple, the financial risks can be comprehended readily. However, complex risk exposures involving substantial sums of money can be very important, yet difficult, to manage, calling for the services of a financial engineer.

MARKETS FOR FINANCIAL DERIVATIVES

As we have seen, futures exchanges arose to solve some of the problems associated with over-the-counter trading of forward contracts, and the futures market grew to dwarf the forward markets that had existed previously. Similarly, the establishment of exchange-traded options led to an explosion of option trading and resulted in option markets that are much larger and more robust than the over-the-counter option markets that came before.

The swaps market, however, is newer than financial futures and exchange-traded options, yet it is strictly an over-the-counter market. Although only about 12 years old, it has grown tremendously and now poses a serious threat to the organized exchanges that trade financial derivatives. In a certain sense, these markets seem to have come full circle: over-the-counter markets gave way to organized exchange trading of futures and options, and the exchanges now appear to be giving way to a new over-the-counter market. Just as organized exchanges grew to avoid the limitations inherent in over-the-counter markets, the new over-the-counter market is emerging to overcome the limitations of exchange-based trading of financial derivatives. This section reviews the market forces that led to the introduction of trading on organized exchanges and now seem to be leading to an increasing role for over-the-counter markets.

EXCHANGE VERSUS OVER-THE-COUNTER MARKETS

We have seen that over-the-counter markets suffer from problems with credit risk when the trading parties do not know and trust each other. Further, liquidity can be low, due to the search costs in finding trading partners willing to take the other side of a desired transaction. Finally, over-the-counter contracts can be difficult to end before the prescribed date.

Organized exchanges have their own weaknesses. First, for some market participants, instruments traded on organized exchanges lack flexibility in the variety of instruments available and the horizon over which they trade. Second, futures and option exchanges are regulated by the government. Even though this regulation may provide some benefits, it also restricts the kinds of trading that can be conducted. Third, complying with the rules of the exchange and the regulations governing exchange trading raises the costs of trading. Fourth, some traders find fault with the public nature of exchange trading. By their very nature, futures and option exchanges are public institutions. Large traders who wish to maintain their privacy have difficulty in executing large transactions on exchanges without calling attention to their trading activity.[3] We consider these issues in turn.

We have seen that organized exchanges for financial derivatives trade contracts that are based on popular cash market goods and that the futures and options contracts have rigid specifications. By creating this homogenous good, the exchange concentrates trading interest and promotes liquidity. Some traders will find the array of exchange-traded instruments unsatisfactory. The instruments available on the exchanges may not have the correct risk exposure characteristics or they may not have the appropriate horizon. Generally, exchange-traded futures and options have only certain months in which they expire, and they do not extend as far into the future as many traders would like. These traders have an incentive to turn to over-the-counter trading to tailor transactions to their exact needs.

Both futures and options exchanges are subject to regulation by the federal government. The Commodity Futures Trading Commission (CFTC) regulates the futures exchanges that trade all futures contracts and options on futures. The Securities Exchange Commission (SEC) regulates the options exchanges. In addition, traders on exchanges are subject to the rules of the exchange, which constitute another layer of regulation. These regulations may enhance the trustworthiness of the market and may make the market function better in some respects, but complying with these regulations involves costs. Today, many large firms that trade financial derivatives actively are seeking to reduce their trading costs by using over-the-counter markets, particularly the swaps market.

Futures and options exchanges require that all trades be publicly executed on the floor of the exchange. Traders at the exchange closely monitor the trading activity of large traders, particularly the trading of investment banking firms such as Salomon Brothers, Merrill Lynch, and Goldman, Sachs. If Merrill Lynch starts to buy, the market may recognize that Merrill is trading and anticipate a very large order. Prices would rise in anticipation of the large order, and the increase in prices would mean that Merrill would have to pay more than expected to complete its purchase. To avoid the price impact of their orders, many large firms seek to arrange privately negotiated transactions away from the exchange. By trading in the over-the-counter market, Merrill might be able to quietly contact a single counterparty that would consummate the entire transaction. By trading in the over-the-counter market, Merrill can potentially avoid the price impact of its large order, reduce its trading costs, and avoid indicating its trading intentions to the market.

The choice of executing a transaction on an exchange or in the over-the-counter market depends on the total costs of securing the desired position. With constantly improving communications and the presence of large firms that understand financial derivatives, many of the largest traders are finding that they can meet their trading objectives in the over-the-counter market. However, even after stressing the current trend of institutions to use the over-the-counter markets, they remain dominant traders on futures and options exchanges as well. The movement of financial institutions away from exchange trading allows smaller traders to have a role on the exchange that is much larger than it would be if institutions traded only on the exchanges.

THE SOCIAL ROLE OF FINANCIAL DERIVATIVES

Two traditional social benefits are associated with financial derivatives. First, as we have already seen, financial derivatives are useful in managing risk. Second, trading financial derivatives generates publicly observable prices that provide information to market observers about the true value of certain assets and the future direction of the economy. Society as a whole benefits from financial derivatives markets in these two ways. Thus, the financial derivatives markets are not merely a gambling den, as some would allege. Although financial derivatives trading *does* provide plenty of opportunity for gambling, these markets confer real benefits to society as well.

From the point of view of society as a whole, the risk management and risk transference functions of financial derivatives provide a substantial benefit. Because financial derivatives are available for risk management, firms can undertake projects that might be impossible without advanced risk management techniques. For example, the pension fund manager discussed earlier in this chapter may be able to reduce the risk of investing in stocks and thereby be able to improve the well-being of the pension fund participants. Similarly, the auto firm that seeks to build a plant in Germany might abandon the project if it were unable to manage the financial risks associated with it. Individuals in the economy also benefit from the risk transference role of financial derivatives. For example, most individuals who want to finance home purchases have a choice of floating rate or fixed rate mortgages. The ability of the financial institution to offer this choice to the borrower depends on the institution's ability to manage its own financial risk through the financial derivatives market.

Financial derivatives markets are instrumental in providing information to society as a whole. The existence of financial derivatives increases trader interest and trading activity in the derivatives instrument and the cash market instrument from which the derivative stems. As a result of greater attention, prices of the derivative and the cash market instrument will be more likely to approximate their true value. Thus, the trading of financial derivatives aids economic agents in **price discovery** – the discovery of accurate price information – because it increases the quantity and quality of information about prices. When parties transact based on accurate prices, economic resources are allocated more efficiently than they would be if prices poorly reflected the economic value of the underlying assets. Further, even mere observers of the markets gain information that is useful in making their own trading decisions. As we will see in later chapters, the prices of financial derivatives give some information about the future direction of interest rates, exchange rates, and the level of inflation. Firms and individuals can use the information discovered in the financial derivatives market to improve the quality of their economic decisions, even if they do not trade financial derivatives themselves.

SUMMARY

This chapter has provided a brief overview of financial derivatives, their markets, and applications. We considered futures, forwards, options, options on futures, and swaps. All of these instruments play an important role in risk management, and we explored some simple examples of how traders can use derivatives to manage risks. Often these risks become complex. Financial engineering is the special branch of finance that creates tailor-made risk management techniques using financial derivatives as building blocks.

Financial derivatives trading began with over-the-counter markets. In the early 1970s, futures and options exchanges developed for financial derivatives, and these exchanges provided a great impetus to the development of markets for financial derivatives. Currently, we are witnessing a re-emergence of over-the-counter markets. We compared the benefits and detriments of exchange trading versus over-the-counter markets. Finally, we considered the social role of financial derivatives and found that these markets contribute to social welfare by providing for a better allocation of resources and more accurate price information on which market participants can base their economic decisions.

QUESTIONS AND PROBLEMS

1. What is the essential difference between a forward contract and a futures contract?

2. Futures and options trade on a variety of agricultural commodities, minerals, and petroleum products. Are these derivative instruments? Could they be considered financial derivatives?

3. Why does owning an option only give rights and no obligations?

4. Explain the difference in rights and obligations between owning a call option and selling a put option.

5. Are swaps ever traded on an organized exchange? Explain.

6. Would all uses of financial derivatives to manage risk normally be considered an application of financial engineering? Explain what makes an application a financial engineering application.

7. List three advantages of exchange trading of financial derivatives relative to over-the-counter trading.

8. Consider again the pension fund manager example of this chapter. How might another trader, in a similar position except that the trader anticipated selling stocks in three months, transact to limit risk?

SUGGESTED READINGS

Brown, K. C., and D. J. Smith. "Forward Swaps, Swap Options, and the Management of Callable Debt." *Journal of Applied Corporate Finance* 2, no. 4 (Winter 1990): 59–71.

Finnerty, J. D. "Financial Engineering in Corporate Finance: An Overview." In *The Handbook of Financial Engineering*, pp. 69–108. New York: Harper Business, 1990.

Kapner, K. R., and J. F. Marshall. *The Swaps Handbook: Swaps and Related Risk Management Instruments.* New York: New York Institute of Finance Corp., 1990.

Kolb, R., *Understanding Futures Markets*, 4th ed. Miami: Kolb Publishing, 1994.

Kolb, R. *Options: An Introduction*, 2nd ed. Miami: Kolb Publishing, 1994.

Kolb, R. *The Financial Derivatives Reader.* Miami: Kolb Publishing, 1992.

Marshall, J. F., and K. R. Kapner. *The Swaps Market.* Miami: Kolb Publishing Company, 1993.

Smith, C. W., Jr., and C. W. Smithson. "Financial Engineering: An Overview." In *The Handbook of Financial Engineering*, pp. 3–29. New York: Harper Business, 1990.

Smith, C. W., Jr., C. W. Smithson, and L. M. Wakeman. "The Market for Interest Rate Swaps." In *The Handbook of Financial Engineering*, pp. 212–229. New York: Harper Business, 1990.

Smith, C. W., Jr., C. W. Smithson, and D. S. Wilford. *Managing Financial Risk.* New York: Harper & Row, Ballinger Division, 1990.

Smith, D. J. "The Arithmetic of Financial Engineering." *Journal of Applied Corporate Finance* 1, no. 4 (Winter 1989): 49–58.

NOTES

1. There are other futures exchanges that do not trade financial futures. These include Commodity Exchange, Inc. (COMEX)

(New York), Minneapolis Grain Exchange, Citrus Associates of the New York Cotton Exchange, Petroleum Associates of the New York Cotton Exchange, and Chicago Rice and Cotton Exchange. In addition, financial futures trade on an ever-increasing number of foreign futures exchanges.

2. There is a notable exception in the forward market for foreign currency, where the forward market is extremely large and overshadows the futures market.

3. Although the identity of traders on futures and options exchanges is not public information, large traders often cannot preserve their anonymity. Traders at the exchange know each other and generally know which traders execute orders for which large firms. Therefore, large transactions executed by employees of a large firm signal the trading intentions of the firm to other traders present at the exchange.

Chapter 2

Futures

OVERVIEW

This chapter explores the futures markets in the United States and the contracts traded on them. Futures markets have a reputation for being incredibly risky. To a large extent, this reputation is justified. As we will see, however, futures contracts may also be used to manage many different kinds of risks. As such, the futures markets play a beneficial role in society by allowing the transference of risk and by providing information about the future direction of prices on many commodities.

The chapter begins by explaining how a futures exchange is organized and how it helps to promote liquidity to attract greater trading volume. After explaining how to read futures price quotations, the chapter focuses on the principles of futures pricing and some of the most important applications of futures for risk management.

THE FUTURES EXCHANGE

A futures exchange is a nonprofit organization composed of members holding seats on the exchange. These seats are traded on an open market, so an individual wishing to become a member of the exchange can do so by buying an existing seat from a member and by meeting other exchange-imposed criteria for financial soundness and ethical reputation. Table 2.1 presents recent prices for

21

■ Table 2.1 ————————————————

SEAT PRICES FOR MAJOR U.S. FUTURES EXCHANGES

Exchange	Last Sale Price
Commodity Exchange of New York	$125,000
Chicago Mercantile Exchange	925,000
Chicago Board of Trade	650,000
New York Mercantile Exchange	555,000
Coffee, Sugar and Cocoa Exchange	130,000

Source: *Futures and Options World,* October, 1994, p. 85.

seats on the more important exchanges. These prices fluctuate quite radically, depending largely on the level of trading activity on the exchange.

The exchange provides a setting in which futures contracts can be traded by its members and other parties who trade through an exchange member. The exchange members participate in committees that govern the exchange and also employ professional managers to execute their directives. So, although the futures exchange is itself a nonprofit corporation, it is constituted to benefit its members. The futures market in the United States is regulated by the Commodity Futures Trading Commission (CFTC), an agency of the U.S. government.

Each exchange determines the kinds of goods that it will trade and the contract specifications for each of the goods. As we will see in more detail later, a great variety of financial futures are traded, and some exchanges tend to specialize in certain segments of the industry.

FUTURES CONTRACTS AND FUTURES TRADING

Each exchange provides a trading floor where all of its contracts are traded. The rules of an exchange require all of its futures contracts to be traded only on the floor of the exchange during its official hours. By specializing in a limited range of commodities and by standardizing contract terms, the futures contract overcomes some of the difficulties noted earlier in the case of forward contracts.

TYPICAL CONTRACT TERMS

The difference between futures contracts and forward contracts can be demonstrated by examining the particular features of a futures contract. For example, the Chicago Board of Trade (CBOT) trades Treasury bond futures that call for the delivery of U.S. Treasury bonds. In brief, the contract specifies that the seller shall deliver $100,000 face value of U.S. Treasury bonds that are not callable and do not mature within 15 years from the delivery date. The terms of the futures contract regulate the way in which the bonds will be delivered (by wire transfer between approved banks) and the timing of delivery (on a business day of the appropriate delivery month, either March, June, September, or December). This standardization of the contract terms means that all of the traders will know immediately the exact characteristics of the good being traded, without negotiation or long discussion. All financial futures also have these closely specified contract conditions. In fact, the only feature of a futures contract that is determined at the time of the trade is the futures price.

ORDER FLOW

Futures contracts are created when an order is executed on the floor of the exchange. The order can originate with a member of the exchange trading for his or her own account in pursuit of profit. Alternatively, it can originate with a trader outside the exchange who enters an order through a broker, who has a member of the exchange execute the trade for the client. These outside orders are transmitted electronically to the floor of the exchange, where actual trading takes place in an area called a pit. A trading **pit** is a particular area of the exchange floor designated for the trading of a particular commodity. It is called a pit because the trading area consists of an oval made up of different levels, like stairs, around a central area. Traders stand on the steps or in the central area of the pit, which allows them to see each other with relative ease.

This physical arrangement highlights a central difference between commodities exchanges and stock exchanges in the United States. In the stock market, there is a specialist for each stock, and every trade on the exchange for a particular stock must go through the specialist for that stock. In the futures market, any trader in the pit may execute a trade with any other trader. The rules of the exchange require that any offer to buy or sell must be made by **open-outcry** to all other traders in the pit. This different form of trading gives rise to the appearance of chaos on the trading floor, because each trader is struggling to gain the attention of other traders.

Once a trade is executed, the information is communicated to the exchange officials who report the transaction over a worldwide electronic communication system. Also, the trader whose order was executed will receive confirmation of the trade.

THE CLEARINGHOUSE AND ITS FUNCTIONS

The trade from an outside party must be executed through a broker, and the broker must, in turn, trade through a member of the exchange. Normally, the two parties to a transaction will be located far apart and will not even know each other. This raises the issue of trust and the question of whether the traders will perform as they have promised. We have already seen that this can be a problem with forward contracts.

To resolve this uncertainty about performance in accordance with the contract terms, each futures exchange has a clearinghouse. The **clearinghouse** is a well-capitalized financial institution that guarantees contract performance to both parties. As soon as the trade is consummated, the clearinghouse interposes itself between the buyer and seller. The clearinghouse acts as a seller to the buyer and as the buyer to the seller. At this point, the original buyer and seller have obligations to the clearinghouse and no obligations to each other. This arrangement is shown in Figure 2.1. In the top portion of the figure, the relationship between the buyer and seller is shown when there is no clearinghouse. The seller is obligated to deliver goods to the buyer, who is obligated to deliver funds to the seller. This arrangement raises the familiar problems of trust between the two parties to the trade. In the lower portion, the role of the clearinghouse is demonstrated. The clearinghouse guarantees that goods will be delivered to the buyer and that funds will be delivered to the seller.

At this point, the traders need to trust only the clearinghouse, instead of each other. Because the clearinghouse has a large supply of capital, there is little need for concern. Also, as the bottom portion of Figure 2.1 shows, the clearinghouse has no net commitment in the futures market. After all the transactions are complet-

■ Figure 2.1

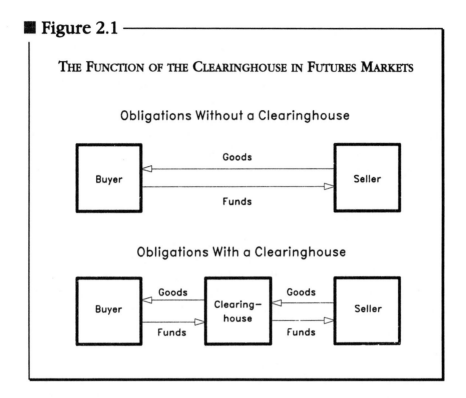

THE FUNCTION OF THE CLEARINGHOUSE IN FUTURES MARKETS

Obligations Without a Clearinghouse

Obligations With a Clearinghouse

ed, the clearinghouse will have neither funds nor goods. It acts only to guarantee performance to both parties.

THE CLEARINGHOUSE AND THE TRADER

While the clearinghouse guarantees performance on all futures contracts, it now has its own risk exposure, because the clearinghouse will suffer if traders default on their obligations. To protect the clearinghouse and the exchange, traders must deposit funds with their brokers to trade futures contracts. This deposit, known as the **margin**, must be in the form of cash or short-term U.S. Treasury securities. This margin acts as a good-faith deposit with the broker. If the trader defaults on his or her obligations, the broker may seize the margin deposit to cover the trading losses. This provides a measure of safety to the broker, the clearinghouse, and the exchange.

This margin deposit, however, is normally quite small relative to the value of the goods being traded. The margin deposit might normally have a value equal to only 5 to 10 percent of the goods represented by the futures contract. Because potential losses on the futures contract could be much larger than this margin deposit, the clearinghouse needs other protection from potential default by the trader. To give this protection, futures exchanges have adopted a system known as **daily settlement** or **marking-to-market**. The policy of daily settlement means that futures traders realize their paper gains and losses in cash on the results of each day's trading. The trader may withdraw the day's gains and must pay the day's losses.

The margin deposit remains with the broker. If the trader fails to settle the day's losses, the broker may seize the margin deposit and liquidate the trader's position, paying the losses out of the margin deposit. This practice limits the exchange's exposure to loss from a trader's default. Essentially, the exchange will lose on the default only if the loss on one day exceeds the amount of the margin. This is unlikely to happen, and even if it did, the amount lost would probably be very small.

FULFILLMENT OF FUTURES CONTRACTS

After executing a futures contract, both the buyer and seller have undertaken specific obligations to the clearinghouse. Fulfillment of those obligations can be accomplished in two basic ways. First, the trader may actually make or take delivery as contemplated in the original contract. Second, a trader who does not wish to make or take delivery can fulfill all obligations by entering a reversing or offsetting trade. In fact, more than 99 percent of all futures contracts are settled by a reversing trade.[1]

DELIVERY

Each futures contract will have its own very specific rules for making and taking delivery. These rules cover the time of delivery, the location of delivery, and the way in which the funds covering the goods will change hands. Some investors, who do not understand the futures market very well, imagine that one could forget about a futures position and wind up with sowbellies on the front lawn. Instead, the delivery process is more complex.

After the clearinghouse interposes itself between the original buyer and seller, each of the trading partners has no obligation to any other trader. As delivery approaches, the clearinghouse supervises the arrangements for delivery. First, the clearinghouse will pair buyers and sellers for the delivery and will identify the two parties to each other. Prior to this time, the two traders had no obligations to each other. Second, the buyer and seller will communicate the relevant information concerning the delivery process to the opposite trading partner and to the clearinghouse. Usually, the seller has the choice of exactly what features the delivered goods will have. For example, in the T-bond contract, many different bonds qualify for delivery, and the seller has the right to choose which bond to deliver. The seller must tell the buyer which bond will be delivered, and the seller must also tell the buyer the name of the bank account to which the funds are to be transmitted. Once the funds have been transmitted to the seller's account and this transaction has been confirmed by the seller's bank, the seller will deliver title to the goods to the buyer.

As long as this transaction is proceeding smoothly, which is usually the case, the clearinghouse has little to do. It acts merely as an overseer. If difficulties arise, or if disputes develop, the clearinghouse must intervene to enforce the rules of the exchange.

REVERSING TRADES

For many commodities, particularly physical commodities, the delivery process can be quite cumbersome. In the case of the bond contract, the seller may not choose to deliver the particular bond that the buyer really wants. To avoid taking delivery most futures traders fulfill their obligations by entering a **reversing trade** prior to the time of delivery. Then if they need to dispose of their supply of the good, or need to acquire the actual good, they do so in the regular spot market, outside the channels of the futures market.

Prior to the initiation of the delivery process, buyers and sellers are not associated with each other, because the clearinghouse has interposed itself between all the pairs of traders. This allows any trader a means to end his or her commitment in the futures market without actually making delivery. Figure 2.2 shows the position of three traders assuming that there is no clearinghouse. At time = 0 trader A buys a futures contract, and trader B is the seller. Later, at time = 1, which is still before delivery, trader A decides to liquidate the original position. Accordingly, he or she sells the identical contract that was purchased at time = 0, to trader C, who buys.

In an important sense, trader A no longer has a position in the futures contract, because he or she will just pass goods from trader B to trader C and will pass funds from trader C to trader B. After time = 1, price fluctuations will not really affect trader A. Traders B and C, however, have a very different perspective. Both have obligations to trader A and expect trader A to perform on the original contracts. This means that trader A is left with duties to perform in the delivery process. As a result, even though no longer having risk exposure, trader A still has obligations.

From the point of view of trader A, all of this is much simpler if there is a clearinghouse, as shown in Figure 2.2. Because the clearinghouse splits apart the original trading partners as soon as the trade is consummated, trader A can now execute a reversing trade that will take him or her out of the market altogether. After the same trades are made, the clearinghouse can recognize that trader A has no position in the futures market, because the trader has bought and sold the identical futures contract. After time = 1, trader C has assumed the position originally held by trader A. As a result, trader B's position is unaffected, and trader A has no further obligations in the futures market.

■ **Figure 2.2**

THE MECHANISM OF THE REVERSING TRADE

It is important to recognize that the reversing trade must be for exactly the same futures contract as originally traded. Otherwise, the trader will have two futures positions rather than none. Also, it should be clear that any trader may execute a reversing trade at any time prior to the contract's expiration. This is exactly what most traders do. As contract expiration approaches, they execute reversing trades to eliminate their futures market commitments. In Figure 2.2, trader C was new to the market, so there are still the same number of futures contracts outstanding. However, if trader C had been executing a reversing trade also, the number of contracts outstanding in the marketplace would have decreased.

FUTURES PRICE QUOTATIONS

Futures price quotations are available daily in *The Wall Street Journal* and other newspapers. Figure 2.3 presents a sample of financial futures price quotations. Although there are far too many different contracts to discuss each in detail, their price quotations are all similar in key respects. For illustrative purposes, we can use the T-bond contract traded by the Chicago Board of Trade. The T-bond quotations are included in Figure 2.3. The first line of the quotation shows the commodity, followed by the exchange where the futures contract is traded, in this case the CBOT. Next the quotations show the amount of good in a single contract. For the T-bond contract, the contract amount is $100,000. The last item in this first line is the method of price quotation. For T-bond futures, the price is quoted in points and 32nds of 100 percent of par. Thus, a quotation of 92-15 means that the futures price is 92 + 15/32 percent of the face value. With a $100,000 face value, the contract price is $92,468.75 = [(92 + 15/32)/100]$100,000. All of this information is important, but it is seriously incomplete. There are additional facts about the T-bond contract that any trader should know before trading T-bond futures, such as the proper way to close a position without delivery, the kinds of T-bonds that are deliverable, and the exact process for making delivery. The CBOT provides all of this detailed information. In the body of the quotation, there is a separate line for each contract maturity. The next contract to come due for delivery is the **nearby contract**. Other contracts, with later delivery dates, are **distant** or **deferred contracts**. The first three columns of figures show the "Open," "High," and "Low" prices for the day's trading.

■ Figure 2.3

FUTURES PRICE QUOTATIONS IN *The Wall Street Journal*

Tuesday, March 28, 1995

Open Interest Reflects Previous Trading Day.

GRAINS AND OILSEEDS

	Open	High	Low	Settle	Change	Lifetime High	Low	Open Interest
CORN (CBT) 5,000 bu.; cents per bu.								
May	247¾	250	247¼	249¼	+ 1	285½	228	106,340
July	254	256¼	253¼	255½	+ 1	285½	232½	110,387
Sept	257½	259½	257	259	+ ½	270½	238	21,181
Dec	261	262½	260¼	262¼	+ ¾	263½	235½	93,118
Mr96	267	268¾	266¼	268¾	+ 1	269¾	249½	8,749
May	271½	272¾	270½	272¾	+ ¾	273	259½	513
July	273¼	274¾	273	274¾	+ ½	275¼	254	4,631
Dec	255	256¼	254½	256	+ ½	258½	239	3,093
Est vol 33,000; vol Mon 28,986; open int 348,012, +372.								
OATS (CBT) 5,000 bu.; cents per bu.								
May	131½	133¾	131	133¾	+ 1½	151	122¼	7,150
July	136¾	139¼	136½	139	+ 1¾	142½	127¼	4,379
Sept	141	143¼	140½	143	+ 2	143¼	132	298
Dec	146¼	148½	146¼	148½	+ 1¾	148½	136	1,317
Est vol 1,000; vol Mon 1,012; open int 13,205, −71.								
SOYBEANS (CBT) 5,000 bu.; cents per bu.								
May	577	59¼	574½	577½	+ ¾	705½	553¼	43,301
July	586½	590	584¾	588¼	+ ¾	706½	559¼	50,186
Aug	591½	594	589½	592½	+ ¾	612	562¾	6,486
Sept	593½	597	592	594½	+ 1	615	564¾	3,823
Nov	601	603½	598¼	602¼	+ 1¼	645	573¼	28,493
Ja96	608	611	607	609½	+ 1¼	621	582¾	1,974
Mar	616½	618	614½	618	+ 1½	629	590½	498
May	....	....	....	620½	+ ½	633	602	103
July	625	627½	625	626¼	+ ½	636¼	599½	764
Nov	608	609	605½	608¼	− ¾	615½	585	1,420
Est vol 33,000; vol Mon 35,068; open int 137,051, −2,732.								
SOYBEAN MEAL (CBT) 100 tons; $ per ton.								
May	165.50	166.70	164.10	165.90	+ .40	207.00	155.30	34,020
July	170.10	171.40	168.60	170.40	+ .60	206.00	159.80	29,911
Aug	171.80	173.00	170.60	172.40	+ .80	182.60	162.10	7,760
Sept	173.80	175.00	172.50	174.30	+ .70	182.70	164.00	5,300
Oct	175.10	176.10	174.10	175.60	+ 1.00	181.80	166.00	8,990
Dec	177.70	179.10	177.00	178.40	+ .60	185.20	169.30	12,367
Ja96	179.00	179.20	178.00	178.70	+ .50	185.20	171.00	723
Est vol 12,000; vol Mon 13,374; open int 99,071, −1,283.								
SOYBEAN OIL (CBT) 60,000 lbs.; cents per lb.								
May	26.52	26.52	26.25	26.29	− .34	28.05	22.85	29,622
July	26.08	26.08	25.84	25.91	− .23	27.85	22.76	21,460
Aug	25.90	25.90	25.75	25.76	− .18	27.20	22.73	8,275
Sept	25.75	25.75	25.62	25.67	− .16	26.80	22.75	6,580
Oct	25.58	25.65	25.50	25.55	− .12	26.60	22.85	6,701
Dec	25.35	25.45	25.25	25.38	− .04	26.30	22.80	13,419
Ja96	25.20	25.20	25.20	25.26	+ .01	26.10	23.20	450
Mar	....	....	25.05			25.80	23.85	259

	Open	High	Low	Settle	Change	Lifetime High	Low	Open Interest
Dec	75.90	76.10	74.70	74.70	− 1.28	79.95	66.25	26,166
Mr96	76.95	76.95	75.80	75.85	− 1.10	80.75	68.80	5,999
May	77.55	77.55	76.65	76.65	− .90	81.30	72.70	1,271
Jly	77.60	77.60	76.90	76.90	− .70	81.50	76.00	199
Est vol 15,000; vol Mon 11,810; open int 78,927, −1,150.								
ORANGE JUICE (CTN) − 15,000 lbs.; cents per lb.								
May	106.00	108.25	105.75	107.35	+ 2.20	126.60	96.65	11,782
July	110.50	112.25	109.75	111.20	+ 2.15	129.00	100.50	5,576
Sept	114.00	115.50	113.75	114.75	+ 2.55	132.00	102.50	4,454
Nov	na	112.50	111.10	112.50	+ 2.35	129.00	105.00	2,316
Ja96	113.50	114.25	112.50	114.20	+ 1.95	129.20	125.50	1,643
Mar	113.25	116.20	113.25	116.20	+ 2.95	130.20	110.00	193
Est vol 4,000; vol Mon 1,016; open int 25,986, +158.								

METALS AND PETROLEUM

	Open	High	Low	Settle	Change	Lifetime High	Low	Open Interest
COPPER-HIGH (Cmx.Div.NYM) − 25,000 lbs.; cents per lb.								
Mar	143.00	143.00	140.80	141.65	−	.75	143.15	76.30	1,740
Apr	141.10	141.10	139.40	139.70	− 1.05	141.70	90.10	1,777
May	138.75	139.40	136.80	137.80	− .95	139.40	76.85	28,601
June	134.70	135.50	134.50	135.00	− 1.05	136.20	106.30	639
July	134.40	134.50	132.30	132.90	− 1.05	134.50	78.00	6,851
Aug	130.60	130.60	130.60	130.65	− 1.10	131.70	111.40	375
Sept	130.00	130.00	128.20	128.45	− 1.10	130.50	79.10	3,428
Oct	....	....	....	127.00	− 1.20	126.90	113.00	423
Nov	....	....	....	125.50	− 1.35	126.00	113.95	291
Dec	125.70	125.70	125.00	124.15	− 1.35	126.10	88.00	3,053
Ja96	....	....	....	122.85	− 1.35	123.50	88.50	224
Mar	....	....	....	120.35	− 1.35	122.00	99.20	1,159
May	....	....	....	117.80	− 1.40	118.50	107.00	369
July	....	....	....	115.80	− 1.40	117.00	105.50	196
Sept	....	....	....	114.60	− 1.40	116.00	105.25	153
Dec	....	....	....	114.10	− 1.40	116.80	112.00	94
Est vol 9,000; vol Mon 7,172; open int 49,377, +121.								
GOLD (Cmx.Div.NYM) − 100 troy oz.; $ per troy oz.								
Mar	....	....	....	383.10	+ .90	385.70	375.20	0
Apr	383.00	383.50	382.00	383.20	+ .90	425.00	374.50	36,192
June	384.50	385.80	384.30	385.50	+ .80	430.00	351.00	46,489
Aug	388.20	389.20	387.80	388.70	+ .80	414.50	380.50	16,560
Oct	....	....	....	392.10	+ .90	419.20	387.20	5,212
Dec	395.00	395.80	394.80	395.60	+ .90	439.50	358.00	13,462
Fb96	....	....	....	399.20	+ 1.00	424.50	393.60	10,283
Apr	....	....	....	402.90	+ 1.10	430.20	398.70	5,576
June	....	....	....	406.70	+ 1.10	447.00	370.90	5,894
Aug	....	....	....	410.40	+ 1.20	423.00	423.00	631
Dec	....	....	....	418.10	+ 1.20	447.50	379.60	3,947
Ju97	....	....	....	430.00	+ 1.30	456.00	429.20	3,002
Dec	....	....	....	442.20	+ 1.50	477.00	402.00	2,882
Ju98	....	....	....	454.60	+ 1.70	489.50	458.50	2,113
Dec	....	....	....	467.00	+ 1.90	505.00	468.00	3,695
Ju99	....	....	....	479.60	+ 2.10	520.00	485.30	3,938
Dec	....	....	....	492.20	+ 2.30	493.50	490.00	1,396

Source: *The Wall Street Journal*, March 29, 1995

The fourth column presents the **settlement price** for the day. In most respects, the settlement price is like a closing price, but there can be important differences. Because every trader marks to the market every day, it is important to have an official price to which the trade must be marked. That is the settlement price, and it is set by the settlement committee of the exchange. If the markets are active at the close of trading, the settlement price will normally be the closing price. However, if a particular contract has not traded for some time prior to the close of the day's trading, the settlement committee may believe that the last trade price is not representative of the actual prevailing price for the contract. In this situation, the settlement committee may establish a price that differs from the last trade price as the settlement price. The "Change" column reports the change in the contract's price from the preceding day's settlement price to the settlement price for the day being reported. The next two columns indicate the highest and lowest prices reached by a contract of a particular maturity since the contract began trading.

The last column shows the **open interest** at the close of the day's trading. The open interest is the number of contracts currently obligated for delivery. If a buyer and seller trade one contract, and neither is making a reversing trade, then the open interest is increased by one contract. For example, the transaction shown in Figure 2.1 creates one contract of open interest, because neither party has any other position in the futures market. The trades shown in Figure 2.2, however, also give rise to just one contract of open interest. When traders A and B trade, they create one contract of open interest. When trader A enters a reversing trade and brings trader C into the market, there is no increase in open interest. In effect, trader C has simply taken the place of trader A.

Every contract begins with zero open interest and ends with zero open interest. When the exchange first permits trading in a given contract maturity, there is no open interest until the first trade is made. At the end of the contract's life, all traders must fulfill their obligations by entering reversing trades or by completing delivery. After this process is complete, there is no longer any open interest. Figure 2.4 shows the typical pattern that the open interest will follow. When the contract is first opened for trading, open interest builds slowly and continues to build. In fact, the nearby contract usually has the largest open interest. As the contract nears maturity, however, the open interest falls off drastically. This is because many traders enter reversing trades to fulfill their commitments without having to incur the expense and bother of actually making delivery. This pattern is very uniform and can be seen clearly from the quotations in Figure 2.3.

The final line of the quotations shows the number of contracts that were estimated to have traded on the day being reported and the actual volume for the preceding day's trading. This line also shows the total open interest, which is simply the sum of the open interest for all of the different contract maturities. The very last item in this line is the change in the open interest since the preceding day.

■ Figure 2.4

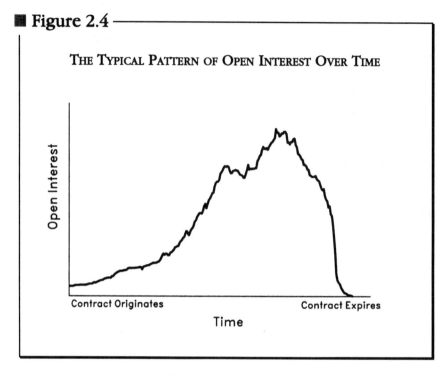

THE TYPICAL PATTERN OF OPEN INTEREST OVER TIME

Open Interest

Contract Originates   Contract Expires

Time

FUTURES PRICING

This section shows that futures prices depend on the cash price of a commodity and the cost of storing the underlying good from the present to the delivery date of the futures contract. This Cost-of-Carry model rests upon the idea of arbitrage, and the model defines the price relationship between the spot price of a good and the futures price that precludes arbitrage. Initially, we assume that futures markets are perfect. In this sanitized framework, we can see more clearly the structure of the pricing relationship defined by the Cost-of-Carry model. Later we relax the assumption of a perfect market to explore the effect of market imperfections on futures prices.

We focus first on gold as an example of a commodity. Even though gold is not a financial asset, its simplicity makes it a useful first example. Gold generates no cash flows, such as coupon payments on bonds or dividend payments on stocks, yet it behaves in most other respects like the financial assets that underlie financial futures contracts. After initially considering gold, we turn our focus to interest rate futures and stock index futures specifically.

THE COST-OF-CARRY MODEL IN PERFECT MARKETS

We begin by using the concept of arbitrage to explore the Cost-of-Carry model or carrying charge theory of futures prices. Carrying charges fall into four basic categories: storage costs, insurance costs, transportation costs, and financing costs. Storage costs include the cost of warehousing the commodity in the appropriate facility. Although storage seems to apply most clearly to physical goods such as wheat or lumber, it is also possible to store financial instruments. In many cases, the owner of a financial instrument will leave the instrument in a bank vault. For many goods in storage, insurance is also necessary. For example, stored lumber should be protected against fire, and stored wheat should be insured against water damage.[2]

The carrying charges also include, in some cases, transportation costs. Wheat on a railroad siding in Kansas must be carried to delivery in two senses. First, it must be stored until the appropriate delivery time for a given futures contract, and second, it must also be physically carried to the appropriate place for delivery. For physical goods, transportation costs between different locations determine price differentials between those locations. Without question, transportation charges play different roles for different commodities. Transporting wheat from Kansas to Chicago could be an important expense. By contrast, delivery of Treasury bills against a futures contract is accomplished by a wire transfer costing only a few dollars. In almost all cases, the most significant carrying charge in the futures market is the financing cost. In most situations, financing the good under storage overwhelms the other costs. For financial futures, storage, insurance, and transportation costs are virtually nil, and we ignore them in the remainder of our discussion.

The carrying charges reflect only the charges involved in carrying a commodity from one time or one place to another and do not include the value of the commodity itself. Thus, if gold costs $400 per ounce and the financing rate is 1 percent per month, the financing charge for carrying the gold forward is $4 per month (1 percent × $400).

Most participants in the futures markets face a financing charge on a short-term basis that is equal to the repo rate, the interest rate on repurchase agreements. In a repurchase agreement, a person sells securities at one time, with the understanding that they will be repurchased at a certain price at a later time. Most repurchase agreements are for one day only and are known, accordingly, as overnight repos. The repo rate is relatively low, exceeding the rate on Treasury bills by only a small amount.[3] The financing cost for such goods is so low because anyone wishing to finance a commodity may offer the commodity itself as collateral for the loan. Further, most of the participants in the market tend to be financial institutions of one type or another who have low financing costs anyway, at least for very short-term obligations.

CASH AND FUTURES PRICING RELATIONSHIPS

The carrying charges just described are important because they play a crucial role in determining pricing relationships between spot and futures prices as well as the relationships among prices of futures contracts of different maturities. For our purposes, assume that the only carrying charge is the financing cost at an interest rate of 10 percent per year. As an example, consider the prices and the accompanying transactions shown in Table 2.2.

The transactions in Table 2.2 represent a successful cash-and-carry arbitrage. This is a cash-and-carry arbitrage because the trader buys the cash good and carries it to the expiration of the futures contract. The trader traded at $t = 0$ to guarantee a riskless profit without investment. There was no investment, because there was no cash flow at $t = 0$. The trader merely borrowed funds to purchase the gold and to carry it forward. The profit in these transactions was certain once the trader made the transactions at $t = 0$. As these transactions show, to prevent arbitrage the futures price of the gold should have been $440 or less. With a futures price of $440, for example, the transactions in Table 2.2 would yield a zero profit. From this example, we can infer the following Cost-of-Carry Rule 1: The futures price must be less than or equal to the spot price of the commodity plus the carrying charges necessary to carry the spot commodity forward to delivery. We can express this rule as follows:

$$F_{0,t} \leq S_0(1+C) \tag{2.1}$$

where

$F_{0,t}$ = the futures price at t = 0 for delivery at time t
S_0 = the spot price at t = 0

◼ Table 2.2

CASH-AND-CARRY GOLD ARBITRAGE TRANSACTIONS

Prices for the Analysis:

Spot price of gold	$400
Future price of gold (for delivery in one year)	$450
Interest rate	10%

Transaction	Cash Flow
t = 0 Borrow $400 for one year at 10%.	+$400
Buy one ounce of gold in the spot market for $400	-$400.
Sell a futures contract for $450	
for delivery of one ounce in one year.	0
Total Cash Flow	**$0**
t = 1 Remove the gold from storage.	$0
Deliver the ounce of gold against the	
futures contract.	+450
Repay loan, including interest.	-440
Total Cash Flow	**+$10**

C = the cost of carry, expressed as a fraction of the spot price, necessary to carry the good forward from the present to the delivery date on the futures

As we have seen, if prices do not conform to Cost-of-Carry Rule 1, a trader can borrow funds, buy the spot commodity with the borrowed funds, sell the futures contract, and carry the commodity forward to deliver against the futures contract. These transactions would generate a certain profit without investment, or an arbitrage profit. The certain profit would be guaranteed by the sale of the futures contract. Also, there would be no investment, because the funds needed to carry out the strategy were borrowed and the cost of using those funds was included in the calculation of the carrying charge. Such opportunities cannot exist in a rational market. The cash-and-carry arbitrage opportunity arises because the spot price is too low relative to the futures price.

We have seen that an arbitrage opportunity arises if the spot price is too low relative to the futures price. As we will now see, the spot price might also be too high relative to the futures price. If the spot price is too high, we have a reverse cash-and-carry arbitrage opportunity. As the name implies, the steps necessary to exploit the arbitrage opportunity are just the opposite of those in the cash-and-carry arbitrage strategy. As an example of the reverse cash-and-carry strategy, consider the prices for gold and the accompanying transactions in Table 2.3.

In these transactions, the arbitrageur sells the gold short. As in the stock market, a short seller borrows the good from another trader and must later repay it. Once the good is borrowed, the short seller sells it and takes the money from the sale. (The transaction is called short selling because one sells a good that he or she does not actually own.) In this example, the short seller has the use of all of the proceeds from the short sale, which are invested at the interest rate of 10 percent. The trader also buys a futures contract to ensure that he or she can acquire the gold needed to repay the lender at the expiration of the futures in one year. Notice that these transactions guarantee an arbitrage profit. Once the transactions at $t = 0$ are completed, the $12 profit at $t = 1$ year is certain. Also, the trader had no net cash flow at $t = 0$, so the strategy required no investment. To make this arbitrage opportunity impossible, the spot and futures prices must obey Cost-of-Carry Rule 2: The futures price must be equal to or greater than the spot price plus the cost of carrying the good to the futures delivery date. We can express this rule mathematically with the notation we introduced earlier:

$$F_{0,t} \geq S_0(1+C) \tag{2.2}$$

If prices do not obey this Cost-of-Carry Rule 2, there will be an arbitrage opportunity. Table 2.4 summarizes the transactions necessary to conduct the cash-and-carry and the reverse cash-and-carry strategies.

To prevent arbitrage, we have seen that the two following rules must hold:

Rule 1. To prevent cash-and-carry arbitrage,

$$F_{0,t} \leq S_0(1+C)$$

Rule 2. To prevent reverse cash-and-carry arbitrage,

$$F_{0,t} \geq S_0(1+C)$$

■ Table 2.3 ———————————————

REVERSE CASH-AND-CARRY GOLD ARBITRAGE TRANSACTIONS

Prices for the Analysis:

Spot price of gold	$420
Future price of gold (for delivery in one year)	$450
Interest rate	10%

Transaction	Cash Flow
t = 0 Sell one ounce of gold short.	+$420
Lend the $420 for one year at 10%.	-$420
Buy one ounce of gold futures for delivery in one year.	0
Total Cash Flow	**$0**
t = 1 Collect proceeds from the loan ($420 X 1.1).	+$462
Accept delivery on the futures contract.	-450
Use gold from futures delivery to repay short sale.	0
Total Cash Flow	**+$12**

Together, equations 2.1 and 2.2 imply Cost-of-Carry Rule 3: The futures price must equal the spot price plus the cost of carrying the spot commodity forward to the delivery date of the futures contract. Expressing Rule 3 mathematically, we have equation 2.3:

$$F_{0,t} = S_0(1+C) \qquad (2.3)$$

■ Table 2.4 ———————————————

TRANSACTIONS FOR ARBITRAGE STRATEGIES

Market	Cash-and-Carry	Reverse Cash-and-Carry
Debt	Borrow funds	Lend short sale proceeds
Physical	Buy asset and store; deliver against futures	Sell asset short; secure proceeds from short sale
Futures	Sell futures	Buy futures; accept delivery; return physical asset to honor short sale commitment

Notice that the relationship of equation 2.3 was derived under the following assumptions: Markets are perfect; that is, they have no transaction costs and no restrictions on the use of proceeds from short sales. It must be acknowledged that this argument explicitly excludes transaction costs. Transaction costs exist on both sides of the market, for purchase or sale of the futures. In many markets, however, transaction costs for short selling are considerably more expensive, which limits the applicability of the reverse cash-and-carry strategy.

In a well-functioning market, the implied repo rate must equal the actual repo rate. As we have seen in this section, deviations from this relationship lead to arbitrage opportunities in a perfect market. We now consider the qualifications to the basic conclusion that are required by market imperfections.

THE COST-OF-CARRY MODEL IN IMPERFECT MARKETS

In real markets, the four market imperfections discussed earlier complicate and disturb the relationship of equation 2.3. (These imperfections were transaction costs, restrictions on short selling, unequal borrowing and lending rates, and lack of storability.) The main effect of these market imperfections is to require adjustments in the identity expressed by equation 2.3. Market imperfections do not invalidate the basic framework we have been building. Instead of being able to state an equality as we did in the perfect markets framework leading to equation 2.3, we will find that market imperfections introduce a certain indeterminacy to the relationship.

For financial futures, there are few effective restrictions on short selling. In addition, the goods are essentially storable. However, we will see that the coupon payments on bonds and dividend payments on stocks make bonds and stocks somewhat less storable than a commodity like gold. In essence, market imperfections frustrate the cash-and-carry and reverse cash-and-carry strategies that we have been considering. We illustrate these effects by considering direct transaction costs.

In actual markets, traders face a variety of direct transaction costs. First, the trader must pay a fee to have an order executed. For a trader off the floor of the exchange, these fees include brokerage commissions and various exchange fees. Even members of the exchange must pay a fee to the exchange for each trade. Second, in every market there is a bid-asked spread. A market maker on the floor of the exchange must try to sell at a higher price (the asked price) than the price at which he or she is willing to buy (the bid price). The difference between the asked price and the bid price is the bid-asked spread. In our discussion, we will assume that these transaction costs are some fixed percentage, T, of the transaction amount. For simplicity, we assume that the transaction costs apply to the spot market but not to the futures market.

To illustrate the impact of transaction costs, we use the same prices with which we began our analysis in perfect markets, but now consider transaction costs of 3 percent. With transaction costs, our previous arbitrage strategy of buying the good and carrying it to delivery will not work. Table 2.5 shows the results of this effort. With transaction costs, the attempted arbitrage results in a certain loss, not an arbitrage profit.

We would have to pay $400 as before to acquire the good, plus transaction costs of 3 percent for a total outlay of $400(1 + T) = $412. We would then have to finance this total until delivery for a cost of $412(1.1) = $453.20. In return, we would only receive $450 upon the delivery of the futures contract. Given these prices, it clearly does not pay to attempt this "cash-and-carry" arbitrage. As Table 2.5 shows, these attempted arbitrage transactions generate a certain loss of $3.20. With transaction costs of 3 percent and the same spot price of $400, the futures price would have to exceed $453.20 to make the arbitrage attractive. To see why this is so, consider the cash outflows and inflows. We pay the spot price plus the transaction costs, $S_0(1 + T)$, to acquire the good. Carrying the good to delivery costs $S_0(1 + T)(1 + C)$. These costs include acquiring the good and carrying it to the delivery date of the futures. In our example, the total cost is

$$S_0(1+T)(1+C) = \$400(1.03)(1.1) = \$453.20$$

Thus, to break even, the futures transaction must yield $453.20. We can write this more formally as

$$F_{0,t} \leq S_0(1+T)(1+C) \tag{2.4}$$

■ Table 2.5

ATTEMPTED CASH-AND-CARRY GOLD ARBITRAGE TRANSACTIONS

Prices for the Analysis:

Spot price of gold	$400
Future price of gold (for delivery in one year)	$450
Interest rate	10%
Transaction cost (T)	3%

Transaction	Cash Flow
t = 0 Borrow $412 for one year at 10%.	+$412
Buy one ounce of gold in the spot market for $400 and pay 3% transaction costs, to total $412	–$412
Sell a futures contract for $450 for delivery of one ounce in one year.	0
Total Cash Flow	**$0**
t = 1 Remove the gold from storage.	$0
Deliver the ounce of gold to close futures contract.	+450.00
Repay loan, including interest	-453.20
Total Cash Flow	**-$3.20**

If prices follow equation 2.4, the cash-and-carry arbitrage opportunity will not be available. Notice that equation 2.4 has the same form as equation 2.1, but equation 2.4 includes transaction costs.

In discussing the Cost-of-Carry model in perfect markets, we saw that, if futures prices are too high relative to spot prices, arbitrage opportunities will be available, as in Table 2.3. We now explore the transactions of Table 2.3, except we include the transaction costs of 3 percent. Table 2.6 shows these transactions. Including transaction costs in the analysis gives a loss on the same transactions that were profitable with no transaction costs. In the transactions of Table 2.3 with the same prices, the profit was $12. For perfect markets, equation 2.2 gave the no-arbitrage conditions for the reverse cash-and-carry arbitrage strategy:

$$F_{0,t} \geq S_0(1+C) \qquad (2.2)$$

Including transaction costs, we have

$$F_{0,t} \geq S_0(1-T)(1+C) \qquad (2.5)$$

Combining equations 2.4 and 2.5 gives

$$S_0(1-T)(1+C) \leq F_{0,t} \leq S_0(1+T)(1+C) \qquad (2.6)$$

Equation 2.6 defines the no-arbitrage bounds – bounds within which the futures price must remain to prevent arbitrage. In general, transaction costs force a loosening of the price relationship in equation 2.3. In perfect markets, equation 2.3 gave an exact equation for the futures price as a function of the spot price and the cost-of-carry. If the futures price deviated from that no-arbitrage price, traders could transact to reap a riskless profit without investment. For a market with transaction costs, equation 2.6 places

■ Table 2.6

ATTEMPTED REVERSE CASH-AND-CARRY GOLD ARBITRAGE

Prices for the Analysis:

Spot price of gold	$420
Future price of gold (for delivery in one year)	$450
Interest rate	10%
Transaction costs (T)	3%

Transaction	Cash Flow
t = 0 Sell one ounce of gold short, paying	
3% transaction costs.	
Receive $420(.97) = $407.40.	+$407.40
Lend the $407.40 for one year at 10%.	−$407.40
Buy one ounce of gold futures for	
delivery in one year.	0
Total Cash Flow	**$0**
t = 1 Collect loan proceeds ($407.40 x 1.1).	+$448.14
Accept gold delivery on the futures contract.	−$450.00
Use gold from futures delivery to	
repay short sale.	0
Total Cash Flow	**−$1.86**

bounds on the futures price. If the futures price goes beyond these boundaries, arbitrage is possible. The futures price can wander within the bounds without offering arbitrage opportunities, however. As an example, consider the bounds implied by the transactions in Table 2.5. With no transaction costs, the futures price must be exactly $440 to exclude arbitrage. With the 3 percent transaction costs on spot market transactions, the futures price can lie between $426.80 and $453.20 without allowing arbitrage, as Table 2.7 shows.

Figure 2.5 illustrates the concept of arbitrage boundaries. The vertical axis graphs futures prices and the horizontal axis shows the time dimension. The solid horizontal line in the graph shows the no-arbitrage condition for a perfect market. In a perfect market, the futures price must exactly equal the spot price times 1 plus the cost of carry, $F_{0,t} = S_0(1 + C)$. With transaction costs, however, we have a lower and an upper bound. If the futures price goes above the upper no-arbitrage bound, there will be a cash-and-carry

---

■ **Table 2.7**

ILLUSTRATION OF NO-ARBITRAGE BOUNDS

Prices for the Analysis:

Spot price of gold	$400
Interest rate	10%
Transaction costs (T)	3%

No-Arbitrage Futures Price in Perfect Markets

$$F_{0,t} = S_0(1 + C) = \$400(1.1) = \$440$$

Upper No-Arbitrage Bound with Transaction Costs

$$F_{0,t} \le S_0(1 + T)(1 + C) = \$400(1.03)(1.1) = \$453.20$$

Lower No-Arbitrage Bound with Transaction Costs

$$F_{0,t} \ge S_0(1 - T)(1 + C) = \$400(.97)(1.1) = \$426.80$$

■ Figure 2.5

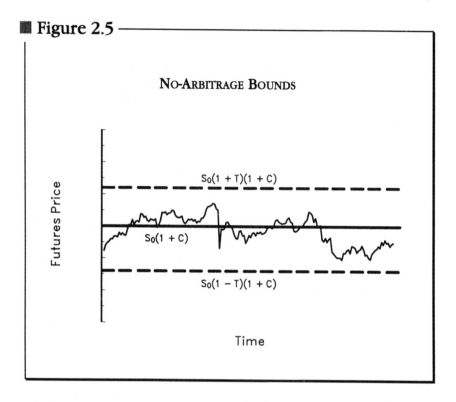

No-Arbitrage Bounds

Futures Price

$S_0(1 + T)(1 + C)$

$S_0(1 + C)$

$S_0(1 - T)(1 + C)$

Time

arbitrage opportunity. This occurs when $F_{0,t} > S_0(1 + T)(1 + C)$. Likewise, if the futures price falls too low, it will be less than the lower no-arbitrage bound. Futures prices that are too low relative to the spot price give rise to a reverse cash-and-carry arbitrage. This opportunity arises when $F_0 < S_0(1 - T)(1 + C)$. Figure 2.5 shows these no-arbitrage boundaries as dotted lines.

If the futures price stays between the bounds, no arbitrage is possible. If the futures price crosses the boundaries, arbitrageurs will flock to the market to exploit the opportunity. For example, if the futures price is too high, traders will buy the spot commodity and sell the futures. This action will raise the price of the spot good relative to the futures price, thereby driving the futures price back within the no-arbitrage boundaries. If the futures price stays within the boundaries, no arbitrage is possible, and the arbitrageurs will not be able to affect the futures price.

From Figure 2.5 we can note three important points. First, the greater the transaction costs, T, the farther apart are the bounds. With higher transaction costs, the arbitrage relationships we have been exploring are less binding on possible prices. Second, we have been assuming that all traders in the market face the same percentage transaction costs, T. Clearly, different traders face different transaction costs. For example, a retail trader, who is not an exchange member, can face transaction costs that are much higher than those for a floor trader. It is easily possible for the retail trader to pay as much as 100 times the exchange and brokerage fees paid by a floor trader. Therefore, Figure 2.5 really pertains to a particular trader, not to every trader in the market. Consider a trader facing higher transaction costs of $2T$ instead of T. For this trader, the no-arbitrage bounds would be twice as wide as those in Figure 2.5. Third, we have seen that market forces exist to keep the futures price within the no-arbitrage bounds and that each trader faces his or her own particular bounds, depending on that trader's transaction costs.

Differences in transaction costs give rise to the concept of quasi-arbitrage. Some traders, such as small retail customers, face full transaction costs. Other traders, such as large financial institutions, have much lower transaction costs. For example, exchange members pay much lower transaction costs than outside traders. Therefore, the quasi-arbitrageur is a potential cash-and-carry or reverse cash-and-carry trader with relatively lower transaction costs. The futures price should stay within the bounds of the lowest transaction cost trader. Once the futures price drifts beyond the bounds of the lowest transaction cost trader, he or she will exploit the arbitrage opportunity. As we have seen, arbitrage activity will drive the futures price back within the no-arbitrage bounds for that trader.

Therefore, in the actual market, we expect to see futures prices within the no-arbitrage bounds of the lowest transaction cost trader. This means that traders with higher transaction costs will not be able to exploit any arbitrage opportunities. If prices start to drift away from the perfect markets equality of equation 2.3, they will be exploited first by the traders with low transaction costs. This exploitation will take place through quasi-arbitrage, because the low transaction cost trader does not face the full transaction costs of an outside trader. Other market imperfections have a similar effect – they widen the no-arbitrage bounds, such as those illustrated in Figure 2.5.

PRICING INTEREST RATE FUTURES CONTRACTS

In this section, we apply the Cost-of-Carry model to interest rate futures under the initial assumption of perfect markets. In addition, we assume that the only carrying charge is the interest rate to finance the holding of a good, and we assume that we can disregard the special features of a given futures contract. For example, we ignore the options that sellers of futures contracts may hold, such as the option to substitute various grades of the commodity at delivery or the option to choose the exact delivery date within the delivery month, and we ignore the differences between forward and futures prices that may result from the daily resettlement cash flows on the futures contract. Later in this chapter, we relax some of these assumptions.

Each interest rate futures contract specifies the maturity of the deliverable bond. For example, the T-bill futures contract requires that a deliverable T-bill must have a maturity of 90–92 days. This requirement applies on the delivery date. As we saw earlier, the cash-and-carry strategy involves selling a futures contract, buying the spot commodity, and storing it until the futures delivery date. Then the trader delivers the good against the futures contract. For example, if the futures price of gold is too high relative to the cash market price of gold, a trader could engage in a cash-and-carry arbitrage. Part of this strategy would involve buying gold, storing it until the futures expiration, and delivering the gold against the futures contract.

To apply this strategy in the interest rate futures market, we must be very careful. For example, if a T-bill futures contract expires in 77 days, we cannot buy a 90-day T-bill and store it for future delivery. If we attempt to do so, we will find ourselves with a 13-day T-bill on the delivery date, which will not be deliverable against the futures contract. Therefore, to apply a cash-and-carry strategy, a trader must buy a bond that will still have or come to have the correct properties on the delivery date. For our T-bill cash-and-carry strategy, the trader must secure a 167-day T-bill to carry for 77 days. Then the bill will have the requisite 90 days remaining until expiration on the delivery date.

We illustrate the cash-and-carry strategy with an example. Consider the data in Table 2.8. The yields used in Table 2.8 are calculated according to the bond pricing formula. The example

▩ Table 2.8

	Futures	Yield According to the Bond Pricing Formula
INTEREST RATE FUTURES AND ARBITRAGE		
Today's Date: January 5		
MAR Contract (Matures in 77 days on March 22)		12.50%
Cash Bills:		
167-day T-bill (Deliverable on MAR futures)		10.00
77-day T-bill		6.00

assumes perfect markets, including the assumption that one can either borrow or lend at any of the riskless rates represented by the T-bill yields. These restrictive assumptions will be relaxed momentarily. The data presented in Table 2.8, and the assumptions just made, mean that an arbitrage opportunity is present. Because the futures contract matures in 77 days, the spot 77-day rate represents the financing cost to acquire the 167-day T-bill, which can be delivered against the MAR futures contract on March 22. This is possible because the T-bill that has 167 days to maturity on January 5 will have exactly 90 days to maturity on March 22.

As the transactions in Table 2.9 indicate, an arbitrage opportunity exists because the prices and interest rates on the three instruments are mutually inconsistent. To implement a cash-and-carry strategy, a trader can sell the MAR futures and acquire the 167-day T-bill on January 5. The trader then holds the bill for delivery against the futures contract. The trader must finance the holding of the bill during the 77-day interval from January 5 to delivery on March 22. To exploit the rate discrepancy, the trader borrows at the short-term rate of 6 percent and uses the proceeds to acquire the long-term T-bill. At the maturity of the futures, the long-term T-bill has the exactly correct maturity and can be delivered against the futures contract. This strategy generates a profit of $2,235 per contract. Relative to the short-term rate, the futures yield and the long-term T-bill yield were too high. In this example, the trader acquires short-term funds at a low rate (6 percent) and reinvests those funds at a higher rate (10 percent). It may appear that this

■ Table 2.9

CASH-AND-CARRY ARBITRAGE TRANSACTIONS

January 5

Borrow $956,750 for 77 days by issuing a 77-day T-bill at 6%.
Buy 167-day T-bill yielding 10% for $956,750.
Sell MAR T-Bill futures contract with a yield of 12.50% for $970.984

March 22

Deliver the originally purchased T-bill against the MAR futures
    contract and collect $970,984.
Repay debt on 77-day T-bill that matures today for $968,749.
Profit:

$$\begin{array}{r} \$970,984 \\ -\$968,749 \\ \hline \$2,235 \end{array}$$

difference generates the arbitrage profit, but that is not completely accurate, as the next example shows.[4]

Consider the same values as shown in Table 2.8, but assume that
the rate on the 77-day T-bill is 8 percent. Now the short-term rate
is too high relative to the long-term rate and the futures yield. To
take advantage of this situation, we reverse the cash-and-carry procedure of Table 2.9, as Table 2.10 shows. In other words, we now
exploit a reverse cash-and-carry strategy. With this new set of rates,
the arbitrage is more complicated, because it involves holding the
T-bill that is delivered on the futures contract. In this situation, the
arbitrageur borrows $955,131 for 167 days at 10 percent and
invests these funds at 8 percent for the 77 days until the MAR
futures matures. The payoff from the 77 day investment of
$955,131 will be $970,894, exactly enough to pay for the delivery
of the T-bill on the futures contract. This bill is held for 90 days
until June 20 when it matures and pays $1 million. On June 20, the
arbitrageur's loan on the 167-day T-bill is also due and equals
$998,308. The trader repays this debt from the $1 million received
on the maturing bill. The strategy yields a profit of $1,692. Notice
in this second example that the trader borrowed at 10 percent and
invested the funds at 8 percent temporarily. This shows that the
entire set of rates must be consistent and that arbitrage opportu-

■ **Table 2.10** ─────────────────────────

REVERSE CASH-AND-CARRY ARBITRAGE TRANSACTIONS

January 5

Borrow $955,131 by issuing a 167-day T-bill at 10%.

Buy a 77-day T-bill yielding 8% for $955,131 that will pay $970,984 on March 22.

Buy one MAR futures contract with a yield of 12.50% for $970,984.

March 22

Collect $970,984 from the maturing 77-day T-bill.

Pay $970,984 and take delivery of a 90-day T-bill from the MAR futures contract.

June

Collect $1,000,000 from the maturing 90-day T-bill that was delivered on the futures contract.

Pay $998,308 debt on the maturing 167-day T-bill.

Profit:

$1,000,000

− $998,308

$1,692

nities need not involve only misalignment between two rates.

From our previous analysis, we know that the reverse cash-and-carry strategy involves selling an asset short and investing the proceeds from the short sale. In our example of Table 2.10, the short sale is the issuance of debt. By issuing debt, the arbitrageur actually sells a bond. A trader can also simulate a short sale by selling from inventory. The same is true for interest rate futures. For example, a bank that holds investments in T-bills can simulate a short sale by selling a T-bill from inventory.

To this point, we have considered a cash-and-carry strategy in Table 2.9 and a reverse cash-and-carry strategy in Table 2.10. These two examples show that there must be a very exact relationship among these rates on the different instruments to exclude arbitrage opportunities. If the yield on the MAR futures is 12.50 percent and the 167-day spot yield is 10 percent, only one yield for the 77-day T-bill will not give rise to an arbitrage opportunity, and that rate is 7.15 percent. To see why that is the case, consider two ways of holding a T-bill investment for the full 167-day period of the examples:

1. hold a 167-day T-bill, or
2. hold a 77-day T-bill followed by a 90-day T-bill that is delivered on the futures contract.

Because these two ways of holding T-bills cover the same time period and have the same risk level, the two positions must have the same yield to avoid arbitrage. For the examples, the necessary yield on the 77-day T-bill can be found by solving for a forward rate. This equation expresses the yield on a long-term instrument as equal to the yield on two short-term positions:

$$(1.10)^{167/360} = (1+x)^{77/360}(1.1250)^{90/360}$$

This equation holds only if the rate, x, on the 77-day T-bill equals 7.1482 percent.

We can also express the same idea in terms of the prices of the bills. To illustrate this point, consider the prices of three securities. The first is a 167-day bill that yields 10 percent and pays $1 upon maturity. The second is a T-bill future with an underlying bill having a $1 face value. With a yield of 12.50 percent, the future's price will be $.970984. Finally, the third instrument matures in 77 days, has a face value of $.970984, and yields 7.1482 percent.

$$P_{167} = \frac{\$1}{(1+r_{167})^{167/360}} = \frac{\$1}{1.1^{167/360}} = .956750$$

$$P_F = \frac{\$1}{(1+r_{fut})^{90/360}} = \frac{\$1}{1.1250^{90/360}} = .970984$$

$$P_{77} = \frac{\$.970984}{(1+r_{77})^{77/360}} = \frac{\$.970984}{1.071482^{77/360}} = .956750$$

The third instrument is peculiar, with its strange face value. However, this is exactly the payoff necessary to pay for delivery on the futures contract in 77 days. Notice also that the 77-day bill and the 167-day bill have the same price. They should, because both prices of $.956750 are the investment now that is necessary to have a $1 payoff in 167 days. The futures yield and the 167-day yield were taken as fixed. The yield on the 77-day bill, 7.1482 percent, is exactly the yield that must prevail if the two strategies are to be equivalent and to prevent arbitrage.

THE FINANCING COST AND THE IMPLIED REPO RATE

With these prices, and continuing to assume that the only carrying cost is the financing charge, we can also infer the implied repo rate. We know that the ratio of the futures price divided by the spot price equals 1 plus the implied repo rate. As we have seen, the correct spot instrument for our example is the 167-day bill, because this bill will have the appropriate delivery characteristics when the futures contract matures. Thus, we have

$$1 + C = \frac{P_F}{P_{167}} = \frac{.970984}{.956750} = 1.014878$$

Thus, the implied repo rate, C, is 1.4878 percent. This covers the cost-of-carry for 77 days from the present to the expiration of the futures. We can annualize this rate as follows:

$$1.014878^{360/77} = 1.071482$$

The annualized repo rate is 7.1482 percent. This exactly matches the interest rate on the 77-day bill that will prevent arbitrage. Therefore, assuming that the interest cost is the only carrying charge, the cost-of-carry equals the implied repo rate. This equivalence between the cost-of-carry and the implied repo rate also leads to two rules for arbitrage.

Rule 1. If the implied repo rate exceeds the financing cost, then exploit a cash-and-carry arbitrage strategy:

Borrow funds
Use the funds to buy the bond in the cash market
Sell futures to cover the cash market bond
Hold the bond and deliver it against the futures at the futures' expiration to secure the arbitrage profit

Rule 2. If the implied repo rate is less than the financing cost, then exploit a reverse cash-and-carry arbitrage strategy:

Buy futures

Sell the cash market bond short
Invest the short sale proceeds until the futures' expiration
Accept delivery on the futures
Repay short sale obligation and keep the arbitrage profit

THE FUTURES YIELD AND THE FORWARD RATE OF INTEREST

We have seen that the futures price of an interest rate futures contract implies a yield on the instrument that underlies the futures contract. We call this implied yield the futures yield. Now we continue to assume that the financing cost is the only carrying charge, that markets are perfect, that we can ignore the options the seller of a futures contract may possess, and that the price difference between forward contracts and futures contracts is negligible. Under these conditions, we can show that the futures yield must equal the forward rate of interest.

We continue to use the T-bill futures contract as our example. The T-bill futures, like many other interest rate futures contracts, has an underlying instrument that will be delivered when the contract expires. The SEP 1996 contract calls for the delivery of a 90-day T-bill that will mature in December 1996. The futures yield covers the 90-day span of time from delivery in September to maturity in December 1996. It is possible to compute forward rates from the term structure. Given the necessary set of spot rates, it is possible to compute a forward rate to cover any given period.

To illustrate the equivalence between futures yields and forward rates under our assumptions, we continue to use our example of a T-bill with a 167-day holding period. Let us assume the following spot yields:

For a 167-day bill	10.0000%
For a 77-day bill	7.1482%

These two spot rates imply a forward rate to cover the period from day 77 to day 167:

$$(1 + r_{0,167})^{167/360} = (1 + r_{0,77})^{77/360}(1 + r_{77,167})^{90/360}$$

Substituting values for the spot bills and solving for the forward rate, $r_{77,167}$, gives

$$(1.10)^{167/360} = (1.071482)^{77/360}(1 + r_{77,167})^{90/360}$$

$$(1 + r_{77,167})^{90/360} = \frac{(1.10)^{167/360}}{(1.071482)^{77/360}} = \frac{1.045205}{1.014877} = 1.02988$$

$$1 + r_{77,167} = 1.1250$$

$$r_{77,167} = .1250$$

Therefore, the forward rate, to cover day 77 to day 167, is 12.50 percent. As we saw earlier, the futures yield is also 12.50 percent for the T-bill futures that expires on day 77. Therefore, the futures yield equals the forward rate for the same period. In deriving this result, we must bear our assumptions in mind: markets are perfect, the financing cost is the only carrying charge, and we can ignore the seller's options and the difference between forward and futures prices.

THE COST-OF-CARRY MODEL FOR T-BOND FUTURES

In this section, we apply the Cost-of-Carry model to the T-bond futures contract. In essence, the same concepts apply, with one difference. The holder of a T-bond receives cash flows from the bond. This affects the cost-of-carry that the holder of the bond actually incurs. For example, assume that the coupon rate on a $100,000 face value T-bond is 8 percent and the trader finances the bond at 8 percent. In this case, the net carrying charge is zero – the earnings offset the financing cost.

To illustrate this idea, let us assume that, on January 5, a T-bond that is deliverable on a futures contract has an 8 percent coupon and costs 100.00. The trader faces a financing rate of 7.1482 percent for the 77 days until the futures contract is deliverable. Because the T-bond has an 8 percent coupon rate, the conversion factor is 1.0 and plays no role.[5]

With an 8 percent coupon, the accrued interest from the date of purchase to the delivery date on the futures is

$$(77/182)(.04)(100,000) = \$1,692$$

Therefore, the invoice amount will be $101,692. If this is the invoice amount in 77 days, the T-bond must cost the present value of that amount, discounted for 77 days at the 77-day rate of 7.1482 percent. This implies a cost for the T-bond of $100,200. If the price is less than $100,200, a cash-and-carry arbitrage strategy will be available. Under these circumstances the cash-and-carry strategy would have the cash flows shown in Table 2.11. The transactions in Table 2.11 show that the futures price must adjust to reflect the accrual of interest. The bond in Table 2.11 had no coupon payment during the 77-day interval, but the same adjustment must be made to account for cash throw-offs that the bondholder receives during the holding period.

INTEREST RATE FUTURES PRICING: AN EXAMPLE

We conclude our discussion of interest rate futures pricing by applying the Cost-of-Carry model to actual market data. For this illustration, we consider the difference between the SEP and DEC 1989 T-bond futures prices. Under the simplifying assumptions made earlier, we would expect these two prices to be closely related by the financing cost of carrying a bond from September to December 1989. We know that market imperfections, the difference between futures and forward prices, and the seller's options might all disturb this relationship. Nonetheless, we expect the main component of this price difference to be tied to the financing cost from September to December.

■ **Table 2.11**

CASH-AND-CARRY TRANSACTIONS FOR A T-BOND

January 5

Borrow $100,200 for 77 days at the 77-day rate of 7.1482 percent.
Buy the 8% T-bond for $100,200.
Sell one T-bond futures contract for $101,692.

March 22

Deliver T-bond; receive invoice amount of $101,692.
Repay loan of $101,692.

Profit: 0

To apply this idea to actual data, we use the SEP 1989 T-bill futures contract to provide a proxy for the financing rate to hold a T-bond from September to December 1989. To accept delivery on the SEP 1989 T-bond futures and carry the delivered bond forward to the December delivery involves paying the invoice price to acquire the bond, financing the bond for three months at the SEP 1989 T-bill rate, receiving the accrued interest on the bond, which we estimate as having an 8 percent coupon rate, and selling the DEC 1989 futures. In a perfect market, this strategy should yield a zero profit. In other words, we expect the quantity

$$F_{0,d} + AI - F_{0,n}(1+C) = 0 \qquad (2.7)$$

where

$F_{0,d}$ = DEC 1989 T-bond futures price

$F_{0,n}$ = SEP 1989 T-bond futures price plus accrued interest due at delivery

C = three-month cost-of-carry estimated from SEP 89 T-bill futures

AI = interest accrued from T-bond in December, estimated at \$2,000 per contract

Figure 2.6 graphs the value of equation 2.7 for a one contract position. In an absolutely perfect market, we expect the value to be zero. As Figure 2.6 shows, it is extremely close to zero. The minimum value is –\$318, and the maximum value is \$105. Thus, the graph of the value of equation 2.7 ranges from –3/10 of 1 percent to +1/10 of 1 percent. These values are all the closer considering the crude estimate of the accrued interest and that we did not even attempt to find the cheapest-to-deliver bond. Presumably, a more exacting analysis would lead to yet smaller discrepancies.

INTEREST RATE FUTURES AND THE YIELD CURVE

The yield curve is extremely important for bond investing and bond portfolio management. The different maturities of bonds and their commensurate yields allows investors to commit their money for different periods of time to take advantage of a particular shape that the yield curve might possess at any given moment.

■ Figure 2.6

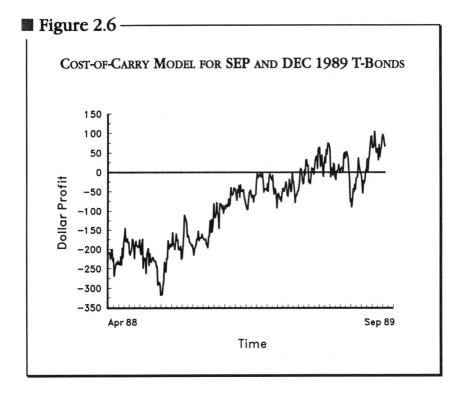

COST-OF-CARRY MODEL FOR **SEP** AND **DEC 1989** T-BONDS

In the interest rate futures markets, the exchanges have made a conscious effort to offer interest-rate futures that cover the yield curve. For example, the International Monetary Market (IMM) of the Chicago Mercantile Exchange (CME) has specialized in the shorter maturity instruments. The IMM currently offers interest rate futures contracts on Treasury bills, bank CDs, and Eurodollar deposits, all with maturities of about three months. By contrast, the Chicago Board of Trade (CBOT) has focused on the longer maturities. The CBOT trades a contract on long-term T-bonds, the most successful futures contract ever introduced. It also offers contracts on 2-, 5-, and 10-year Treasury notes.

To illustrate the connection between the yield curve and interest rate futures, we will focus on the IMM's T-bill contract. This contract calls for the delivery of T-bills with a face value of $1 million having 90 days to maturity at the time of delivery. Prices for the T-bill futures are quoted according to a system known as the IMM Index. The IMM Index is simply the discount yield on the T-bill futures subtracted from 100. So, for example, a quoted settlement value of 94.00 means that the futures yield would be 6 percent. To contract for delivery of a 90-day T-bill with a futures price of 94.00, for example, a trader would have to agree to pay a price that was commensurate with a discount yield of 6 percent.

As we noted before in our discussion of arbitrage, an important relationship between yields is implied by futures prices and the yields on spot market instruments. Essentially, interest rate futures yields may be interpreted as forward rates of interest. For example, the yield of the March 1996 T-bill futures contract is the forward rate of interest for a 90-day T-bill to run from March to June 1996. In other words, if we calculated from the spot market the forward rate for the same period as that covered by the March 1996 T-bill futures contract, we should find a result that almost exactly matches the yield on the T-bill futures.

If that were not the case and markets were perfect, it would be possible to generate arbitrage profits. This would be accomplished by buying and selling spot market T-bills and T-bill futures to take advantage of the yield discrepancy. In fact, if markets were perfect and included in this is the opportunity for unrestricted short selling, the forward rates of interest and the yield on the futures contract would have to be exactly equal. Actual markets, however, are not perfect, so the relationship would not have to hold exactly. If we take into account transaction costs, though, the difference between the forward rate of interest calculated from the spot market and the rate of interest implied by the futures contract would still have to be very close.

STOCK INDEX FUTURES PRICES

Like most financial futures, stock index futures essentially trade in a full-carry market. Therefore, the Cost-of-Carry model provides a virtually complete understanding of stock index futures pricing. When the conditions of the Cost-of-Carry model are violated, arbitrage opportunities arise. For a cash-and-carry strategy, a trader would buy the stocks that underlie the futures contract and sell the futures. The trader would then carry these stocks until the futures expiration. The cash-and-carry strategy is attractive when stocks are priced too low relative to the futures. In a reverse cash-and-carry strategy, the trader would sell the stocks short and invest the proceeds, in addition to buying the futures. The reverse cash-and-carry strategy is attractive when stocks are priced too high relative to the futures. Thus, any discrepancy between the futures and cash market prices would lead to a profit at the expiration of the futures simply by exploiting the appropriate strategy.

THE COST-OF-CARRY MODEL FOR STOCK INDEX FUTURES

Applying equation 2.3 to stock index futures involves the complication of dividends. Holding the stocks gives the owner dividends; however, each of the indexes is simply a price index. The value of the index at any time depends solely on the prices of the stocks, not the dividends that the underlying stocks might pay. Because the futures prices are tied directly to the index values, the futures prices do not include dividends.

To fit stock index futures, equation 2.3 must be adjusted to include the dividends that would be received between the present and the expiration of the futures. In essence, the chance to receive dividends lowers the cost of carrying the stocks. Carrying stocks requires that a trader finance the purchase price of the stock from the present until the futures expiration. However, the trader will receive dividends from the stock, which will reduce the value of the stocks. This contrasts directly with the cost-of-carry for holding a commodity like gold. As we have seen, gold generates no cash flows, so the cost-of-carry for gold is essentially the financing cost. For stocks, the cost-of-carry is the financing cost for the stock less the dividends received while the stock is carried.

As an example, assume the present is time zero and a trader decides to engage in a self-financing cash-and-carry transaction. The trader decides to buy and hold one share of Widget, Inc., currently trading for $100. Therefore, the trader borrows $100 and buys the stock. We assume that the stock will pay a $2 dividend in six months, and the trader will invest the proceeds for the remaining six months at a rate of 10 percent. Table 2.12 shows the trader's cash flows. In Table 2.12, a trader borrows funds, buys and holds a stock, receives and invests a dividend, and liquidates the portfolio after one year. At the outset, the stock costs $100, but its value in a year, P_1, is unknown. From Table 2.12, the trader's cash inflow after one year is the future value of the dividend, $2.10, plus the current value of the stock, P_1, less the repayment of the loan, $110.

■ **Table 2.12**

CASH FLOWS FROM CARRYING STOCK

t = 0

Borrow $100 for one year at 10%.	+ 100
Buy one share of Widget, Inc.	– 100

t = 6 months

Receive dividend of $2.	+ $2
Invest $2 for 6 months at 10%.	– $2

t = 1 year

Collect proceeds of $2.10 from dividend investment.	+ 2.10
Sell Widget, Inc., for P1.	+ P_1
Repay debt.	– 110.00

Total Profit: P_1 + $2.10 – $110.00

From this example, we can generalize to understand the total cash inflows from a cash-and-carry strategy. First, the cash-and-carry strategy will return the future value of the stock, P_1, at the horizon of the carrying period. Second, at the end of the carrying period, the cash-and-carry strategy will return the future value of the dividends – the dividend plus interest from the time of receipt to the horizon. Against these inflows, the cash-and-carry trader must pay the financing cost for the stock purchase.

We can now determine the futures price that is consistent with the cash-and-carry strategy. From the arguments advanced earlier, we know that equation 2.3 holds as an equality with perfect markets and unrestricted short selling. The cash-and-carry trading opportunity requires that the futures price must be less than or equal to the cash inflows at the futures expiration. Similarly, the reverse cash-and-carry trading opportunity requires that the futures price must equal or exceed the cash inflows at the futures expiration. Therefore, the stock index futures price must equal the cost of the stocks underlying the stock index, plus the cost of carrying those stocks to expiration, $S_0(1 + C)$, minus the future value of all dividends to be received, $D_i(1 + r_i)$. The future value of dividends is measured at the time the futures contract expires. More formally,

$$F_{0,t} = S_0(1+C) - \sum_{i=1}^{N} D_i(1+r_i)$$

where

$F_{0,t}$	=	the stock index futures price at $t = 0$ for a futures contract that expires at time t
S_0	=	the value of the stocks underlying the stock index at $t = 0$
C	=	the percentage cost of carrying the stocks from $t = 0$ to the expiration at time t
D_i	=	the Ith dividend
r_i	=	the interest earned on carrying the Ith dividend from its time of receipt until the futures expiration at time t

FAIR VALUE FOR STOCK INDEX FUTURES

A stock index futures price has its fair value when the futures price fits the Cost-of-Carry model. In this section we consider a simplified example of determining the fair value of a stock index futures contract. We consider a futures contract on an equally weighted index, and for simplicity we assume that there are only two stocks. Table 2.13 provides the information that we will need.

Based on the data in Table 2.13, the index value is 110.56, as given by

$$\frac{P_A + P_B}{\text{Index Divisor}} = \frac{115 + 84}{1.8} = 110.56$$

The cost of buying the stocks underlying the portfolio is simply the sum of the prices of Stocks A and B, or $199. For carrying the stocks to expiration, the interest cost will be 10 percent for 76 days or 2.11 percent. Therefore, the cost of buying and carrying the stocks to expiration is $199(1.0211) = $203.20. Offsetting this cost will be the dividends received and the interest earned on the dividends. For the stocks, the future value of the dividends at expiration will be

For Stock A:	$1.50(1.0164) = $1.52
For Stock B:	$1.00(1.0108) = $1.01

■ Table 2.13

INFORMATION FOR COMPUTING FAIR VALUE

Today's date:	July 6
Futures expiration:	September 20
Days until expiration:	76
Index:	Equally weighted index of two stocks
Index divisor:	1.80
Interest rates:	All interest rates are 10 %

Stock A

Today's price:	$115
Projected dividends:	$1.50 on July 23
Days dividend will be invested:	59
r_A:	.10(59/360) = .0164

Stock B

Today's price:	$84
Projected dividends:	$1.00 on August 12
Days dividend will be invested:	39
r_B:	.10(39/360) = .0108

Therefore, the entire cost of buying the stocks and carrying them to expiration is the purchase price of the stocks plus interest less the future value of the dividends measured at expiration:

$$\$203.20 - \$1.52 - \$1.01 = \$200.67$$

In the Cost-of-Carry model, we know that the futures price must equal this entire cost-of-carry. However, the futures price is expressed in index units, not the dollars of the actual stock prices. To find the fair value for the futures price, this cash value of $200.67 must be converted into index units by dividing by the index divisor, 200.67/1.8 = 111.48. Hence, the fair value for the futures contract is 111.48. Because it conforms to the Cost-of-Carry model, this fair value for the futures price is the price that precludes arbitrage profits from both the cash-and-carry and reverse cash-and-carry strategies.

INDEX ARBITRAGE AND PROGRAM TRADING

In the preceding section we saw how to derive the fair value futures price from the Cost-of-Carry model. From our earlier discussion, we know that deviations from the theoretical price of the Cost-of-Carry model give rise to arbitrage opportunities. If the futures price exceeds its fair value, traders will engage in cash-and-carry arbitrage. If the futures price falls below its fair value, traders can exploit the pricing discrepancy through a reverse cash-and-carry trading strategy. These cash-and-carry strategies in stock index futures are called index arbitrage. This section presents an example of index arbitrage using a simplified index with only two stocks. Because index arbitrage can require trading in many stocks, it is often implemented by using computer programs to automate the trading. Computer-directed index arbitrage is called program trading.

INDEX ARBITRAGE

Table 2.13 gave values for stocks A and B, and we saw how to compute the fair value of a stock index futures contract based on an index composed of those two stocks. With the values in Table 2.13, the cash market index value is 110.56, and the fair value for the futures contract is 111.48, where both values are expressed in index points. If the futures price exceeds the fair value, cash-and-carry index arbitrage is possible. A futures price below its fair value creates an opportunity for reverse cash-and-carry index arbitrage.

To illustrate cash-and-carry index arbitrage, assume that the data of Table 2.13 hold, but that the futures price is 115.00. Because this price exceeds the fair value, an index arbitrageur would trade as shown in Table 2.14. At the outset on July 6, the trader borrows the money necessary to purchase the stocks in the index, buys the stocks, and sells the futures. On July 23 and August 12, the trader receives dividends from the two stocks and invests the dividends to the expiration date at 10 percent. Like all stock index futures, our simple example uses cash settlement. Therefore, at expiration on September 20, the final futures settlement price is set equal to the cash market index value. This ensures that the futures and cash prices converge and that the basis – the cash price minus the futures price – goes to zero.[6]

■ Table 2.14 ─────────────

CASH-AND-CARRY INDEX ARBITRAGE

Date	Cash Market	Futures Market
July 6	Borrow $199 for 76 days at 10%. Buy Stock A and Stock B for a total outlay of $199.	Sell one SEP index futures contract for 115.00.
July 23	Receive dividend of $1.50 from Stock A and invest for 59 days at 10%.	
Aug 12	Receive dividend of $1.00 from Stock B and invest for 39 days at 10%.	
Sept 20	**For illustrative purposes, assume any values for stock prices at expiration. We assume that stock prices did not change. Therefore, the index value is still 110.56.**	
	Receive proceeds from invested dividends of $1.52 and $1.01. Sell Stock A for $115 and Stock B for $84. Total proceeds are $201.53. Repay debt of $203.20.	At expiration, the futures price is set equal to the spot index value of 110.56. This gives a profit of 4.44 index units. In dollar terms, this is 4.44 index units times the index divisor of 1.8.
	Loss: $1.67	Profit: $7.99

Total Profit: $7.99 - $1.67 = $6.32

The profits or losses from the transactions in Table 2.14 do not depend on the prices that prevail at expiration on September 20. Instead, the profits come from a discrepancy between the current futures price and its fair value. To illustrate the profits, we assume that the stock prices do not change. Therefore, the cash market index is at 110.56 at expiration. As Table 2.14 shows, these transactions give a profit of $6.32.

This will be the profit no matter what happens to stock prices between July 6 and September 20. For example, assume the prices of Stocks A and B both rose by $5, to $120 and $89, respectively. The cash market cash flows will then come from the sale of the shares, the future value of the dividends, and the debt repayment:

Sale of Stock A	+120.00
Sale of Stock B	+89.00
Future value of dividends on Stock A	+1.52
Future value of dividends on Stock B	+1.01
Debt repayment	-203.20
Futures profit/loss	-2.01

On the futures transaction, the index value at expiration will then equal 116.11 = (120 + 89)/1.8. This gives a futures loss of 1.11 index points, or $2.01. Taking all of these cash flows together, the profit is still $6.32. The profit will be the same no matter what happens to stock prices.

If the futures price is too low relative to the fair value, arbitrageurs can engage in reverse cash-and-carry transactions. For example, assume that the futures price is 105.00, well below its fair value of 111.48. Now the arbitrageur will trade as shown in Table 2.15. Essentially, the transactions in Table 2.15 are just the opposite of those in Table 2.14. The most important difference is that the trader sells stock short. Having sold the stock short, the trader must pay the dividends on the stocks as they come due.

The transactions give the trader a net profit of $11.68. Again, this profit does not depend upon the actual stock prices that prevail at expiration. Instead, the profit comes from the discrepancy between the actual futures price of 105.00 and the fair value of 111.48. Once the trader initiates the transactions in Table 2.15, the profit will depend only on the discrepancy between the fair value and the prevailing futures price. The profit will equal the error in the futures price times the index divisor: (111.48 - 105.00)1.8 = $11.68.[7]

PROGRAM TRADING

We have illustrated the cash-and-carry and reverse cash-and-carry transactions with a hypothetical two-stock index futures contract, but real stock index futures trading involves many more stocks. The MMI is smallest with 20 stocks, while the S&P 500 contains (of course) 500 stocks, and the NYSE index has about 1,700 underlying stocks. Exploitation of index arbitrage opportunities with actual stock index futures requires trading the futures and simultaneously buying or selling the entire collection of stocks that underlie the index.

■ Table 2.15

REVERSE CASH-AND-CARRY INDEX ARBITRAGE

Date	Cash Market	Futures Market
July 6	Sell Stock A and Stock B for a total of $199. Lend $199 for 76 days at 10%	Buy one SEP index futures contract for 105.00.
July 23	Borrow $1.50 for 59 days at 10% and pay dividend of $1.50 on Stock A	
Aug 12	Borrow $1.00 for 39 days at 10% and pay dividend of $1.00 on Stock B	
Sept 20	For illustrative purposes, assume any values for stock prices at expiration. We assume that stock prices did not change. Therefore, the index value is still 110.56.	
	Receive proceeds from investment of $203.20. Repay $1.52 and $1.01 on money borrowed to pay dividends on Stocks A and B. Buy Stock A for $115 and Stock B for $84. Return stocks to repay short sale.	At expiration, the futures price is set equal to the spot index value of 110.56. This gives a profit of 5.56 index units. In dollar terms, this is 5.56 index units times the index divisor of 1.8.
	Profit: $1.67	Profit: $10.01

Total Profit: $1.67 + $10.01 = $11.68

If we focus on the S&P 500 futures contract, we can see that the transactions of Tables 2.14 and 2.15 call for the buying or selling of 500 stocks. The success of the arbitrage depends upon identifying the misalignment between the futures price and the fair futures price. However, at a given moment the fair futures price depends upon the current price of 500 different stocks. Identifying an index arbitrage opportunity requires the ability to instantly find pricing discrepancies between the futures price and the fair futures price reflecting 500 different stocks. In addition, exploiting the arbitrage opportunity requires trading 500 stocks at the prices that created the arbitrage opportunity. Enter the computer!

Large financial institutions can communicate orders to trade stock via their computer for very rapid execution. Faced with a cash-and-carry arbitrage opportunity, one of these large traders could execute a computer order to buy every stock represented in the S&P 500. Simultaneously, the institution would sell the S&P 500 futures contract. The use of computers to execute large and complicated stock market orders is called **program trading**. Although computers are used for other kinds of stock market transactions, index arbitrage is the main application of program trading. Often index arbitrage and program trading are used interchangeably.

PROGRAM TRADING AND STOCK MARKET VOLATILITY

Program trading strategies can lead to massive orders to buy or sell stocks, and some observers have maintained that program trading may have led to increasing stock market volatility and may even have played a role in market disruptions, such as the crash of October 1987. These issues are highly controversial and the subject of continuing investigation. Therefore, the following summary of current thinking must be regarded as provisional.

General Stock Market Volatility There has been a general impression of increased volatility in the stock market. This view has been strengthened by occurrences such as the October 1987 crash and the frequency of days with 50-point swings in the Dow. However, most studies of stock market volatility conclude that volatility in the 1980s (the period of stock index futures trading) was not noticeably more volatile than other periods. So, there does not seem to be a general increase in the overall volatility in the stock market.

Episodic Volatility Even though overall volatility may not have increased, some scholars have been concerned that short-term volatility may be higher due to stock index futures trading. For example, the massive orders associated with program trading might lead to temporary episodes of extremely high volatility, even though the month-to-month volatility shows no real change. This concern focuses on the volatility for a period of a day or even an hour, and these bursts of volatility have become known as **episodic volatility** or **jump volatility**. The bulk of evidence suggests a connection between stock index futures trading and jump volatility. However, the evidence does not suggest that the temporary increase in volatility associated with futures trading impairs the functioning of the stock market.[8] As we noted at the beginning of this discussion, these issues of stock market volatility and the role of futures markets in contributing to volatility remain very controversial.

PREDICTING DIVIDEND PAYMENTS AND INVESTMENT RATES

In the example of computing fair value from Table 2.13, we assumed certainty about the amount, timing, and investment rates for the dividends on Stocks A and B. In the actual market, these quantities are highly predictable, but they are not certain. Dividend amounts and payment dates can be predicted based on the past policy of the firm. However, these quantities are far from certain until the dividend announcement date when the firm announces the amount and payment date of the dividend. In practice, there is quite a bit of variability in the payment of dividends depending on the time of year. Further, dividends tend to cluster on certain days in early March, June, September, and December.[9]

In actual practice, traders follow the dividend practices of firms to project the dividends that the stocks underlying an index will pay each day. This problem varies in difficulty from one index to the next. The MMI has only 20 very large firms with relatively stable dividend policies. By contrast, the NYSE index has about 1,700 firms. Many of these firms are small and may have irregular dividend payment patterns. Therefore, it is more difficult to predict the exact dividend stream for the NYSE or the S&P 500 index. Although the difficulties in predicting dividends may introduce some uncertainties into the cost-of-carry calculations, projections of dividends prove to be quite accurate in practice.

In our example of computing the fair value of a stock index futures contract and in our arbitrage examples, we also assumed that dividends could be invested at a known rate. In practice, it is difficult to know the exact rate that will be received on invested dividends. Knowing the exact rate to be received on invested dividends is difficult, but good predictions are possible. For the most part, the futures expiration date is not very distant, so the current short-term interest rate can provide a good estimate of the investment rate for dividends.

MARKET IMPERFECTIONS AND STOCK INDEX FUTURES PRICES

Earlier, we saw that four different types of market imperfections could affect the pricing of futures contracts, and we also saw that the effect of these market imperfections is to create a band of no-arbitrage prices within which the futures price must fall. In this section we consider these imperfections briefly in the context of stock index futures.

Direct transaction costs affect stock index futures trading to a considerable extent. Relative to many goods, transaction costs for stocks are low in percentage terms. Nonetheless, stock traders face commissions, exchange fees, and a bid-asked spread. In general, these costs may be about one-half of 1 percent for stock market transactions. Even with such modest transaction costs, we cannot expect the Cost-of-Carry model to hold as an exact equality. Instead, these transactions costs will lead to a no-arbitrage band of permissible stock index futures prices.

Unequal borrowing and lending costs, margins, and restrictions on short selling all play a role in stock index futures pricing. In the stock market, the restrictions on short selling are quite explicit. The Federal Reserve Board will not allow a trader to use more than 50 percent of the proceeds from a short sale. The short seller's broker may restrict that usage to an even smaller percentage. As we have seen, these factors all force slight discrepancies in the Cost-of-Carry model. The pricing relationship of equation 2.8 holds as an approximation, not with exactitude. Thus, these market imperfections create a no-arbitrage band of permissible futures prices. However, a highly competitive trading environment and low transaction costs keep this no-arbitrage band quite tight around the perfect markets theoretical fair value of equation 2.8.

Because the stocks of the MMI, S&P 500, and NYSE indexes are so widely held by financial institutions with low transaction costs, quasi-arbitrage is a dominant feature of stock index futures trading. As an example of the importance of quasi-arbitrage, consider the differential use of short sale proceeds for a retail customer and a pension fund with a large stock portfolio. Assume that the retail customer must sell a stock short through a broker. This customer will be able to use only half of the proceeds of the short sale. By contrast, we will assume that the pension fund already owns the

stocks necessary to sell short for the reverse cash-and-carry transaction. In this situation, the pension fund can simulate a short sale
by selling a portion of its stock portfolio. Because the pension fund
is actually selling stocks, not technically selling short, it receives
the full use of its proceeds. However, selling stocks from a portfolio is a perfect substitute for an actual short sale. Thus, the pension
fund faces substantially lower transaction costs than the retail customer for engaging in reverse cash-and-carry arbitrage. A similar
conclusion emerges from considering program trading. A small
retail trader faces enormous transaction costs in attempting to
engage in index arbitrage. The quasi-arbitrage opportunities
enjoyed by financial institutions ensure that no individual could
ever engage in index arbitrage.

SUMMARY

This chapter attempted to give a general introduction to futures
markets. It distinguished futures and forward contracts by noting
the differences in their cash flow commitments. We then examined the institutional features of futures markets, including the
flow of orders, the role of the clearinghouse, and the fulfillment of
commitments in the futures market.

Futures pricing was also explored in this chapter, with a focus
on two widely accepted models of the relationship between
futures and spot prices. One model views futures prices as being
equal to expected future spot prices. The second model uses arbitrage concepts to express a cost-of-carry relationship. If this cost-
of-carry relationship is violated, arbitrage opportunities will exist.
Although there are many different kinds of futures contracts,
including those on agricultural commodities and metals, the chapter emphasized financial futures – particularly interest rate and
stock index futures.

QUESTIONS AND PROBLEMS

1. What are the two major cash flow differences between futures
and forward contracts?
2. What problems with forward contracts are resolved by futures
contracts?
3. What are the two most important functions of the clearinghouse
of a futures exchange?

4. What is the investment for a trader who purchases a futures contract? Justify your answer.

5. What are the two ways to fulfill a futures contract commitment? Which is used more frequently? Why?

6. Explain why the futures price might reasonably be thought to equal the expected future spot price.

7. Assume that you believe the futures prices for corn are too low relative to wheat prices. Explain how you could take advantage of this belief.

8. Which is likely to have a greater variance – the basis or the cash price of a good? Why?

9. According to a widely held belief, an upward sloping yield curve generally implies that spot interest rates were expected to rise. If this is so, does it also imply that futures prices are expected to rise? Does this suggest a trading strategy? Explain.

10. Assume that you are a bond portfolio manager and that you anticipate an infusion of investable funds in three months. How could you use the futures market to hedge against unexpected changes in interest rates?

11. Assume that the spot corn price is $3.50, that it costs $.017 cents to store a bushel of corn for one month, and that the relevant cost of financing is 1 percent per month. If a corn futures contract matures in six months and the current futures price for this contract is $3.95 per bushel, explain how you would respond. Explain your transactions for one contract, assuming 5,000 bushels per contract and assuming that all storage costs must be paid at the outset of the transaction.

Suggested Readings

Chance, D. M. "The Effect of Margins on the Volatility of Stock and Derivative Markets: A Review of the Evidence." *Monograph Series in Finance and Economics* 2 (1990).

Clark, T., and M. Gibson. "Program Trading." *Quantitative International Investing: A Handbook of Analytical and Modeling Techniques and Strategies,* pp. 61–74. Chicago: Probus Publishing Company, 1990.

Edwards, F. R. "Does Futures Trading Increase Stock Market Volatility?" *Financial Analysts Journal* 44, no. 1 (January–February 1988): 63–69.

Gastineau, G. L. "Arbitrage, Program Trading, and the Tail of the Dog." *The Institutional Investor Focus on Investment Management*, pp. 101–113, Cambridge. MA: Ballinger Publishing Company, 1989.

Hsieh, D. A., and M. H. Miller. "Margin Regulation and Stock Market Volatility." *Margins and Market Integrity*, pp. 319–364. Chicago: Probus Publishing Company, 1991.

Kawaller, I. G., and T. W. Koch. "Managing Cash Flow Risk in Stock Index Futures: The Tail Hedge." *The Handbook of Derivative Instruments*, pp. 257-266. Chicago: Probus Publishing Company, 1991.

Kolb, R. *Understanding Futures Markets*, 4th ed. Miami: Kolb Publishing Company, 1994.

Kolb, R. *The Financial Derivatives Reader*. Miami: Kolb Publishing Company, 1992.

Morris, C. S., "Coordinating Circuit Breakers in Stock and Futures Markets." Federal Reserve Bank of Kansas City *Economic Review* (March–April 1990): 35–48.

Rendleman, R., and C. Carabini. "The Efficiency of the Treasury Bill Futures Market." *Journal of Finance* 34, no. 4 (September 1979): 895–914.

Tosini, P. A. "Stock Index Futures and Stock Market Activity in October 1987." *Financial Analysts Journal* 44, no. 1 (January–February 1988): 28-37.

Zurack, M. "Establishing an Arbitrage Program: Stock Index Arbitrage." *The Institutional Investor Focus on Investment Management*, pp. 115–132. Cambridge, MA: Ballinger Publishing Company, 1989.

NOTES

1. By contrast, more than 90 percent of foreign exchange forward contracts are completed by actual delivery.

2. In many cases, the owner of these goods will choose to insure these goods for himself or herself. Nonetheless, there is an implicit cost of insurance even when the owner self-insures.

3. For a very informative and readable account of repurchase agreements, see Bowsher, "Repurchase Agreements," *Instruments of the Money Market* (Richmond, Va.: Federal Reserve Bank of Richmond, 1981).

4. For studies of this approach to pricing T-bill futures, see I. Kawaller and T. Koch, "Cash-and-Carry Trading and the Pricing

of Treasury Bill Futures," *The Journal of Futures Markets* 4, no. 2 (Fall 1984): 115-123.

5. The T-bond futures contract is quite complex, and our discussion abstracts from many of its features. For a comprehensive discussion of the features of the contract, see R. W. Kolb, *Understanding Futures Markets,* 3rd ed. (Miami: Kolb Publishing, 1991).

6. Trading for the S&P 500 and the NYSE futures contracts ends on one day, and the final settlement price is set at the next day's opening price.

7. These calculations are sometimes off by a penny or two due to rounding.

8. For a discussion of stock index futures and stock market volatility with references to many specific studies, see R. W. Kolb, *Understanding Futures Markets,* 4th ed. (Miami: Kolb Publishing, 1994).

9. G. Gastineau and A. Madansky, "S&P 500 Stock Index Futures Evaluation Tables," *Financial Analysts Journal* 39, no. 6 (November-December 1983): 68-76, were among the first to recognize the importance of the daily dividend flows for stock index futures pricing.

Chapter 3

Options

OVERVIEW

Options markets are very diverse and have their own particular jargon. As a consequence, understanding options requires a grasp of the institutional details and terminology employed in the market. The chapter begins with a discussion of the institutional background of options markets, including the kinds of contracts traded and the price quotations for various options.

The successful option trader must also understand the pricing relationships that prevail in the options market. For example, how much should an option to buy IBM at $100 be worth if IBM is selling at $120? With IBM trading at $120, how much more would an option be worth if it required a payment of only $90 instead of $100? Similarly, how much would an option to sell IBM for $115 be worth if IBM is trading at $120? These are the kinds of questions that prospective option investors need to have answered. Fortunately, the pricing principles for options are well developed. The particular answers to these questions may sometimes be surprising, but they are very logical upon reflection.

For a potential speculator in options, these pricing relationships are of the greatest importance. As in the futures market, much option speculation relies on techniques of **spreading**, which involves trading two or more related options to create a single position. This chapter examines some of the speculative strategies that investors might utilize. However, options are also important for hedging, and the use of options for risk control is a well-defined area of study that is also very important for understanding and utilizing options markets. For example, options contracts on stock indexes have gained wide acceptance among portfolio managers as a potential tool for controlling the risk of their equity portfolios.

One of the more recent developments in options is the trading of options on futures contracts. For example, a trader can buy an option that allows him or her to enter the futures contract at a particular price, no matter what the market of the futures contract might be. Obviously, this kind of instrument involving both options and futures contracts is more complicated than an option or a futures contract alone. Nonetheless, these options on futures have already received a wide acceptance for some contracts.

As a result of the proliferation of these contracts, there are many ways to contract for the same good. This is very clear in the case of foreign currencies. For example, there are futures contracts on foreign currencies, such as the deutsche mark. There are also options on marks, and even an option on the mark futures contract. The chapter concludes by exploring options on futures in general, and the variety of instruments traded on foreign currencies, including futures, options, and options on futures.

CALL AND PUT OPTIONS

As discussed in Chapter 1, there are two major classes of options, call options and put options. Ownership of a **call option** gives the owner the right to buy a particular good at a certain price, with that right lasting until a particular date. Ownership of a **put option** gives the owner the right to sell a particular good at a specified price, with that right lasting until a particular date. For every option, there is both a buyer and a seller. In the case of a call option, the seller receives a payment from the buyer and gives the buyer the option of buying a particular good from the seller at a certain price, with that right lasting until a particular date. Similarly, the seller of a put option receives a payment from the buyer. The buyer then has the right to sell a particular good to the seller at a certain price for a specified period of time.

In all cases, ownership of an option involves the right, but not the obligation, to make a certain transaction. The owner of a call option may, for example, buy the good at the contracted price during the life of the option, but there is no obligation to do so. Likewise, the owner of a put option may sell the good under the terms of the option contract, but there is no obligation to do so. Selling an option does commit the seller to specific obligations. The seller of a call option receives a payment from the buyer, and in exchange for this payment, the seller of the call option (or simply, the call) must be ready to sell the given good to the owner of the call, if the owner of the call so wishes. The discretion to engage in further transactions always lies with the owner or buyer of an option. Option sellers have no such discretion. They have obligated themselves to perform in certain ways if the owners of the options so desire. Later in this chapter we will see the conditions under which buyers and sellers find it reasonable to act in different ways.

OPTION TERMINOLOGY

A great deal of special terminology is associated with the options market. The seller of an option is also known as the **writer** of an option, and the act of selling an option is called **writing an option**. The owner of the call who takes advantage of the option is said to **exercise** the option. An owner would exercise a call option by buying a good under the terms of an option contract. Each option contract stipulates a price that will be paid if the option is exercised, and this price is known as the **exercise price, strike price,** or the **striking price**. In our first example of the call option to buy IBM at $100 when it is selling at $120, the exercise price would be $100, because this is the amount that must be paid at exercise.

Every option involves a payment from the buyer to the seller. This payment is simply the price of the option, but it is also called the **option premium**. Also, every option traded on an exchange is valid for only a limited period of time. For example, an option on IBM might be valid only through August of the present year. The option has no validity after its **expiration date** or **maturity**. This special terminology is used widely in the options market and throughout the rest of this chapter.

TYPES OF OPTIONS

Many different kinds of options are traded actively on a variety of option exchanges. Perhaps the best known among these are options on individual stocks. However, options also trade on stock indexes, interest rate instruments, precious metals indexes, foreign currencies, and futures contracts. Table 3.1 lists the major option exchanges in the United States and the instruments that they trade.

■ **Table 3.1**

MAJOR U.S. OPTIONS EXCHANGES AND GOODS TRADED

American Stock Exchange	Stocks; options on individual stocks and stock indexes
Chicago Board of Trade	Futures; options on futures, precious metals, stock indexes, and debt instruments
Chicago Board Options Exchange	Options on individual stocks, stock indexes, and Treasury securities
Chicago Mercantile Exchange	Futures and options on futures
Coffee, Sugar and Cocoa Exchange	Futures and options on futures
Commodity Exchange (COMEX)	Futures and options on futures
Kansas City Board of Trade	Futures and options on futures
MidAmerica Commodity Exchange	Futures and options on futures
Minneapolis Grain Exchange	Futures and options on futures
New York Cotton Exchange	Futures and options on futures
New York Futures Exchange	Futures and options on stock indexes
New York Mercantile Exchange	Futures and options on futures
New York Stock Exchange	Stocks and options on individual stocks and a stock index
Pacific Stock Exchange	Options on individual stocks and a stock index
Philadelphia Stock Exchange	Stocks, futures, and options on individual stocks, currencies, and stock indexes

OPTION QUOTATIONS

No matter what the exchange or the good underlying the option, the quotations are similar. Because the market for individual stocks is the oldest and has the most overall trading activity, we will use the quotations for IBM to illustrate the basic features of the prices. Figure 3.1 shows the quotations for call and put options on individual stocks from *The Wall Street Journal*, including options on IBM in particular. Options on IBM trade on the Chicago Board Options Exchange (CBOE) and the quotations pertain to the close of trading on the previous trading day.

Beneath the identifier "IBM," the quotations list the closing price of IBM stock for the day, while the second column lists the various striking prices or exercise prices that are available for IBM. The striking prices are kept fairly near the prevailing price of the stock. As the stock price fluctuates, new striking prices are opened for trading, at intervals of $5. As a consequence, volatile stocks are likely to have a greater range of striking prices available for trading at any one time. Each contract is written on 100 shares, but the prices quoted are on a per-share basis. Upon payment, the owner of the call would have the right to purchase 100 shares of IBM for the exercise price of, we assume, $100 per share, and this right would last until the expiration date. For the purchaser of the option, the total price to acquire a share of IBM would be the option premium plus the exercise price. The option writer would receive the premium as soon as the contract is initiated, and this amount belongs to the option writer no matter what develops. However, the option writer is obligated to sell 100 shares of IBM to the call purchaser for $100 per share, if the option purchaser chooses to exercise the option. However, the purchaser must exercise the option before it expires.[1]

Obviously, the right to buy IBM at $100 per share, when the market price of IBM is above $100, is very valuable. By contrast, there is also a put option traded on IBM, which allows the owner to sell a share of IBM for, we assume, $100. Investors are not willing to pay very much for the right to sell IBM at $100 via an options contract if it could be sold for more than $100 in the marketplace.

A number of important features about options can be illustrated from price quotations, such as those shown in Figure 3.1. First, for any given expiration, the lower the striking price for a call, the greater will be the price. Similarly, the longer the time to expira-

■ Figure 3.1

QUOTATIONS FOR OPTIONS ON INDIVIDUAL STOCKS

LISTED OPTION QUOTATIONS

Tuesday, March 28, 1995

Composite volume and close for actively traded equity and LEAPS, or long-term options, with results for the corresponding put or call contract. Volume figures are unofficial. Open interest is total outstanding for all exchanges and reflects previous trading day. Close when possible is shown for the underlying stock on primary market. **CB**-Chicago Board Options Exchange. **AM**-American Stock Exchange. **PB**-Philadelphia Stock Exchange. **PC**-Pacific Stock Exchange. **NY**-New York Stock Exchange. **XC**-Composite. **p**-Put.

MOST ACTIVE CONTRACTS

Option/Strike		Vol	Exch	Last	Net Chg	a-Close	Open Int	Option/Strike		Vol	Exch	Last	Net Chg	a-Close	Open Int
Olicom	Apr 10	p18,187	CB	5⁄16	...	11⅛	277	Intel	Apr 80	2,268	AM	9	+ 7⁄8	88½	9,628
MicrTc	Apr 70	5,741	XC	15	+ 4	84½	9,226	I B M	Apr 85	2,179	CB	17⁄16	− ¼	84½	15,065
MicrTc	Apr 75	5,658	XC	11	+ 3½	84½	6,568	Intel	Apr 80	p 2,097	AM	¼	− 3⁄16	88½	6,366
MicrTc	Apr 85	5,104	XC	4	+ 1⅞	84½	2,287	D S C	Apr 30	2,052	AM	4⅞	+ ½	34½	2,189
MicrTc	Apr 80	4,696	XC	7¼	+ 3⅛	84½	5,449	LDDS	Sep 25	2,025	PC	3⅛	− 5⁄8	25⅜	3,019
Dig Eq	Apr 35	4,381	XC	3⅜	+ 1	38	8,042	Carmrk	May 15	2,010	XC	5	+ 7⁄8	19¾	440
TelMex	Apr 30	3,911	XC	13⁄16	− 5⁄16	28⅜	36,397	IntrDig	Apr 15	1,992	PC	1¼	+ 3⁄8	12⅝	9,286
Dig Eq	Jul 35	3,412	XC	5¼	+ 1¼	38	3,205	Teldyn	May 25	1,911	CB	2½	...	26⅜	...
Biogen	Apr 40	3,306	XC	3	+ 2	42	2,391	Motrla	Apr 55	1,867	AM	3	+ ⅛	56⅜	17,383
LDDS	Sep 30	3,135	PC	13⁄16	− ¼	25⅜	7,705	TelMex	Apr 30	1,861	XC	2¹⁄16	− 7⁄16	28⅜	6,997
Compaq	Apr 35	2,873	PC	15⁄16	+ 1⁄16	35	21,284	Intel	Apr 75	1,844	AM	14	+ 7⁄8	88½	10,735
Intel	Apr 85	2,787	AM	4⅞	+ ¾	88½	11,106	Motrla	Apr 60	1,793	AM	5⁄8	...	56⅜	20,806
Intel	Apr 90	2,781	AM	2	+ 3⁄8	88½	3,348	WelptH	Apr 35	1,766	XC	1¼	+ ¼	34⅜	1,391
Intel	Apr 85	p 2,555	AM	1¹⁄16	− 5⁄16	88½	2,783	CalGlf	Apr 15	p 1,653	XC	1⅛	− ¼	14¼	4,122
Cisco	Apr 40	2,545	XC	4	+ 5⁄16	39⅛	6,442	Intel	May 80	1,627	AM	9¾	+ ¾	88½	2,080
TelMex	Apr 35	2,478	XC	⅛	...	28⅜	8,230	Limltd	May 17½	1,601	CB	4½	+ 2⅛	22½	3,019
Ph Mor	Apr 65	2,420	AM	5⁄16	...	67½	1,644	Amgen	Apr 70	1,572	AM	1¹³⁄16	+ 5⁄8	69¾	10,947
MicrTc	Apr 80	p 2,382	XC	2¼	− 1⅜	84½	935	GTelev	Apr 15	1,554	XC	1¹³⁄16	...	16⅝	9,831
IntrDig	Apr 12½	2,346	PC	2⅛	+ ½	12⅝	13,860	QuakrO	May 45	1,455	PB	7⁄16	− 3⁄16	34	989
MicrTc	Jul 80	2,324	XC	11⅛	+ 2⅛	84½	1,209	Chrysr	Apr 40	1,446	CB	7⁄8	+ 3⁄16	39⅛	8,552

Option/Strike	Exp.	−Call− Vol. Last	−Put− Vol. Last	Option/Strike	Exp.	−Call− Vol. Last	−Put− Vol. Last	Option/Strike	Exp.	−Call− Vol. Last	−Put− Vol. Last
ADC Tel 35	May	88 2½	... ...	53⅜	50 Apr	... ...	52 1¹⁄16	39⅛	40 May	488 1⅜	69 2
ADT 10	Jun	130 2⅜	... ...	53⅜	55 Apr	213 ½	15 2⁹⁄16	39⅛	40 Jul	386 2¼	77 2⅞
AGCO 30	May	35 2	... ...	53⅜	55 May	109 1¼	12 3⅜	39⅛	45 Apr	32 ⅛	3 6
ALC Cm 30	Jun	57 5	5 1¼	53⅜	55 Jul	40 1⅞	10 4⅝	39⅛	45 May	104 5⁄16	¼ 6½
34	35 Apr	... ...	481 1¹⁵⁄16	BanySy	17½ Nov	50 2	... ...	39⅛	45 Jul	127 ¹¹⁄16	... ...
34	35 May	757 1⅝	... ...	Barnet	40 Apr	203 5¼	... ...	39⅛	50 Apr	... ...	30 11⅛
A M R 60	May	46 6½	20 9⁄16	45	40 May	200 5½	... ...	39⅛	50 Jul	1031 ½	10 11¾
65¼	65 Apr	72 1¾	... ...	45	45 Apr	5 13¾	30 13⁄16	CinBel	22½ Apr	15 ⅛	... ...
65¼	65 May	1066 2¾	... ...	BarickG	20 Apr	93 4	50 ¹⁄16	21¾	22½ May	50 5⁄16	... ...
65¼	65 Aug	66 4⅝	16 2⅞	24	20 Oct	... ...	31 ½	CircaPh	20 May	70 5⁄8	10 2
A S A 45	Apr	178 1¾	251 3⅜	24	22½ Apr	377 1¹¹⁄16	270 4	18⅛	20 Oct	98 1¹³⁄16	... ...
46⅛	45 May	60 2¹⁄16	... ...	24	22½ May	46 2¹⁄16	... ...	CirCty	22½ Apr	50 3	... ...
46⅛	50 Apr	10 ¼	100 3⅞	24	25 Apr	1303 5⁄8	9 1½	Circus	22½ Jun	... ...	30 ¹⁄16
46⅛	50 May	218 5⁄8	... ...	24	25 May	45 3⁄4	... ...	32¼	25 Jun	46 7⅜	4 ⅛
46⅛	50 Aug	89 1⁹⁄16	1 4⅝	24	25 Jul	102 1⁵⁄16	14 2¼	32¼	30 Apr	238 2⁹⁄16	20 ⅜
46⅛	55 May	100 ⅛	1 8¾	24	25 Oct	165 2⅛	... ...	32¼	30 May	222 3	... ...
AST Rs 15	Apr	62 1½	10 ⅛	BattlM	10 Apr	116 7⁄8	20 3⁄16	32¼	30 Jun	208 3½	35 ⅞
16½	15 May	68 1⅝	5 ½	10¾	10 Jul	31 1½	... ...	32¼	30 Sep	50 4½	... ...
AT&T 50	Apr	76 2¾	30 3⁄16	10¾	12½ Apr	104 ⅛	... ...	32¼	35 Apr	92 ⅝	... ...
52⅜	50 May	43 3⅜	212 ⅞	10¾	12½ Jul	30 ¾	... ...	32¼	35 May	48 1³⁄16	10 3½
52⅜	50 Jul	45 3¾	30 1³⁄16	BausLm	35 Apr	18 1¹⁄16	90 ⅞	32¼	35 Jun	101 1¼	50 3⅜
52⅜	50 Oct	... ...	152 1½	35	35 Jul	... ...	120 1½	32¼	35 Sep	86 2¼	... ...
52⅜	55 Apr	119 3⁄16	5 2¾	35⅛	40 Jul	118 ⅞	2 4¾	Cirrus	40 Apr	80 ¾	5 2⅝
52⅜	55 Jul	74 1	65 3¼	Baxter	30 May	50 4¾	... ...	Cisco	25 Apr	50 13⅞	... ...
52⅜	55 Oct	114 1¾	... ...	BayNtw	25 Jun	5 13¾	66 ⅛	39⅛	30 Apr	93 9	5 ¹⁄16
Abbt L 30	May	100 7½	... ...	38⅜	30 Apr	143 8¼	30 ¼	39⅛	35 Apr	1349 4¼	1256 ¹⁄16
37⅜	35 Apr	355 2½	... ...	38⅜	35 Apr	240 3¾	1 ⅜	39⅛	35 May	284 4⅞	235 ⁷⁄16
37⅜	35 Aug	6 3⅝	1025 ¾	38⅜	35 May	101 4⅜	27 ½	39⅛	35 Jul	618 5⅝	184 1⅛
37⅜	40 May	77 ¼	... ...	38⅜	35 Jun	52 5⅛	40 1³⁄16	39⅛	35 Oct	43 7	11 1⅞
37⅜	40 Aug	1046 1	... ...	38⅜	40 Apr	144 ⅝	... ...	39⅛	40 Apr	2545 ¾	208 19⁄16
37⅜	40 Nov	14 1½	30 3¼	38⅜	40 May	283 1½	66 2¹¹⁄16	39⅛	40 Jul	1215 1⅝	474 2¾
Aclaim 15	May	... ...	30 1	38⅜	40 Jun	70 2	78 3¼	39⅛	40 Jul	970 2⁷⁄16	106 2¾
15½	17½ Apr	81 3⁄8	... ...	38⅜	40 Sep	205 3⅜	10 4¼	39⅛	40 Oct	88 3¾	30 3½
15½	20 Apr	90 ⅛	... ...	38⅜	40 Jun	35 5	... ...	Citicp	40 Apr	103 4⅛	87 ¾
Adaptc 30	Apr	722 6¾	... ...	Baybks	60 Jun	35 5	... ...	44⅛	40 Oct	10 5½	224 1½
35⅞	35 Apr	273 2½	... ...	BedBth	22½ Apr	10 1¹¹⁄16	80 ⅞	44⅛	40 Apr	84 ½	240 1¾
35⅞	40 Apr	81 5⁄8	... ...	23¼	25 Apr	61 5⁄8	5 2	44⅛	45 Jul	363 1¹⁄16	8 2⅜
35⅞	40 Jul	30 2¹⁵⁄16	2 5⅞	BellAtl	55 Apr	70 ½	2 1¼	44⅛	45 Oct	... ...	485 3¼
AdobeS 40	Apr	46 10⅜	... ...	55	55 Oct	124 2½	2 2⅝	44⅛	50 Jul	257 ⁷⁄16	... ...
50¼	40 Oct	... ...	28 1½	55	60 Oct	353 9⁄16	... ...	ClarkE	55 Apr	40 1¼	... ...
				BellSo	55 Apr	34 5⅜	2 ⅛				

Source: *The Wall Street Journal*, March 29, 1995

tion, the higher will be the price of an option. The same relationship holds true for put options. As we will see in the section on option pricing, there are very clear reasons why these kinds of pricing relationships must obtain in the marketplace.

OPTION PRICING

Option pricing affords one of the showcase results of research in modern finance. The pricing models that have been developed for options perform very well, and a study of these models is very useful for the trader. In fact, traders on the options exchanges have immediate access to the information provided by option pricing models through machines located on the floors of the exchanges.

Prices of options on stocks without cash dividends depend upon five factors:

Stock Price	S
Exercise Price	E
Time until Expiration	T
Volatility of the Underlying Stock	σ
Risk-Free Interest Rate	R_f

Initially, it will be very useful to consider the effects of just the first three factors, the stock price (S), the exercise price (E), and the time until expiration (T). Later, we will consider the more complicated situations that arise from taking into account different interest rate environments and different risk levels.

For a call option, we can express the call price as a function of the stock price, the exercise price, and the time until expiration using this compact notation:

$$C(S, E, T)$$

For example, the equation

$$C(\$120, \$100, \$.25) = \$22.75$$

says that a call option on a share trading at $120, with an exercise price of $100, and one-quarter of a year to expiration has a price of $22.75.

THE PRICING OF CALL OPTIONS AT EXPIRATION

The term **at expiration** refers to the moment just prior to expiration. If the option is not exercised at this time, it will expire immediately and have no value. The value of options at expiration is an important topic because many of the complications that ordinarily affect option prices disappear when the option is about to expire. With this terminology in mind, let us consider the value of a call option at expiration, where $T = 0$. In this case, only two possibilities may arise regarding the relationship between the exercise price (E) and the stock price (S). Either $S > E$ or $S \leq E$. If the stock price is less than or equal to the exercise price $(S \leq E)$, the call option will have no value. To see why this is the case, consider a call option with an exercise price of $80 on a stock trading at $70. Because the option is about to expire, the owner of the option has only two alternatives. The option may be exercised or it may be allowed to expire.[2] If the option is exercised in this situation, the holder of the option must pay the exercise price of $80 and receive a stock trading in the market for only $70. In this situation, it does not pay to exercise the option and the owner will allow it to expire worthless. Accordingly, this option has no value and its market price will be zero. Employing our notation, we can say

$$\text{If } S \leq E, \ C(S, E, 0) = (\tag{3.1}$$

If an option is at expiration and the stock price is less than or equal to the exercise price, the call option has no value. This equation simply summarizes the conclusion we have already reached.

The second possible relationship that could obtain between the stock price and the exercise price at expiration is for the stock price to exceed the exercise price $(S > E)$. Again, in our notation,

$$\text{If } S > E, \ C(S, E, 0) = S - \tag{3.2}$$

If the stock price is greater than the exercise price, the call option must have a price equal to the difference between the stock price and the exercise price.

If this relationship did not hold, there would be arbitrage opportunities. Assume for the moment that the stock price is $50 and the exercise price is $40. If the option were selling for $5, an arbitrageur would make the following trades:

Transaction	Cash Flow
Buy a call option	-$5
Exercise the option	-40
Sell the stock	50
Net Cash Flow	$5

As these transactions indicate, if the call price is less than the difference between the stock price and the exercise price, there will be an arbitrage opportunity.

What if the price of the call option is greater than the difference between the stock price and the exercise price? Continuing to use our example of a stock priced at $50 and the exercise price of the option being $40, assume now that the call price is $15. Faced with these prices, an arbitrageur would make the following transactions:

Transaction	Cash Flow
Sell a call option	+$15
Sell the stock	-50
Initial Cash Flow	-$35

The owner of this call option must then immediately exercise the option or allow it to expire. If the option is exercised, the seller of the call has these additional transactions:

Transaction	Cash Flow
Deliver stock	0
Collect exercise price	+40
Total Cash Flow	$5

In this case, there is still a profit of $5. Alternatively, the owner of the option may allow the option to expire. In that event, the arbitrageur would simply sell the stock as soon as the option expires and receive $50. In this case the profit would be $15, because the arbitrageur simply keeps the option premium. In this second situation, in which the call price is greater than the stock price minus the exercise price, the holder of the call option would exercise the option. The important point is to see that the arbitrageur would make a profit no matter what the holder of the call might do.

At expiration, if the stock price exceeds the exercise price, the price of the call must equal the difference between the stock price and the exercise price. Combining these two relationships allows us to state the first basic principle of option pricing:

$$C(S, E, 0) = \max(0, S - E)$$

(3.3)

At expiration, a call option must have a value that is equal to zero or to the difference between the stock price and the exercise price, whichever is greater. This condition must hold, otherwise there will be arbitrage opportunities awaiting exploitation.[3]

OPTION VALUES AND PROFITS AT EXPIRATION

In this discussion, it is important to keep separate the option's value or price and the profit or loss that a trader might experience. The value of options at expiration can be shown very easily by considering a concrete example. Consider both a call and a put option, with each having a striking price of $100. Figure 3.2 shows the value of these options at expiration for various stock prices. The graph shows the value of call and put options at expiration on the vertical axis as a function of the stock price, which is shown on the horizontal axis. The call price is shown as a solid line, and the put price is shown as a dotted line.

If the stock price is less than or equal to the exercise price of $100, the value of the call must be zero, as is shown in Figure 3.2. For stock prices above the exercise price, the call price equals the difference between the stock price and the exercise price. This is reflected by the fact that the graph of the call option's value rises at a 45 degree angle for stock prices above $100. The graph presents a similar analysis for a put option. Although we have not discussed the pricing of put options in any detail, the reader can reach the conclusion that this is the correct graph by the same kind of argument that was given earlier for call options.

Now consider the same situation, with put and call options each having an exercise price of $100, but assume that trades had taken place for the options with a premium of $5 on both the put and the call options. Knowing the price that was paid allows us to calculate the profits and losses at expiration for the sellers and buyers of both the put and call options. Alternative outcomes for all of these trading parties are shown in Figure 3.3. The top panel shows the profit and loss positions for the call option. The solid line pertains to the buyer of the call, and the dotted line to the seller.[4] For any stock price less than or equal to the exercise price of $100, the

■ Figure 3.2

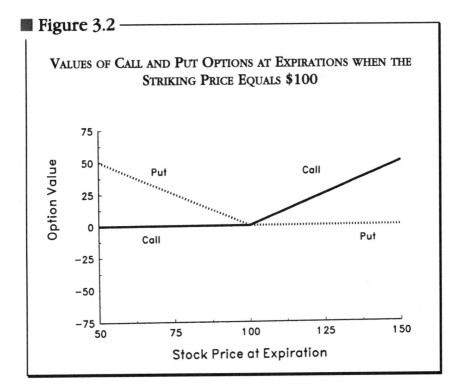

VALUES OF CALL AND PUT OPTIONS AT EXPIRATIONS WHEN THE
STRIKING PRICE EQUALS $100

option will expire worthless and the purchaser of the call will lose
the full purchase price. If the stock price exceeds $100, reaching
$105 say, the owner of the call will exercise the call, paying $100
for the share and receiving a share worth $105. With a share price
of $105, the call owner breaks even exactly. The entire cash flow
has been the $5 for the option plus the $100 exercise price. This
total outflow of $105 is exactly matched by the receipt of the share
that is worth $105. For the call owner, any stock price less than
$100 results in the loss of the total amount paid for the option. For
stock prices greater than the exercise price, the call owner will
exercise the option. The call owner may still lose money even with
exercise. In this example, the stock price must be greater than
$105 to generate any net profit for the call owner.

For the writer of the call, the profit picture is exactly opposite
that of the call owner's. The best situation for the writer of the call
is for the stock price to stay at or below $100. In this situation, the
call writer keeps the entire option premium and the call option
will not be exercised. If the stock price is $105, the option may be

■ **Figure 3.3** ───────────────────────

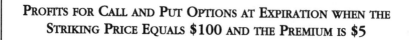

PROFITS FOR CALL AND PUT OPTIONS AT EXPIRATION WHEN THE STRIKING PRICE EQUALS $100 AND THE PREMIUM IS $5

exercised and the writer of the call must deliver shares now worth $105 and receive only $100 for them. At this point, the loss on the exercise exactly equals the premium that was already received, so the call writer breaks even. If the stock price is greater than $105, the call writer will have a net loss. Notice that the buyer's profits exactly mirror the seller's losses and vice versa. This emphasizes that the options market is a zero-sum game. That is, the buyer's gains are the seller's losses and vice versa. If we add up all of the gains and losses in the options market, ignoring transaction costs, the total will equal zero.

The second panel of Figure 3.3 shows the profit and loss positions for the put traders. A put buyer who pays $5 for a put with an exercise price of $100 will break even at $95. The writer of a put also breaks even at $95. These graphs indicate the wide variety of possible profit-and-loss patterns that traders may create by using the options market. This kind of graph is useful for analyzing a wide variety of market strategies.

THE PRICING OF A CALL OPTION WITH A ZERO EXERCISE PRICE AND INFINITE TIME UNTIL EXPIRATION

It may appear unimportant to consider an option with a zero exercise price and an infinite time until expiration, because such options are not traded in the options market. However, this kind of option represents an extreme situation, and as such, it can be used to set boundaries on possible option prices. An option on a stock that has a zero exercise price and an infinite time to maturity can be surrendered at any time, without any cost, for the stock itself. Because such an option can be transformed into the stock without cost, it must have a value as great as the stock itself. Similarly, an option on a good can never be worth more than the good itself. This allows us to state a second principle of option pricing:

$$C(S, 0, \infty) = S \qquad (3.4)$$

A call option with a zero exercise price and an infinite time to maturity must sell for the same price as the stock. Together, these first two principles allow us to specify the upper and lower possible bounds for the price of a call option as a function of the stock price, the exercise price, and the time to expiration. These boundaries are shown in Figure 3.4. If the call has a zero exercise price and an infinite maturity, the call price must equal the stock price, and this situation is shown as the 45 degree line from the origin. This represents the upper bound for an option's price. Alternatively, if the option is at expiration, the price of the option must lie along the horizontal axis from the origin to the point at which the stock price equals the exercise price ($S = E$), and then upward at a 45 degree angle. If the stock price is less than or equal to the exercise price, the call price must be zero, as shown in the graph. If the stock price exceeds the exercise price, the option must trade for a price that is equal to the difference between the stock price and the exercise price. Other options such as those with some time remaining until expiration and with positive exercise prices would have to lie in the shaded region between these two extremes. To further our understanding of option pricing, we need to consider other factors that put tighter restrictions on the permissible values of option prices.

■ **Figure 3.4**

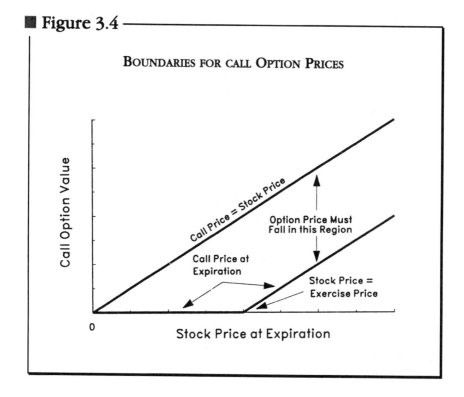

BOUNDARIES FOR CALL OPTION PRICES

Call Option Value

Call Price = Stock Price

Option Price Must
Fall in this Region

Call Price at
Expiration

Stock Price =
Exercise Price

0

Stock Price at Expiration

RELATIONSHIPS BETWEEN CALL OPTION PRICES

Numerous striking prices and expiration dates are available for options on the same stock. Not surprisingly, there are definite relationships that must be maintained between these different kinds of options, if there are not to be arbitrage opportunities:

$$\text{If } E_1 < E_2, \ C(S,E_1,T) \geq C(S,E_2,T) \tag{3.5}$$

If two call options are alike, except that the exercise price of the first is less than that of the second, then the option with the lower exercise price must have a price that is equal to or greater than the price of the option with the higher exercise price.

In this situation, both options allow the owner of the option to acquire the same share of stock for the same period of time. However, the option with the lower exercise price allows the owner of that option to acquire the stock for a lower price. Therefore, the option with the lower exercise price should have a greater value. To see why this rule must hold, imagine a situation in which two options are alike, except the first has an exercise price of $100 and sells for $10. The second option has an exercise price of $90 and a premium of $5. The profit-and-loss graphs for both options are shown in Figure 3.5. The option with the $90 exercise price has a much better profit-and-loss profile than the option with the $100 exercise price. No matter what the stock price might be at expiration, the option with the $90 exercise price will perform better.

This is already an impossible pricing situation, because it represents a disequilibrium result. With these prices, all participants in the market would want the option with the exercise price of $90. This would cause the price of the option with the $100 exercise price to fall until investors were willing to hold it, too. But this could occur only if it were not inferior to the option with the $90 exercise price.

The same point can be made in the following context, because the profit-and-loss opportunities shown in the first panel of Figure 3.5 create an arbitrage opportunity. Faced with these prices, the arbitrageur would simply transact as follows:

Transaction	**Cash Flow**
Sell the option with the $100 exercise price	$10
Buy the option with the $90 exercise price	-5
Net Cash Flow	$5

■ **Figure 3.5**

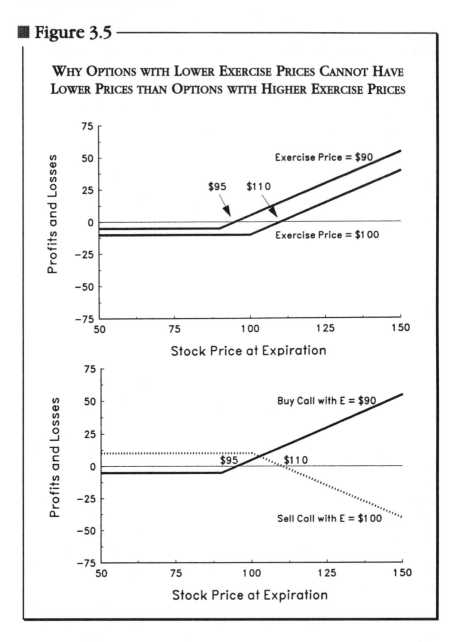

WHY OPTIONS WITH LOWER EXERCISE PRICES CANNOT HAVE
LOWER PRICES THAN OPTIONS WITH HIGHER EXERCISE PRICES

This gives a combined position that is graphed in the second panel of Figure 3.5. Here, the sale of the option with the $100 striking price is shown as the dotted line. To see why this is a good transaction to make, consider the profit and loss position on each option and the overall position for alternative stock prices that might prevail at expiration:

Stock Price at Expiration	Profit or Loss on the Option Position		
	For E = $90	For E = $100	For Both
80	-$5	+$10	+$5
90	-5	+10	+5
95	0	+10	+10
100	+5	+10	+15
105	+10	+5	+15
110	+15	0	+15
115	+20	-5	+15

For any stock price, there will be some profit. If the stock price is $90 or less, the profit will be $5 from the options position, plus the net cash inflow of $5 that was received when the position was initiated. As the stock price at expiration goes from $90 to $100, the profit goes up, until the maximum profit of $15 on the options position is achieved at a stock price of $100. When stock prices at expiration are greater than $100, the profit on the options position remains at $15.

With the prices in the example, it is possible to trade to guarantee a total profit of at least $10 and perhaps as much as $20. This was accomplished without risk or investment, so it is an example of arbitrage. If option prices are to be rational, they cannot allow arbitrage. To eliminate the arbitrage opportunity, the price of the option with a striking price of $90 must be at least as large as the price of the option with the striking price of $100.[5]

A similar principle refers to the expiration date:

$$\text{If } T_1 > T_2, \ C(S, T_1, E) \geq C(S, T_2, E) \tag{3.6}$$

If two options are otherwise alike, the option with the longer time to expiration must sell for an amount equal to or greater than the option that expires earlier.

Intuitively, this principle must hold, because the option with the longer time until expiration gives the investor all of the advantages that the one with a shorter time to expiration offers. But the option with the longer time to expiration also gives the investor the chance to wait longer before exercising the option or before the option expires. In some circumstances, the extra time for the option to run will have positive value.[6]

If the option with the longer period to expiration sold for less than the option with the shorter time to expiration, there would also be an arbitrage opportunity. To conduct the arbitrage, assume that two options are written on the same stock with a striking price of $100. Let the first option have a time to expiration of six months and assume it trades for $8, while the second option has three months to expiration and trades for $10. In this situation, the arbitrageur would make the following transactions:

Transaction	Cash Flow
Buy the six-month option for $8	–$8
Sell the three-month option for $10	+$10
Net Cash Flow	$2

By buying the longer maturity option and selling the shorter maturity option, the option trader receives a net cash flow of $2. However, there might appear to be some risk, because the option that was sold might be exercised. To see that the trader's position is secure, consider that if the option that is sold is exercised against the arbitrageur, he or she can simply exercise the six-month option that was purchased and use the stock that is received to deliver on the three-month option. This will guarantee that the $2 can be kept, so there will be a $2 profit no matter what happens to the stock price. Because this profit is certain and was earned without investment, it is an arbitrage profit.[7] The option with the longer time to expiration cannot be worth less than the option with the shorter time to expiration. Otherwise, there will be arbitrage opportunities.

Generally, the option with the longer time to expiration will actually be worth more than the option with the shorter time to expiration. We have already seen that any option must be worth at least the difference between the stock price and the exercise price ($S - E$) at expiration. If the stock price is greater than the exercise price ($S > E$), the call option is said to be **in-the-money**, but if the stock price is less than the exercise price ($S < E$), the option is **out-of-the-money**. If the stock price equals, or nearly equals, the exercise price ($S = E$), the option is **at-the-money**. Prior to expiration, an in-the-money option will normally be worth more than $S - E$. This difference ($S - E$) is known as the **intrinsic value** of the option, which is simply the value of the option if it were exercised immediately. An in-the-money option prior to expiration can be worth more than $S - E$, because the value of being able to wait to exercise normally has value. If the option is exercised prior to expiration, the trader will receive only the amount $S - E$ for the option. By selling the option in the market, the trader will get the market price of the option, which normally exceeds $S - E$. So it generally will not pay to exercise an option early.[8]

Thus far, we have set bounds for option prices and we have established relationships between pairs of options, as shown in Figure 3.6. There, the two options, C_1 and C_2, are alike except that option C_1 has a lower exercise price. Accordingly, the price of C_1 is more tightly bounded than that of option C_2. The two options in

■ Figure 3.6

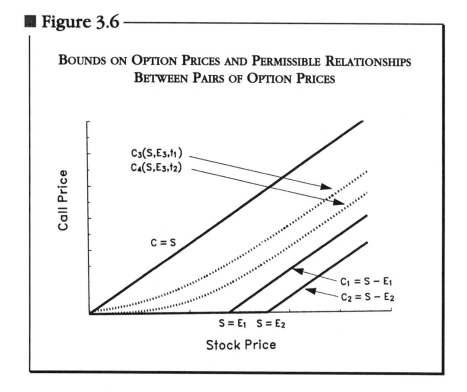

BOUNDS ON OPTION PRICES AND PERMISSIBLE RELATIONSHIPS
BETWEEN PAIRS OF OPTION PRICES

$C_3(S,E_3,t_1)$
$C_4(S,E_3,t_2)$

$C = S$

$C_1 = S - E_1$
$C_2 = S - E_2$

$S = E_1$ $S = E_2$

Stock Price

Call Price

the second pair, C_3 and C_4, differ only in the time to expiration. Consistent with this, the price of the option with the longer time to expiration, C_4, has a higher price. Even though we can now put bounds on the overall price of options and establish which of two options should have the higher price, we need to be able to put further restrictions on the price of a call option. To do this, we need to consider the impact of interest rates.

CALL OPTION PRICES AND INTEREST RATES

Assume that a stock now sells for $100 in the marketplace and that over the next year its value can change by 10 percent in either direction. For a round lot of 100 shares, the value one year from now will be either $9,000 or $11,000. Assume also that the risk-free rate of interest is 12 percent and that a call option exists on this stock with a striking price of $100 per share and an expiration date one year from now. With these facts in mind, imagine two portfolios constructed in the following way:

Portfolio A: 100 shares of stock, current value $10,000.

Portfolio B: A $10,000 pure discount bond maturing in one year, with a current value of $8,929, which is consistent with the 12 percent interest rate. One option contract, with an exercise price of $100 per share, or $10,000 for the entire contract.

Which portfolio is more valuable, and what does this tell us about the price of the call option? In one year, the stock price for the round lot will be either $11,000 if the price goes up by 10 percent, or $9,000 if the price goes down by 10 percent. This result is shown for Portfolio A in Table 3.2. For Portfolio B, there are both bonds and the call option to consider. As is also shown in Table 3.2, the bonds will mature in one year and will be worth $10,000 no matter what happens to the stock price. The stock price will have a strong effect on the value of the call option, however. If the stock price goes up by 10 percent, the call option will be worth exactly $1,000, the difference between the stock price and the exercise price $(S - E)$. If the stock price goes down by 10 percent, the option will expire worthless. So, if the stock price goes down, Portfolio B will be worth $10,000, whereas if the stock price goes up, Portfolio B will be worth $11,000.

In this situation, Portfolio B is clearly the better portfolio to

▪ Table 3.2

PORTFOLIO VALUES IN ONE YEAR

Stock Price:

	Rises 10%	Falls 10%
Portfolio A		
Stock	$11,000	$9,000
Portfolio B		
Maturing Bond	10,000	10,000
Call Option	1,000	0

hold. If the stock price goes down, Portfolio B is worth $1,000 more than Portfolio A. But if the stock price goes up, Portfolios A and B have the same value. An investor could never do worse by holding Portfolio B, and there is some chance to do better. Therefore, the value of Portfolio B must be at least as great as the value of Portfolio A.

This tells us something very important about the price of the option. Because Portfolio B is sure to perform at least as well as Portfolio A, it must cost at least as much. Further, we know that the value of Portfolio A is $10,000, so the price of Portfolio B must be at least $10,000. The bonds in Portfolio B cost $8,929, so the option must cost at least $1,071. This means that the value of the call must be worth at least as much as the stock price minus the present value of the exercise price. If the call did not meet this condition, any investor would prefer to purchase Portfolio B in the example, rather than Portfolio A. Further, there would be an arbitrage opportunity.[9] Previously, we were able to say only that the price of the call must be either zero or $S - E$ at expiration. Based on the reasoning from the example, we can now say the following:

$$C \geq S - \text{Present Value}(E) \qquad (3.7)$$

The call price must be greater than or equal to the stock price minus the present value of the exercise price. This substantially tightens the bounds that we can put on the value of a call option.[10]

As the next example indicates, it must also be true that the higher the interest rate, the higher will be the value of the call option, if everything else is held constant. In the previous example, the interest rate was 12 percent, and we were able to conclude that the price of the call option must be at least $1,071, because:

$$C \geq \$10,000 - \frac{\$10,000}{(1.12)} = \$1,071$$

For the same portfolio, imagine that the interest rate had been 20 percent rather than 12 percent. In that case, the value of the call option must have been at least $1,667, as is shown by the following equation:

$$C \geq \$10,000 - \frac{\$10,000}{(1.20)} = \$1,667$$

From this line of reasoning, we can assert the following principle:

$$\text{If } R_{f1} > R_{f2}, \; C(S, E, T, R_{f1}) \geq C(S, E, T, R_{f2}) \qquad (3.8)$$

Other things being equal, the higher the risk-free rate of interest, the greater must be the price of a call option.

Prices of Call Options and the Riskiness of Stocks

Surprisingly enough, the riskier the stock on which an option is written, the greater will be the value of the call option. This principle can also be illustrated by an example. Consider a stock trading at $10,000 that will experience either a 10 percent price rise or a 10 percent price decline over the next year. As in our earlier example of Table 3.2, a call option on such a stock with an exercise price of $10,000 and a risk-free interest rate of 12 percent, would be worth at least $1,071. Now consider a new stock, which trades at $10,000, but that will experience either a 20 percent price increase or a 20 percent price decrease over the next year. If we hold the other factors constant, by assuming that interest rates are 12 percent per year, and focus on an option with a striking price of $10,000, what can we say about the value of the call option?

As Table 3.3 shows, the call option on the stock that will go up or down by 10 percent must be worth at least $1,071. If the stock price goes down, the call will be worth zero. If the stock price goes up, the call will be worth $1,000. In the bottom panel of Table 3.3,

■ **Table 3.3** ——————————————————————

PORTFOLIO VALUES IN ONE YEAR

	Stock Price: Rises 10%	Stock Price: Falls 10%
Portfolio B		
Maturing Bond	$10,000	$10,000
Call Option	1,000	0

	Stock Price: Rises 10%	Stock Price: Falls 10%
Portfolio A		
Stock	$12,000	$8,000
Portfolio B		
Maturing Bond	10,000	10,000
Call Option	2,000	0

the stock will go up or down by 20 percent. If the stock price goes down, the call in this case will be worth zero. This is the same result as the call in the top panel. If prices go up, the call in the bottom panel will be worth $2,000, which is the difference between the exercise price and the stock price.

In this scenario, any investor would prefer the option in the bottom panel, because it cannot perform worse than the call in the top panel, and it might perform better if the stock price goes up. This means that the value of the call in the bottom panel must be at least as much as the value of the call in the top panel, but it will probably be worth more. The only difference between the two cases is the risk level of the stock. In the top panel, the stock will move up or down by 10 percent, but the stock in the bottom panel is riskier, because it will move 20 percent. By reflecting on this example, we can derive the following principle:

$$\text{If } \sigma_1 > \sigma_2, C(S, E, T, R_f, \sigma_1) \geq C(S, E, T, R_f), \quad (3.9)$$

Other things being equal, a call option on a riskier good will be worth at least as much as a call option on a less risky good.

CALL OPTIONS AS INSURANCE POLICIES

In Table 3.2, the call option will be worth either $1,000 or zero in one year, and the value of that option must be at least $1,071. At first glance, it is a terrible investment to pay $1,071 or more for something that will be worth either zero or $1,000 in a year. However, the option offers more than a simple investment opportunity; it also involves an insurance policy. The insurance character of the option can be seen by comparing the payoffs from Portfolio A and Portfolio B. If the stock price goes down by 10 percent, Portfolio A will be worth $9,000 and Portfolio B will be worth $10,000. If the stock price goes up by 10 percent, both portfolios will be worth $11,000. Holding the option insures that the worst outcome from the investment will be $10,000. This is considerably safer than holding the stock alone. Under these circumstances, it would make sense to pay $1,071 or more for an option that has a maximum payoff of $1,000. Part of the benefit from holding the option portfolio is the insurance that the total payoff from the portfolio will be at least $10,000. This also makes sense of the fact that the riskier the stock, the more the option will be worth. This relationship results, because the riskier the stock, the more valuable will be an insurance policy against particularly bad outcomes.

Previously we said that the price of the option must be at least as great as the stock price minus the present value of the exercise price. However, this formulation neglects the value of the insurance policy inherent in the option. If we take that into account, we can say that the value of the option must be equal to the stock price minus the exercise price, plus the value of the insurance policy inherent in the option. Or, where the value of the insurance policy is denoted *by I*, the value of the call option is given by

$$C(S, E, T, R_f, \sigma) = S - \text{Present Value}(E) + I \qquad (3.10)$$

However, we have no way, thus far, of putting a numerical value on the insurance policy denoted by *I*. That task requires an examination of the option pricing model.

THE OPTION PRICING MODEL

To this point, by a process of reasoning about option prices and finding the boundaries for option prices that rule out arbitrage opportunities, we have learned a great deal about call option prices and the relationship of these prices to other variables. In the preceding discussion, we identified five variables that affect the value of a call option. In the following list, a plus sign (+) by a variable indicates that the price of a call option is larger the larger is the value of the associated variable:

+	Stock Price	S
–	Exercise Price	E
+	Time to Expiration	T
+	Risk-Free Interest Rate	R_f
+	Variability of the Stock's Returns	σ

Even though we now know the basic factors that affect the prices of call options and the direction of their influence, there is still a great deal to learn. For example, in exploring the bounds of option pricing, we considered an example in which the stock price could move by 10 percent up or down in a year. This is obviously a great simplification of reality. In a given period of time, stock prices can take on a virtually infinite number of values. Also, stock prices change continuously for all practical purposes. To be able to put an exact price on a call option requires a much more realistic model of stock price behavior.

This is exactly the approach that was taken by Fischer Black and Myron Scholes as they developed the option pricing model (OPM).[11] Their model applies to European options on non-dividend paying stocks, strictly speaking, although adjustments can be made to the model to deal with other cases.[12] The mathematics of the model are extremely complex, but they were able to derive their model by assuming that stock prices follow a certain kind of path through time called a stochastic process. A **stochastic process** is simply a mathematical description of the change in the value of some variable through time. The particular stochastic process used by Black and Scholes is known as a **Wiener process**. The key features of the Wiener process are that the variable changes continuously through time and that the changes that it might make over any given time interval are distributed normally. Figure 3.7 shows a graph of the path that stock prices might follow if they followed a Wiener process.

Essentially, the difference between our discussion to this point and the achievement of the OPM is that the OPM gives a mathe-

■ **Figure 3.7**

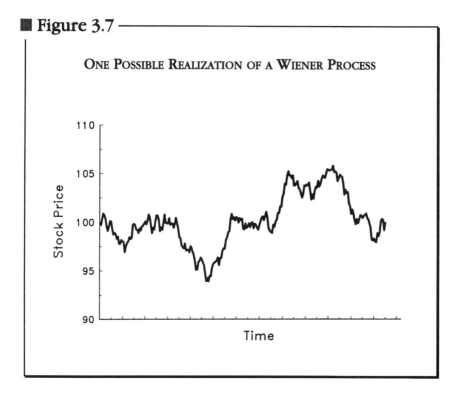

ONE POSSIBLE REALIZATION OF A WIENER PROCESS

matical expression to the value of the call option. Whereas we were unable to say what the call price should equal, Black and Scholes present a theoretical formula for the price of a call option. If we know the values of the five variables listed earlier, we can use the OPM to calculate the theoretical price of an option. Further, even though we cannot consider the mathematics that Black and Scholes used, we can understand how to calculate option values according to their model, and we can understand the relationship between the OPM and the conclusions we have reached in previous sections.

The formula for the Black–Scholes OPM is given by

$$C = SN(d_1) - Ee^{-R_f T} N(d_2) \tag{3.11}$$

where

$$d_1 = \frac{\ln(S/E) + \left[R_f + (1/2)\sigma^2\right]T}{\sigma\sqrt{T}}$$

$$d_2 = d_1 - \sigma\sqrt{T}$$

$N(d_1)$, $N(d_2)$	=	cumulative normal probability values of d_1 and d_2
S	=	stock price
E	=	exercise price
R_f	=	the risk-free rate of interest
σ	=	instantaneous variance rate of the stock's return
T	=	time to expiration of the option

The most difficult part of this formula to understand is the use of the normal cumulative probability function. However, this is exactly the part of the OPM that takes account of the risk and allows the model to give such good results for option prices. The best way to understand the application of the model is with an example. Let us assume values for the five parameters and calculate the Black-Scholes value for an option. For purposes of the example, assume the following:

$$
\begin{aligned}
S &= \$100 \\
E &= \$100 \\
T &= 1 \text{ year} \\
R_f &= 12 \text{ percent} \\
\sigma &= 10 \text{ percent}
\end{aligned}
$$

These values make it possible to calculate the Black-Scholes theoretical option value, and the first task is to calculate values for d_1 and d_2.

$$
\begin{aligned}
d_1 &= \frac{\ln(S/E) + \left[R_f + (1/2)\sigma^2\right]T}{\sigma\sqrt{T}} \\
&= \frac{\ln(100/100) + \left[.12 + 1/2(.01)\right]1}{(.1)(1)} = \frac{0 + .1250}{.1} \\
&= 1.25 \\
d_2 &= d_1 - \sigma\sqrt{T} \\
&= 1.25 - (.1)(1) = 1.15
\end{aligned}
$$

Having calculated the values of d_1 and d_2, the next step is to calculate the cumulative normal probability values of these two results. Essentially, these two values are simply z-scores from the normal probability function, such as the one shown in Figure 3.8. In this graph the two values of interest, 1.15

■ Figure 3.8

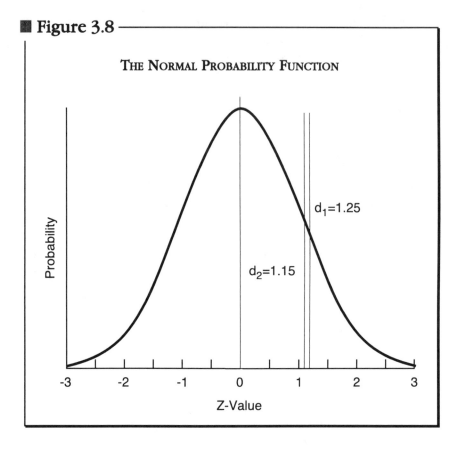

THE NORMAL PROBABILITY FUNCTION

d_1=1.25

d_2=1.15

Probability

Z-Value

-3 -2 -1 0 1 2 3

and 1.25, are shown. In calculating the cumulative normal probability values of d_1 = 1.25 and d_2 = 1.15, we simply need to determine the proportion of the area under the curve that lies to the left of the value in question. For example, if we were interested in a z-score of 0.00, we would know that 50 percent of the area under the curve lies to the left of a z-score of 0.00. This is because the normal probability distribution is symmetrical about its mean, and we know that the z-scores are standardized so that they have a mean of 0.00.

Because the standardized normal probability distribution is so important and so widely used, tables of its values are included in virtually every statistics textbook. A typical table appears as the Appendix to this text. As is shown, the probability of drawing a value from this distribution that is less than or equal to d_1 = 1.25 is .8944. So, the two values we seek are

$$N(d_1) = N(1.25) = .8944$$

$$N(d_2) = N(1.15) = .8749$$

Returning to the OPM, we can now make the final calculation:

$$C = SN(d_1) - Ee^{-R_fT}N(d_2)$$
$$C = \$100(.8944) - \$100e^{-(.12)(1)}(.8749)$$
$$= \$89.44 - \$100(.8869)(.8749)$$
$$= \$89.44 - \$77.60$$
$$= \$11.84$$

In this calculation, the term $e^{-R_fT} = .8869$ is simply the discounting factor for continuous time with an interest rate of 12 percent and a period of one year. So, according to the OPM, the call option should be worth \$11.84.

The calculation of the value of this option by the OPM corresponds very closely to our earlier example from Table 3.2. There we concluded that an option with similar characteristics must be worth at least \$10.71. The result from the OPM is consistent with our earlier analysis, but it is much more exact. The difference between the OPM value of \$11.84 and the minimum value of \$10.71 is due to the value of the insurance policy that we were unable to capture without the sophisticated approach of the OPM.[13]

Also, it should be clear that the OPM result is very close to the result that we reached by just a process of reasoning. We were able to conclude that

$$C = S - \text{Present Value}(E) + I \qquad (3.12)$$

and the OPM says that

$$C = SN(d_1) - Ee^{-R_fT}N(d_2)$$

The term, Ee^{-R_fT} is simply the present value of the exercise price when continuous discounting is used. This means that the OPM is saying

$$C = SN(d_1) - \text{Present Value}(E)N(d_2)$$

The terms involving the cumulative probability function are the terms that take account of risk. Coupled with the rest of the formula, they capture the value of the insurance policy. If the stock involved no risk, the calculated values for d_1 and d_2 would be very large and the subsequent calculated cumulative functions would both approach a value of 1. If $N(d_1)$ and $N(d_2)$ both equal 1, the OPM could be simplified to

$$C = S - \text{Present Value}(E)$$

which is very close to the result we were able to reach without the OPM. This expression simply does not reflect the value of the option as an insurance policy, a value we know it has and that we can measure by using the OPM.

Upon first acquaintance with the OPM, many people think that it is too complicated to be useful. Nothing could be further from the truth. Of all of the models in finance, the OPM is among those receiving the widest acceptance by actual investors. For example, machines on the floor of the CBOE give traders OPM prices for all options using instantaneously updated information on all of the parameters in the model. Further, most investment banking houses have staffs that specialize in options and use the OPM on a daily basis. Finally, the OPM has achieved such widespread acceptance that some calculator manufacturers have even made special modules to allow their calculators to calculate OPM values automatically.

This widespread acceptance is due in large part to the very good results of the OPM. The Black-Scholes theoretical model price is usually very close to the market price of the option. Without doubt, the OPM has contributed greatly to our understanding of option pricing, and many traders use it as a key tool in their trading strategies.

THE VALUATION OF PUT OPTIONS

Although the OPM pertains specifically to call options, it can also be used to price put options, through the principle of put-call parity.[14] Assume that an investor makes the following transactions and that the put and call options are on the same stock:

Buy one share of stock $S = \$100$
Buy one put option with price $P = ?$, $E = \$100$, and $T = 1$ year
Sell one call option with price $C = \$11.84$, $E = \$100$, and $T = 1$ year

At expiration, the stock price could have many different values, some of which are shown in Table 3.4. The interesting feature about this portfolio is that its value will be the same, $\$100 = E$, no matter what the stock price is at expiration. Consistent with Table 3.4, no matter what the stock price at expiration might be, the value of the entire portfolio will be $\$100 = E$. Holding these three instruments in the way indicated gives a risk-free investment that will pay $\$100 = E$ at expiration, so the value of the whole portfolio must equal the present value of the riskless payoff at expiration. This means that we can write

$$S - C + P = \frac{E}{\left(1 + R_f\right)^T} \tag{3.13}$$

The value of the put-call portfolio equals the present value of the exercise price discounted at the risk-free rate.

Because it is possible to know all of the other values, except for the price of the put, P, we can use this put-call parity relationship to calculate P. To see how this is done, let us assume, as before, that $R_f = 12$ percent and that the call value is $\$11.84$, as was calculated according to the OPM. Rearranging the put-call parity formula gives a put value of $\$1.13$:

■ **Table 3.4** ────────────────────────────────────

POSSIBLE OUTCOMES FOR PUT-CALL PARITY PORTFOLIO

Stock Price	Call Value	Put Value	Portfolio Value
$80	$0	$20	$100
90	0	10	100
100	0	0	100
110	-10	0	100
120	-20	0	100

$$P = \frac{E}{\left(1+R_f\right)^T} - S + C$$

$$P = \frac{\$100}{(1.12)} - \$100 + \$11.84 = \$1.13$$

SPECULATING WITH OPTIONS

Many option traders are attracted to the market by the exciting speculative opportunities that options offer. Relative to stocks, options offer a great deal of leverage. A given percentage change in the stock price will cause a much greater percentage change in the price of the option.

Using the example of the option worth $11.84, consider the effect of a sudden 10 percent change in the price of the stock. If the stock price changes by 1 percent, the option price will change by 7.52 percent in the same direction. The following call values were calculated from the Black-Scholes formula, assuming only that the stock price had changed as indicated:

Original Values	Stock Price Increase 1%	Stock Price Decrease 1%
$S = \$100$	$S = \$101$	$S = \$99$
$C = \$11.84$	$C = \$12.73$	$C = \$10.95$

This leverage means that trading options can give investors much more price action for a given investment than simply holding the stock. It also means that options can be much riskier than holding stock. Even though options can be risky as investments, they need not be. In fact, options can be used to take very low risk speculative positions by using options in combinations. The combinations are virtually endless, including strips, straps, spreads, and straddles. We discuss these in Chapter 5.

HEDGING WITH OPTIONS

As we have seen with futures, very risky financial instruments can be used to control risk. One of the most important applications of options is their use as a hedging vehicle. Once again, the OPM gives important insights into this process.

To illustrate the idea of hedging with options, let us use our original example of a stock selling at $100 and having a standard deviation of 10 percent. Recall that a call option with an exercise price of $100 and a time to expiration of one year would sell for $11.84. Recall, too, that a sudden 1 percent price rise in the stock from $100 to $101 would drive the option price to $12.73. If the stock price and the option price are so intimately related, it should be possible to use options to offset risk inherent in the stock. This possibility is shown in Table 3.5.

Consider an original portfolio composed of 8,944 shares of stock selling at $100 per share and assume that a trader sells 100 call option contracts, or options on 10,000 shares, at $11.84. In the table, this short position in the option is indicated by a minus sign. That entire portfolio would have a value of $776,000. Now consider the effect of a 1 percent change in the price of the stock. If the stock price increases by 1 percent to $101, the shares will be worth $903,344. The option price will increase from $11.84 to $12.73. But this portfolio involves a short position in 10,000 options, so this creates a loss of $8,900. After these two effects are taken into

■ Table 3.5

A HEDGED PORTFOLIO

Original Portfolio	**S=$100**	**C=$11.84**	
8,944 shares of stock			$894,400
A short position for options on 10,000 shares			-$118,400
(100 contracts)		**Total Value**	$776,000
Stock Price Rises by 1%	**S=$101**	**C=$12.73**	
8,944 shares of stock			$903,344
A short position for options on 10,000 shares			-$127,300
(100 contracts)		**Total Value**	$776,044
Stock Price Falls by 1%	**S=$99**	**C=$10.95**	
8,944 shares of stock			$885,456
A short position for options on 10,000 shares			-$109,500
(100 contracts)		**Total Value**	$775,956

account, the value of the whole portfolio will be $776,044. This is virtually identical to the original value.

On the other hand, if the stock price falls by 1 percent, there will be a loss on the stock of $8,944. The price of the option will fall from $11.84 to $10.95, and this means that the entire drop in price for the 10,000 options will be $8,900. Taking both of these effects into account, the portfolio will then be worth $775,956. As this example indicates, the overall value of the portfolio will not change no matter what happens to the stock price. If the stock price increases, there is an offsetting loss on the option. Likewise, if the stock price falls, there will be an offsetting gain on the option.

In this example, holding .8944 shares of stock for each option sold short will give a perfect hedge. The value of the entire portfolio will be insensitive to any change in the stock price. How can we know exactly the right number of options to trade to give this result? The careful reader might recall the number .8944. When the value of this call option was calculated, we saw that $N(d_1) =$ .8944. This value gives the appropriate hedge ratio to construct a perfect hedge, and the principle can be summarized by the following rule: A portfolio composed of a short position of one option and a long position of $N(d_1)$ shares of the stock will have a total value that will not fluctuate as the share price fluctuates.

Alternatively, to hedge a long position of one share in a stock, sell a number of options equal to $1/N(d_1)$. This hedge will hold for infinitesimal changes in the stock price. In the preceding example, the hedge was not quite perfect because the change in the stock price was discrete. Actually, the value of the portfolio fluctuates by only .00057. Also, a change in the stock price will change the value of $N(d_1)$, because the value of $d1$ will change. This means that the hedge must be adjusted periodically as the stock price changes if it is to be kept perfect.

OPTIONS ON FUTURES

To this point, we have considered options that are written directly on a substantial underlying good. We now consider options on futures. A trader who buys a call option on a futures contract pays the option price. In return, the call owner receives the right to exercise his or her option and assume a long position in the futures contract. For the call owner, exercise makes sense only if the futures price exceeds the exercise price on the option. A call owner who exercises receives a long position in the futures contract and a cash payment that equals the difference between the futures price at the time of exercise and the exercise price. The seller of a call is subject to the exercise decision of the call holder. If the call holder exercises, the call seller receives a short position in the futures contract and pays the call holder the difference between the current futures price and the exercise price. As an example, assume that a trader buys a call option on the December wheat futures with an exercise price of $3.50. Later, the futures price is $3.75, and the call holder exercises. Upon exercise, the call holder receives a long position in the futures contract with a contract price of $3.75. In addition, the call holder receives $.25 per bushel, or $1,250 on one contract. The seller of this call must pay the call holder $1,250 and accept a short position in the futures contract with a contract price of $3.75.

At this point, both traders have completed all transactions related to the futures option. However, the call owner holds a long position in the futures and the call seller holds a short position in the futures, both at a contract price of $3.75. At this point, neither trader has a profit or loss on the futures. They can both offset their futures position to avoid any future obligations. Alternatively, they can maintain their positions and hope to profit from subsequent movements in the futures price.

For a put, the buyer of a futures option acquires the right to force the seller of the put to assume a long futures position and pay the long put trader the difference between the exercise price of the option and the futures price at the time of exercise. As an example, assume a trader buys a put option with an exercise price of $3.80. Later, when the futures price is $3.75, the put owner can exercise. The seller then receives a long position in the futures at the current futures price of $3.75. In addition, the seller pays the put owner the difference between the futures price and the exercise price. In this example, the futures price is $3.75 and the exercise price is $3.80. Therefore, the put seller pays the put buyer $.05 per bushel, or $250 on a 5,000 bushel contract. The buyer of a put receives a short position in the futures. Both the long and short put traders now hold futures positions at \$3.75, the market price prevailing at the time of exercise. They may offset their futures positions to avoid further profits or losses, or they may maintain the futures position in pursuit of profit.[15]

The pricing of options on futures relies on the Cost-of-Carry model for futures pricing that we considered in Chapter 2. There we saw that in a perfect market the Cost-of-Carry model implies

$$F_{0,t} = S_0 e^{ct} \tag{3.14}$$

Because we continue to assume perfect markets, our analysis of options on futures focuses on futures contracts that can be adequately described by the Cost-of-Carry model. For the most part, this model works well for precious metal and financial futures. By contrast, the model does not describe agricultural and energy futures very well. To see this, note that the Cost-of-Carry model implies that the futures price must always exceed the cash price. This condition is often violated by agricultural goods and by energy products, such as oil.[16]

When the Cost-of-Carry model applies, we can treat a futures contract as an asset that pays a continuous dividend at the risk-free rate.[17] In terms of our notation for the continuous dividend version of the Black-Scholes model, $\delta = r$. In this case, the futures rate equals the cost-of-carry. The only cost of carrying the commodity is the interest cost. Applying the continuous dividend version of the Black-Scholes model to a futures contract, F, gives the value of a call option on a futures, C^f:

$$C^f = e^{-rt} \left[FN\left(d_1^f\right) - EN\left(d_2^f\right) \right.$$
$$d_1^f = \frac{\ln(F/E) + \left(.5\sigma^2\right)t}{\sigma\sqrt{t}}$$
$$d_2^f = d_1^f - \sigma\sqrt{t} \tag{3.15}$$

To see why this model is correct, assume for the moment that there is no risk. From our previous discussions, we know that the $N(\cdot)$ terms drop out from the Black-Scholes model under conditions of certainty. In that case, the payoff at expiration is just the difference between the futures price at the time the call is purchased and the exercise price of the call:

$$C^f = [S - E]e^{-rt}$$

The value of the call at time zero must be the present value of the certain payoff at expiration.

Now we introduce risk and consider an example of a European futures option. Assume a wheat futures contract trades at \$3.50 per bushel and the corresponding futures options have a striking price of \$3.45 and expire in 47 days. The standard deviation of the futures price is .23. The interest rate is 9 percent, which equals the cost-of-carry. With these values, the call price is \$.1395 and the put price is \$.0901 per bushel. With a contract size of 5,000 bushels, the two contracts cost \$697.50 and \$450.50, respectively.

Thus far, we have considered only European futures options. Because futures options are generally American, they can be exercised any time. This makes them extremely difficult to price. Essentially, an American futures option consists of an infinite series of European options. In essence, the American futures option has an exercise price equal to the explicit amount that must be paid, plus the sacrifice of the remaining European options in the series. Because the American futures option must be analyzed as an infinite series of European options, there is no closed-form solution for the value of the American futures option. Instead, we must approximate the value of the American futures option. The value of an American futures option is given by

$$C = FW_1 - EW_2 \tag{3.16}$$

where

W_1, W_2 = "weighting factors comprised of infinite sums of the products of discount factors and conditional probability terms that reflect, at each instant, the present value of the exercise value conditioned on the probability that exercise did not occur at a previous instant."[18]

Because W_1 *and* W_2 are sums of an infinite series, the value of the call must be estimated instead of being computed exactly. However, we can compute the estimate to a very high degree of accuracy. In every instance, the value of the American futures option should equal or exceed the value of the corresponding European futures option.

With futures options, there is always the prospect of early exercise, whether the good on which the futures contract is written pays dividends or not. For a call option on a non-dividend paying stock, early exercise never makes sense. An owner who exercises receives the intrinsic value, $S - E$. In effect, this means that the owner throws away the time value of the option. If the underlying stock pays a dividend, early exercise is sometimes reasonable. When a stock pays a dividend, the value of the share drops by the amount of the dividend. In this case, value is "leaking out" of the underlying good, so it may be wise to exercise before expiration.

Similarly, it may be wise to exercise futures options before expiration. Consider a call option with an exercise price $E = \$50$ and a futures contract with a price $F = \$100$. Assume for the moment that the futures price will not change anymore, and consider whether the call owner should exercise early or wait until expiration. With these data, the owner should exercise early. By doing so, the owner receives $50 immediately. After exercising, the trader can earn interest on $50 until the expiration date. In short, the benefit of early exercise on a futures option is that exercise provides an immediate payment of $F - E$. The value of the early exercise is the interest that can be earned between the time of exercise and the expiration date:

$$[F - E]e^{rt}$$

In this example, we have assumed that the futures price does not change. In that circumstance, it was clearly wise to exercise early to capture the interest on the mark to market payment $F - E$. However, in the normal event, the futures price can fluctuate. Therefore, early exercise discards the option's value over and above the intrinsic value $F - E$. As a consequence, early exercise of a futures option has a benefit and a cost:

Benefit: Use of the funds $F - E$ until expiration
Cost: Sacrifice of option value over and above intrinsic value $F - E$

Figure 3.9 illustrates the differences between the pricing of American and European futures call options. Consider a futures

■ **Figure 3.9** ────────────

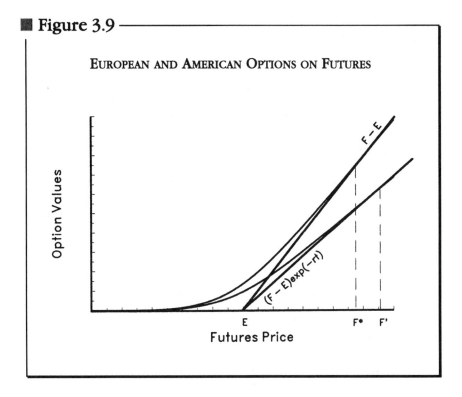

EUROPEAN AND AMERICAN OPTIONS ON FUTURES

call with exercise price E. Figure 3.9 shows how the prices of otherwise identical American and European options vary as a function of the futures price, F. We already observed that the minimum price for a European futures call option is $(F - E)e^{rt}$. In Figure 3.9, the European option attains this minimum when its price touches the line designated as $(F - E)e^{rt}$. This happens when the futures price *reaches* F', which is equivalent to $N(d_1^f)$ and $N(d_2^f)$ both equaling 1.0 in equation 3.15. In economic terms, this situation arises when it is certain that the option will remain in-the-money. In that case, the option will pay $F - E$ at maturity. Before maturity, its price must equal the present value of $F - E$, or $(F - E)e^{-rt}$.

The American futures option price must equal or exceed the corresponding European futures call price shown in Figure 3.9.[19] The difference between the American and European futures option prices is the early exercise premium. It is the extra value the American futures option has because it can be exercised before expiration. In the figure, the American futures option attains an important level of F^*, at which the American futures option has no excess value above its intrinsic value. When the futures price is F^*, the intrinsic value of the American futures option is $F^* - E$ and its market value should be the same.

Following Whaley, we call F^* the critical futures price.[20] This is a critical price because it is the point at which the option price reaches a price that justifies immediate exercise. We can compute the critical price using various sophisticated methods. For any futures price above F^*, the value of the American futures option equals its intrinsic value. Therefore, the owner of the call option should exercise the option at any futures price above F^* and invest the proceeds to earn interest. For any futures price below F^*, the option should not be exercised because the option will still have value above its intrinsic value. At F^*, the owner is indifferent about exercising.[21]

Foreign Currency Options

The many different kinds of futures and options come together in the foreign currency market, because it is only in foreign exchange in which all four kinds of speculative contracts discussed in the last two chapters are traded. In this section, we focus on the German mark, where we find

- an option on the German mark itself,
- a forward contract on the German mark,
- a German mark futures contract, and
- an option on the German mark futures contract.

Figure 3.10 presents quotations for all four instruments. To see how to read these quotations, note the following facts. In the quotations, the spot price of the German mark is shown in the first column for the Philadelphia Exchange options. The German mark option trades on the Philadelphia Exchange and the contract size is 62,500 marks, with the quotations being shown in one-hundredths of a cent per mark. The striking prices are shown in half-cent intervals. The figure also shows prices for options on the futures contract. These instruments act as a combination of the option and the futures. When a futures option is exercised, the exercising party receives a futures position and a cash payment from the original seller of the futures option.

By now the reader will suspect that there are likely to be lawlike relationships among the prices of these diverse instruments. In

■ **Figure 3.10**

QUOTATIONS FOR CURRENCY FORWARDS, FUTURES, OPTIONS AND FUTURES OPTIONS

FORWARDS

Germany (Mark)	.7207	.7110	1.3875	1.4065
30-Day Forward	.7211	.7120	1.3867	1.4046
90-Day Forward	.7226	.7134	1.3838	1.4017
180-Day Forward	.7251	.7157	1.3790	1.3972

FUTURES

DEUTSCHEMARK (CME) — 125,000 marks; $ per mark

June	.7135	.7239	.7124	.7224	+ .0099	97448	.5980	53,973
Sept	.7187	.7250	.7179	.7249	+ .0101	.7415	.6290	1,851
Dec	.7247	.7280	.7247	.7275	+ .0103	.7400	.6580	370

Est vol 25,790; vol Mon 27,671; open int 56,240, +1,118.

OPTIONS

62,500 German Marks-cents per unit.

65½	Apr	...	...	10	0.01
66	Apr	...	...	2	0.02
66	Jun	11	5.80	10	0.25
68	Apr	...	...	130	0.07
68	Jun	...	...	6	0.60
69	Apr	...	...	12	0.11
69	May	...	...	30	0.45
69	Jun	...	...	100	0.78
69½	Jun	...	...	5	1.02
70	Apr	...	...	1658	0.30
70	Jun	...	...	6	1.10
70½	Jun	...	...	160	1.35
71	Apr	...	...	20	0.56
71	May	...	...	13	1.21
71	Jun	3	2.42	15	1.47
71½	Apr	5	1.14	5	0.97
72	Apr	40	1.04	20	1.26
72	May	180	1.61	...	...
72	Jun	37	2.12	5	2.11
72½	Jun	19	1.90	...	...
73	Apr	20	0.64	...	...
73	Jun	44	1.64	2	2.40
73½	May	30	0.95	...	...
74	Apr	45	0.37	...	...
74	Jun	11	1.26	...	...

FUTURES OPTIONS

DEUTSCHEMARK (CME)
125,000 marks; cents per mark

Strike	Calls—Settle			Puts—Settle		
Price	Apr	May	Jun	Apr	May	Jun
7100	1.60	2.12	2.56	0.36	0.89	1.33
7150	1.27	1.82	2.29	0.53	1.09	1.56
7200	0.97	1.57	2.02	0.73	1.33	1.78
7250	0.74	1.33	1.78	1.00	1.59	2.04
7300	0.52	1.12	1.56	1.28	1.87	2.31
7350	0.40	0.94	1.37	1.66	2.19	2.62

Est vol 6,229   Mon 3,470 calls 3,109 puts
Op int Mon   108,446 calls 95,928 puts

Source: *The Wall Street Journal*, March 29, 1995.

fact, we observed the relationships between futures and forward prices. For the sake of convenience, assume that the futures and options contracts are all written for 1 million marks and that all prices are quoted in U.S. dollars per mark. We also assume that both options and the futures contract expire in four months and we assume that the risk-free interest rate is 1 percent per month.

To illustrate the pricing relationships between futures and options, consider a portfolio constructed by buying one call option and selling one put option, each with an exercise price of $.31 and the same expiration date in four months. The value of this option portfolio at expiration depends on the value of the German mark at the time of expiration. If the mark is worth $.31 or less at expiration, the call expires worthless. For values of the mark above $.31, the call option increases in value. The short put position has no value unless the mark is worth less than $.31 at expiration. However, for each cent the mark falls below $.31 at expiration, there is a one cent contribution to profit on the short put position. Considering the entire portfolio, there will be a positive value to the long call/short put portfolio if the mark lies above $.31 when the options expire. However, if the spot price of the mark is worth less than $.31 at expiration, the portfolio will have a negative value. Notice that we have focused on the terminal value of the portfolio so far, and we have ignored the cost of the combined call and put portfolio.

Now we need to compare the terminal value of this two-option portfolio with the futures contract. In Figure 3.11 we assume that a futures contract is available at a price of $.33. There is no cost for entering a futures contract, except for the transaction costs, which we ignore. Therefore, the line for the futures contract in Figure 3.11 shows the profit or loss that will be realized on the futures at its expiration, which we assume is the same expiration date that prevailed for the options.

As the graph shows, no matter what the value of the mark might be at expiration, the option portfolio will have a value that exceeds the profit or loss for the futures. For example, if the mark is at $.33 at expiration, the futures contract will have no value, but the option portfolio will be worth $.02 per mark. If the mark is worth $.31 at the expiration date in March, the options portfolio will be worthless, but the futures contract will show a loss of $.02 per mark. No matter what the mark is worth at expiration, the options portfolio will perform $.02 better than the futures contract.

Because the options portfolio will always perform better, it must be priced higher than the futures contract. Otherwise, all traders would prefer the options portfolio. In fact, because we know exactly how much better the options portfolio will perform at

■ Figure 3.11

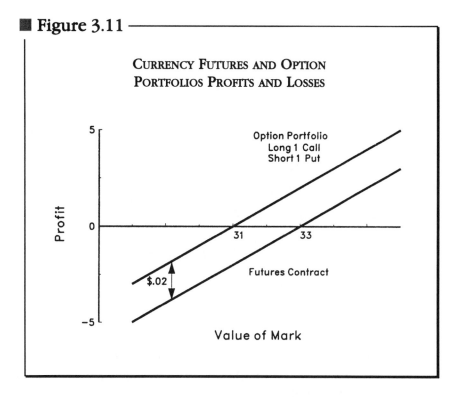

CURRENCY FUTURES AND OPTION
PORTFOLIOS PROFITS AND LOSSES

Option Portfolio
Long 1 Call
Short 1 Put

Profit

0

31   33

$.02

Futures Contract

Value of Mark

expiration, we can calculate how much more the options portfolio will be worth than the futures contract. If the current price of the futures contract is $.33, it costs nothing to enter the futures contract at that price. The options portfolio is certain to pay off $.02 per mark better than the futures contract at expiration, so it has a positive value. This must be the case because the futures contract costs nothing to enter.

How much will the options portfolio be worth? Using our assumption of the contract size being 1 million marks, what will be the difference in the dollar payoffs between the futures position and the options portfolio at maturity? With a payoff difference of $.02 per mark, the difference in the payoffs between the futures and options portfolio must be a total of $20,000, because we are assuming a contract size of 1 million marks. In mathematical terms, the difference in the payoffs can be represented as

$$F - E = \$20,000$$

where

E = $310,000, the exercise price for a contract on 1 million marks

F = $330,000, the total futures price for 1 million marks

By acquiring the options portfolio rather than the futures contract, the investor is certain to receive $20,000 more at expiration than the futures contract holder will receive. Because this $20,000 incremental payoff is certain and the price of the futures contract is zero, the holder of the options portfolio must be willing to pay the present value of that future payoff. In other words, the options portfolio must be worth the present value of the $20,000 that will be received in June. That means the price of the options portfolio must equal the present value of the difference between the futures price and the exercise price on the options:

$$C - P = \frac{F - E}{(1 + R_f)^T}$$ (3.17)

In our example, the difference $F - E$ is $20,000, so the cost of the options portfolio must be the present value of $20,000 discounted at the risk-free rate. Assuming that the interest rate is 1 percent per month and that the expiration is four months away, the total cost of the options portfolio should be $20,000/(1.01)[4] or $19,220. This gives us a technique for establishing a relationship between futures and option prices.[22]

Another way to see the same point is to assume that a trader makes the following transactions:

Buy one call
Sell one put
Sell one futures

We now consider the payoffs on this three-asset portfolio for different values of the German mark at the expiration of the three instruments. First, if the mark is worth $.31, the two options are both worthless and a short futures position is worth $.02, so the total portfolio is worth $.02. If the mark is worth $.33 at expiration, the futures profit is zero, the short put expires worthless, and the long call is worth $.02, for a total portfolio value of $.02. In fact, for any value of the German mark, the portfolio is worth $.02. Therefore, we see that a long call/short put/short futures simulates a risk-free pure discount instrument that pays the futures contract price less the common option exercise price. It may seem surprising that options and futures, instruments known for their riskiness, can be combined to create a risk-free investment. However, Chapter 5 explores the combinations of different instruments that can be created to tailor risk positions in an amazing variety of ways.

SUMMARY

This chapter presented an overview of the options market in the United States. Option trading on organized exchanges began in 1973 with the introduction of options on individual stocks. Since that time, option markets in the United States have expanded greatly with options on metals, stock and other indexes, foreign currencies, and options on futures contracts.

Options can be classified as put or call options, each of which may be bought or sold. Ownership of a call option confers the right to buy a given good at a specified price for a specified period of time. Selling a call option confers those same rights to the owner of a call option in exchange for a payment from the call option purchaser. Ownership of a put option permits the sale of a good at a specified price for a specified period of time. Selling a put option gives those rights to the buyer in exchange for a payment from the buyer.

The theory of option pricing is very well developed. Starting merely from the assumption that options should be priced in a way that allows no arbitrage opportunities, it is possible to bound option prices very closely. Essentially, it can be shown using the no-arbitrage condition that call option prices are a function of the stock price, the exercise price of the option, the time to expiration, the interest rate, and the risk level of the good underlying the option. Additionally, Black and Scholes developed an option pricing model that gives an exact price for a call option as a function of the same five variables. Even though their model is a theoretical model, it has been shown to accord very well with option prices that are actually observed in the market.

Options are useful financial instruments for both speculation and hedging. For example, an investor expecting a stock price to increase can profit from being correct by buying a call option or selling a put option on that stock. By speculating with options, it is possible to achieve more leverage than by merely trading the stock itself. Options are useful for controlling risk as well, because the careful combination of options and positions in the underlying good can provide virtually any degree of risk that is desired. Further, combinations of options themselves widen the range of payoff possibilities available to the investor.

QUESTIONS AND PROBLEMS

1. Respond to the following claim: "Buying a call option is very dangerous because it commits the owner to purchasing a stock at a later date. At that time the stock may be undesirable. Therefore, owning a call option is a risky position."

2. "I bought a call option with an exercise price of $110 on IBM when IBM was at $108 and I paid $6 per share for the option. Now the option is about to expire and IBM is trading at $112. There's no point in exercising the option, because I will wind up paying a total of $116 for the shares – $6 I already spent for the option plus the $110 exercise price." Is this line of reasoning correct? Explain.

3. What is the value of a call option on a share of stock if the exercise price of the call is $0 and its expiration date is infinite? Explain.

4. Why is the value of a call option at expiration equal to the maximum of zero or the stock price minus the exercise price?

5. Two call options on the same stock have the following features. The first has an exercise price of $60, a time to expiration of three months, and a premium of $5. The second has an exercise price of $60, a time to expiration of six months, and a premium of $4. What should you do in this situation? Explain exactly, assuming that you transact for just one option. What is your profit or loss at the expiration of the nearby option if the stock is at $55, $60, or $65?

6. Two call options are identical except that they are written on two different stocks with different risk levels. Which will be worth more? Why?

7. Explain why owning a bond is like a short position in a put option.

8. Why does ownership of a convertible bond have features of a call option?

9. Assume the following: a stock is selling for $100, a call option with an exercise price of $90 is trading for $6 and matures in one month, and the interest rate is 1 percent per month. What should you do? Explain your transactions.

10. Consider a German mark futures contract with a current price of $.35 per mark. There are also put and call options on the mark with the same expiration date in three months that happen to have a striking price of $.35. You buy a call and sell a put. How much should your combined option position cost? Explain. What if the interest rate were 1 percent per month and the striking prices were $.40? How much should the option position be worth then?

11. Two call options on the same stock expire in two months. One has an exercise price of $55 and a price of $5. The other has an exercise price of $50 and a price of $4. What transactions would you make to exploit this situation?

SUGGESTED READINGS

Abken, P. A. "Interest-Rate Caps, Collars, and Floors." Federal Reserve Bank of Atlanta *Economic Review* (November–December 1989): 2–23.

Black, F. "Fact and Fantasy in the Use of Options." *Financial Analysts Journal* 31, no. 4 (July–August 1975): 36–72.

Black, F. "How to Use the Holes in Black-Scholes." *Journal of Applied Corporate Finance* 1, no. 4 (Winter 1989): 67–73.

Black, F., and M. Scholes. "The Pricing of Options and Corporate Liabilities." *Journal of Political Economy* (1973): 637–654.

Giddy, I. "Foreign Exchange Options." *Journal of Futures Markets* 3, no. 2 (1983): 143–166.

Jarrow, R. A., and A. Rudd. *Option Pricing.* Homewood, IL: Richard D. Irwin, 1983.

Kolb, R. *Options: An Introduction*, 2d ed. Miami: Kolb Publishing, 1994.

Kolb, R. *The Financial Derivatives Reader.* Miami: Kolb Publishing, 1992.

Leong, K. S. "Volatility and Option Pricing." *The Handbook of Derivative Instruments*, pp. 113–127. Chicago: Probus Publishing Company, 1991.

Merton, R. C. "Theory of Rational Option Pricing." *Bell Journal of Economics and Management Science* (1973): 141–183.

NOTES

1. In the place of some prices, the letters r and s appear. An r indicates that a particular option was not traded on the day being reported. An s indicates that no option with those characteristics is being made available for trading by the exchange.

2. We are assuming that it is too late to sell the option, because expiration is imminent.

3. Most of the principles indicated here were originally proven rigorously by Robert C. Merton, "Theory of Rational Option Pricing," *Bell Journal of Economics and Management Science* (1973): 141–183.

4. Throughout this chapter, solid lines are used to indicate long positions and dashed lines are used to indicate short positions.

5. There is still an interesting result to be noted here. If the prices are equal, a trader could buy the option with the lower striking price and sell the one with the higher striking price. This strategy would not guarantee a profit, but it could not lose. Further, there would be some situations in which it would pay off. For this reason, options with lower exercise prices almost always sell for higher, not just equal, prices, as the quotations from *The Wall Street Journal* make clear.

6. Strictly speaking, this argument holds for **American options**. An American option allows exercise at any time until maturity. By contrast, a **European option** allows exercise only at maturity. Thus, an American option gives all the advantages of the European option, plus it allows the possibility of early exercise. For this reason, an American option must always have a value at least as great as a European option, other factors being equal.

7. This result requires that the six-month option be an American option so that it could be exercised at will prior to expiration.

8. In the case of a dividend-paying stock, this will not always be true.

9. The arbitrage transactions would involve buying Portfolio B and selling Portfolio A short. Assume that the price of the call option

is $1,000 and try to work out the transactions and the arbitrage profit that must result.

10. Strictly speaking, this condition will hold necessarily if at least one of two conditions is met. First, the equation holds if the stock underlying the option pays no dividends. Second, the equation holds if the option is a European option. A European option can be exercised only at the expiration of the option. As these two restrictions imply, the equation might fail depending upon the cash flows associated with the stock before expiration. The complications these interim cash flows present are beyond the scope of this text.

11. See Fischer Black and Myron Scholes, "The Pricing of Options and Corporate Liabilities," *Journal of Political Economy* (1973): 637–654.

12. These adjustments and further developments of the OPM are beyond the scope of this text. The interested student should see Robert A. Jarrow and Andrew Rudd, *Option Pricing* (Homewood, IL: Richard D. Irwin, 1983), for a complete exposition of these other developments.

13. Actually, part of the difference is due to the discounting method. Had our example used continuous discounting at 12 percent, we would have found that the value of the option had to be at least as great as $100 – $100 (.8869) = $11.31. This is much closer to the OPM value of $11.84.

14. The put-call parity relationship was first derived by Hans Stoll, "The Relationship between Put and Call Option Prices," *The Journal of Finance* (December 1969): 802–824.

15. Two books discuss options on futures in great detail: John W. Labuszewski and Jeanne Cairns Sinquefield, *Inside the Commodity Options Market* (New York: Wiley, 1985); and John W. Labuszewski and John E. Nyhoff, *Trading Options on Futures* (New York: Wiley, 1988).

16. If we define the net cost-of-carry to include all benefits that come from holding the commodity, we can specify a revised Cost-of-Carry model that fits more commodities. These benefits of holding the physical good are known as the **convenience yield**. However, this strategy merely saves the model by stipulating that apparent discrepancies in the model equal the unobservable convenience yield. For applying the option model, we would then need to measure the convenience yield, which appears difficult at best.

17. Fischer Black, "The Pricing of Commodity Contracts," *Journal of Financial Economics* 3 (1976): 167–179, was the first to develop a pricing model for options on futures.

18. K. Shastri and K. Tandon, "An Empirical Test of a Valuation Model for American Options on Futures Contracts," *Journal of Financial and Quantitative Analysis* 21, no. 4 (December 1986): 377–392.

19. In Figure 3.9, we indicate the special number e by the notation "exp."

20. R. Whaley, "Valuation of American Futures Options: Theory and Empirical Tests," *Journal of Finance* (March 1986): 127–150. Figure 3.9 is based on a figure in Whaley's paper. See also Robert E. Whaley, "On Valuing American Futures Options," *Financial Analysts Journal* 42, no. 3 (May–June 1986): 49–59.

21. Giovanni Barone-Adesi and Robert E. Whaley, "Efficient Analytical Approximation of American Option Values," *Journal of Finance* 42, no. 2 (June 1987): 301–320, show how to find the critical futures price efficiently. Gerald D. Gay, Robert W. Kolb, and Kenneth Yung, "Trader Rationality in the Exercise of Futures Options," *Journal of Financial Economics* 23, no. 2 (August 1989): 339–362, examine the correspondence between actual exercise behavior and the guidance provided by the Barone-Adesi and Whaley model. In general, Gay, Kolb, and Yung find very few instances in which traders exercise when they should not. However, in many instances traders should have exercised but did not. There are rare occasions of traders exercising when they should not have with these exercises resulting in large losses.

22. For more on the relationships between options and futures on foreign currencies, see I. Giddy, "Foreign Exchange Options," *The Journal of Futures Markets* (1983): 143–166.

■ Chapter 4

The Swaps Market

Overview

A **swap** is an agreement between two or more parties to exchange sets of cash flows over a period in the future. For example, Party A might agree to pay a fixed rate of interest on $1 million each year for five years to Party B. In return, Party B might pay a floating rate of interest on $1 million each year for five years. The parties that agree to the swap are known as **counterparties**. The cash flows that the counterparties make are generally tied to the value of debt instruments or to the value of foreign currencies. Therefore, the two basic kinds of swaps are **interest rate swaps** and **currency swaps**.

This chapter provides a basic introduction to the swaps market. As we will see, the swaps market has grown rapidly in the last few years, because it provides firms that face financial risks with a flexible way to manage that risk. We will explore the risk management motivation that has led to this phenomenal growth in some detail.

A significant industry has arisen to facilitate swap transactions. This chapter considers the role of **swap facilitators** – economic agents who help counterparties identify each other and consummate swap transactions. Swap facilitators, who are either brokers or dealers, may function as agents that identify and bring prospective counterparties into contact with each other. Alternatively, swap dealers may actually transact for their own account to help complete the swap.

By taking part in swap transactions, swap dealers expose themselves to financial risk. This risk can be serious, because it is exactly the risk that the swap counterparties are trying to avoid. Therefore, the swap dealer has two key problems. First, the swap dealer must price the swap to provide a reward for his or her services in bearing risk. Second, the swap dealer essentially has a portfolio of swaps that results from numerous transactions in the swaps market and, therefore, the problem of managing a swap portfolio. We explore how swap dealers price their swap transactions and manage the risk inherent in their swap portfolios.

THE SWAPS MARKET

In this section we consider the special features of the swaps market. For purposes of comparison, we begin by summarizing some of the key features of futures and options markets. Against this background, we focus on the most important features of the swap product. The section concludes with a brief summary of the development of the swaps market.

REVIEW OF FUTURES AND OPTIONS MARKET FEATURES

In Chapters 2 and 3, we explored the futures and options markets. In Chapter 2 we observed that futures contracts trade exclusively in markets operated by futures exchanges and regulated by the Commodity Futures Trading Commission. Chapter 3 focused on exchange-traded options. Again, this portion of the options market is highly formalized with the options exchanges playing a major role in the market, and the options exchanges are regulated by the Securities and Exchange Commission (SEC).

Futures markets trade highly standardized contracts, and the options traded on exchanges also have highly specified contract terms that cannot be altered. For example, the S&P 500 futures contract is based on a particular set of stocks, for a particular dollar amount, with only four fixed maturity dates per year. In addition, futures and exchange-traded options generally have a fairly short horizon. In many cases, futures contracts are listed only about one to two years before they expire. Even when it is possible to trade futures for expiration in three years or more, the markets do not become liquid until the contract comes much closer to expiration. For exchange-traded stock options, the longest time to maturity is generally less than one year. These futures and options cannot provide a means of dealing with risks that extend farther into the future than the expiration of the contracts that are traded. For example, if a firm faces interest rate risk for a 10-year horizon associated with a major building project, the futures market allows risk management only for the horizon of futures contracts currently being traded, which is about 3 years.

In summary, the futures and options markets that we have explored are regulated markets, and they are dominated by the exchanges where trading takes place. The futures and options contracts are highly standardized; they are limited to relatively few goods; and they have a few fixed expirations per year. In addition, the horizon over which they trade is often much shorter than the risk horizon that businesses face.

CHARACTERISTICS OF THE SWAPS MARKET

In large part, the swaps market has emerged because swaps escape many of the limitations inherent in futures and exchange-traded options markets. Swaps, of course, have some limitations of their own.

Swaps are custom tailored to the needs of the counterparties. If they wish, the potential counterparties can start with a blank sheet of paper and develop a contract that is completely dedicated to meeting their particular needs. Thus, swap agreements are more likely to meet the specific needs of the counterparties than exchange-traded instruments. The counterparties can select the dollar amount that they wish to swap, without regard to some fixed contract terms, such as those that prevail in exchange-traded instruments. Similarly, the swap counterparties choose the exact maturity that they need, rather than having to fit their needs to the offerings available on an exchange. This is very important in the swaps market, because this flexibility allows the counterparties to deal with much longer horizons than can be addressed through exchange-traded instruments.

On futures and options exchanges, major financial institutions are readily identifiable. For example, in a futures pit, traders will be able to discern the activity of particular firms, because traders know who represents which firm. Therefore, exchange trading necessarily involves a certain loss of privacy. In the swaps market, by contrast, only the counterparties know that the swap takes place. Thus, the swaps market affords a privacy that cannot be obtained in exchange trading.[1]

We have noted that the futures and options exchanges are subject to considerable government regulation. By contrast, the swaps market has virtually no government regulation. As we will see later, swaps are similar to futures. The swaps market feared that the Commodity Futures Trading Commission might attempt to assert regulatory authority over the swaps market on the grounds that swaps are really futures. However, the Commodity Futures Trading Commission has formally announced that it will not seek jurisdiction over the swaps market. This means that the swaps market is likely to remain free of federal regulation for the foreseeable future. For the most part, participants in the swaps market are thankful to avoid regulation.

The swaps market also has some inherent limitations. First, to consummate a swap transaction, one potential counterparty must find a counterparty that is willing to take the opposite side of a transaction. If one party needs a specific maturity or a certain pattern of cash flows, it can be very difficult to find a willing counterparty. Second, because a swap agreement is a contract between two counterparties, the swap cannot be altered or terminated early without the agreement of both parties. Third, for futures and exchange-traded options, the exchanges effectively guarantee performance on the contracts for all parties. By its very nature, the swaps market has no such guarantor. As a consequence, parties to the swap must be certain of the creditworthiness of their counterparties.

As we will see later in this chapter, the swaps market has developed mechanisms to deal with these three limitations. The problem of potential default is perhaps the most important. Assessing the financial credibility of a counterparty is difficult and expensive. Therefore, participation in the swaps market is effectively limited to firms and institutions that either engage in frequent swap transactions or have access to major swap facilitators that can advise on creditworthiness. In effect, the swaps market is virtually limited to firms and financial institutions, and there are few or no individual transactors in the market.

PLAIN VANILLA SWAPS

In this section we analyze the different kinds of swaps that are available, and we show how swaps can help corporations manage various types of risk exposure. We begin by considering the mechanics of the simplest kinds of swaps. A **plain vanilla swap**, the simplest kind, can be an interest rate swap or a foreign currency swap.

INTEREST RATE SWAPS

In a plain vanilla interest rate swap, one counterparty has an initial position in a fixed rate debt instrument, while the other counterparty has an initial position in a floating rate obligation. In this initial position, the party with the floating rate obligation is exposed to changes in interest rates. By swapping the floating rate obligation, this counterparty eliminates exposure to changing interest rates. For the party with a fixed rate obligation, the interest rate swap increases the interest rate sensitivity. (Later, we explore the motivation that these counterparties might have for taking their respective positions. First, however, we need to understand the transactions.)

To see the nature of the plain vanilla interest rate swap most clearly, we use an example. We assume that the swap covers a five-year period and involves annual payments on a $1 million principal amount. Let us assume that Party A agrees to pay a fixed rate of 12 percent to Party B. In return, Party B agrees to pay a floating rate of LIBOR + 3 percent to Party A. LIBOR stands for "London Interbank Offered Rate," a base rate at which large international banks lend funds to each other. Floating rates in the swaps market are most often set as equaling LIBOR plus some additional amount. Figure 4.1 shows the basic features of this transaction. Party A pays 12 percent of $1 million, or $120,000, each year to Party B. Party B makes a payment to Party A in return, but the actual amount of the payments depends on movement in LIBOR.

Conceptually, the two parties also exchange the principal amount of $1 million. However, actually making the transaction of sending each other $1 million would not make practical sense. As a consequence, principal amounts are generally not exchanged. Instead, the principal plays a conceptual role in determining the

■ **Figure 4.1**

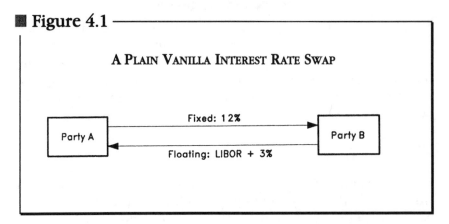

A Plain Vanilla Interest Rate Swap

amount of the interest payments. Because the principal is not actually exchanged, it is called a **notional principal**, an amount used as a base for computations, but not an amount that is actually transferred from one party to another. In our example, the notional principal is $1 million, and knowing that amount lets us compute the actual dollar amount of the cash flows that the two parties make to each other each year.

Let us assume that the LIBOR is 10 percent at the time of the first payment. This means that Party A will be obligated to pay $120,000 to Party B. Party B will owe $130,000 to Party A. Offsetting the two mutual obligations, Party B owes $10,000 to Party A. Generally, only the **net payment**, the difference between the two obligations, actually takes place. Again, this practice avoids unnecessary payments.[2]

Foreign Currency Swaps

In a currency swap, one party holds one currency and desires a different currency. The swap arises when one party provides a certain principal in one currency to its counterparty in exchange for an equivalent amount of a different currency. For example, Party C may have German marks and be anxious to swap those marks for U.S. dollars. Similarly, Party D may hold U.S. dollars and be willing to exchange those dollars for German marks. With these needs, Parties C and D may be able to engage in a currency swap.

A plain vanilla currency swap involves three different sets of cash flows. First, at the initiation of the swap, the two parties actually do exchange cash. The entire motivation for the currency swap is the actual need for funds denominated in a different currency. This differs from the interest rate swap, in which both parties deal in dollars and can pay the net amount. Second, the parties make periodic interest payments to each other during the life of the swap agreement. Third, at the termination of the swap, the parties again exchange the principal.

As an example, let us assume that the current spot exchange rate between German marks and U.S. dollars is 2.5 marks per dollar. Therefore, the mark is worth $.40. We assume that the U.S. interest rate is 10 percent and the German interest rate is 8 percent. Party C holds 25 million marks and wishes to exchange those marks for dollars. In return for the marks, Party D would pay $10 million to Party C at the initiation of the swap. We also assume that the term of the swap is seven years and the parties will make annual interest payments. With the interest rates in our example, Party D will pay 8 percent interest on the 25 million marks it received, so the annual payment from Party D to Party C will be 2 million marks. Party C received $10 million dollars and will pay interest at 10 percent, so Party C will pay $1 million each year to Party D.

In actual practice, the parties will make only net payments. For example, assume that at year 1 the spot exchange rate between the dollar and mark is 2.2222 marks per dollar, so the mark is worth $.45. Valuing the obligations in dollars at this exchange rate, Party C owes $1 million and Party D owes $900,000 (2 million marks times $.45). Thus, Party C would pay the $100,000 difference. At other times, the exchange rate could be different, and the net payment would reflect that different exchange rate.

At the end of seven years, the two parties again exchange principal. In our example, Party C would pay $10 million and Party D would pay 25 million marks. This final payment terminates the currency swap. Figure 4.2 shows the first element of the swap, which is the initial exchange of principal. Figure 4.3 represents the payment of interest, and in our example there would be seven of these payments, one for each year of the swap. Finally, Figure 4.4 shows the second exchange of principal that completes the swap.

SUMMARY

In this section we considered the transactions involved in plain vanilla interest rate and currency swaps. As we saw for an interest rate swap, the essential feature is the transformation of a fixed rate

■ **Figure 4.2**

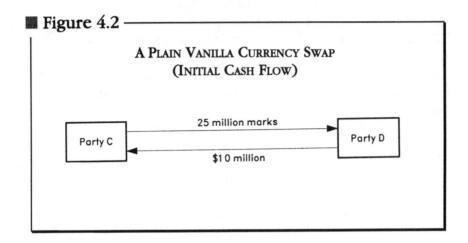

A PLAIN VANILLA CURRENCY SWAP
(INITIAL CASH FLOW)

■ **Figure 4.3**

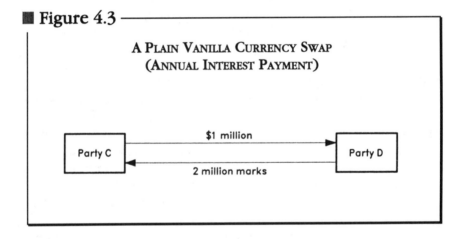

A PLAIN VANILLA CURRENCY SWAP
(ANNUAL INTEREST PAYMENT)

■ **Figure 4.4**

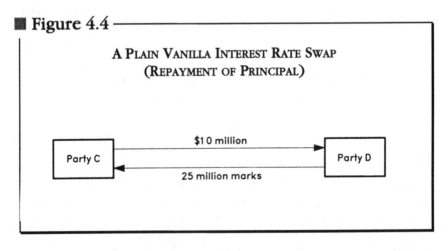

A PLAIN VANILLA INTEREST RATE SWAP
(REPAYMENT OF PRINCIPAL)

obligation to a floating rate obligation for one party and a complementary transformation of a floating rate obligation to a fixed rate obligation for the other party. In a currency swap, the two parties exchange currencies to obtain access to a foreign currency that better meets their business needs. To this point, we have focused only on the elementary transactions involved in simple swaps; we have not considered the motivation that leads to swap agreements.

MOTIVATIONS FOR SWAPS

In our example of a plain vanilla swap, we saw that one party begins with a fixed rate obligation and seeks a floating rate obligation. The second party exchanges a floating rate for a fixed rate obligation. For this swap to occur, the two parties have to be seeking exactly the opposite goals.

There are two basic motivations that we consider in this section. First, the normal commercial operations of some firms naturally lead to interest rate and currency risk positions of a certain type. Second, some firms may have certain advantages in acquiring specific types of financing. Firms can borrow in the form that is cheapest and use swaps to change the characteristics of the borrowing to one that meets the firm's specific needs. In this section we consider several simple examples of motivations for swaps.

COMMERCIAL NEEDS

As an example of a prime candidate for an interest rate swap, consider a typical savings and loan association. Savings and loan associations accept deposits and lend those funds for long-term mortgages. Because depositors can withdraw their funds on short notice, deposit rates must adjust to changing interest rate conditions. Most mortgagors wish to borrow at a fixed rate for a long time. As a result, the savings and loan association can be left with floating rate liabilities and fixed rate assets. This means that the savings and loan is vulnerable to rising rates. If rates rise, the savings and loan will be forced to increase the rate it pays on deposits, but it cannot increase the interest rate it charges on the mortgages that have already been issued.

To escape this interest rate risk, the savings and loan might use the swap market to transform its fixed rate assets into floating rate assets or transform its floating rate liabilities into fixed rate liabilities. Let us assume that the savings and loan wishes to transform a fixed rate mortgage into an asset that pays a floating rate of interest. In terms of our interest rate swap example, the savings and loan association is like Party A – in exchange for the fixed rate mortgage that it holds, it wants to pay a fixed rate of interest and receive a floating rate of interest. Engaging in a swap as Party A did will help the association to resolve its interest rate risk.

To make the discussion more concrete, we extend our example of the plain vanilla interest rate swap. We assume that the savings and loan association has just loaned $1 million for five years at 12 percent with annual payments, and we assume that the savings and loan pays a deposit rate that equals LIBOR plus 1 percent. With these rates, the association will lose money if LIBOR exceeds 11 percent, and this danger prompts the association to consider an interest rate swap.

Figure 4.5 shows our original plain vanilla interest rate swap with the additional information about the savings and loan that we have just elaborated. In the figure, Party A is the savings and loan association, and it receives payments at a fixed rate of 12 percent on the mortgage. After it enters the swap, the association also pays 12 percent on a notional principal of $1 million. In effect, it receives mortgage payments and passes them through to Party B under the swap agreement. Under the swap agreement, Party A receives a floating rate of LIBOR plus 3 percent. From this cash inflow, the association pays its depositors LIBOR plus 1 percent. This leaves a periodic inflow to the association of 2 percent, which is the spread that it makes on the loan.

In our example, the association now has a fixed rate inflow of 2 percent, and it has succeeded in avoiding its exposure to interest rate risk. No matter what happens to the level of interest rates, the association will enjoy a net cash inflow of 2 percent on $1 million. This example clarifies how the savings association has a strong motivation to enter the swaps market. From the very nature of the savings and loan industry, the association finds itself with a risk exposure to rising interest rates. However, by engaging in an interest rate swap, the association can secure a fixed rate position.

COMPARATIVE ADVANTAGE

In many situations, one firm may have better access to the capital market than another firm.[3] For example, a U.S. firm may be able to

■ **Figure 4.5**

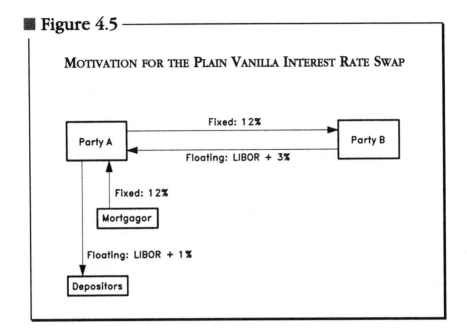

MOTIVATION FOR THE PLAIN VANILLA INTEREST RATE SWAP

borrow easily in the United States, but it might not have such favorable access to the capital market in Germany. Similarly, a German firm may have good borrowing opportunities domestically but poor opportunities in the United States.

Table 4.1 presents borrowing rates for Parties C and D, the firms of our plain vanilla currency swap example. In the plain vanilla example, we assumed that, for each currency, both parties faced the same rate. We now assume that Party C is a German firm with access to marks at a rate of 7 percent, whereas the U.S. firm, Party D, must pay 8 percent to borrow marks. On the other hand, Party D can borrow dollars at 9 percent, whereas the German Party C must pay 10 percent for its dollar borrowings.

As the table shows, Party C enjoys a comparative advantage in borrowing marks and Party D has a comparative advantage in borrowing dollars. These rates raise the possibility that each firm can exploit its comparative advantage and share the gains by reducing overall borrowing costs. This possibility is shown in Figures 4.6–4.8, which parallel Figures 4.2–4.4.

Figure 4.6 resembles Figure 4.2, but it provides more information. In Figure 4.6, Party C borrows 25 million marks from a third party lender at its borrowing rate of 7 percent, while Party D borrows $10 million from a fourth party at 9 percent. After these bor-

■ Table 4.1 —————————————————————

Borrowing Rates for Two Firms in Two Currencies

Firm	U.S. Dollar Rate	German Mark Rate
Party C	10%	7%
Party D	9%	8%

rowings, both parties have the funds to engage in the plain vanilla currency swap that we have already analyzed. To initiate the swap, Party C forwards the 25 million marks it has just borrowed to Party D, which reciprocates with the $10 million it has borrowed. In effect, the two parties have made independent borrowings and then exchanged the proceeds. For this reason, currency swaps are also known as an **exchange of borrowings**.

Figure 4.7 shows the same swap terms we have already analyzed. Party C pays interest payments at a rate of 10 percent on the $10 million it received from Party D, and Party D pays 2 million marks

■ Figure 4.6 —————————————————————

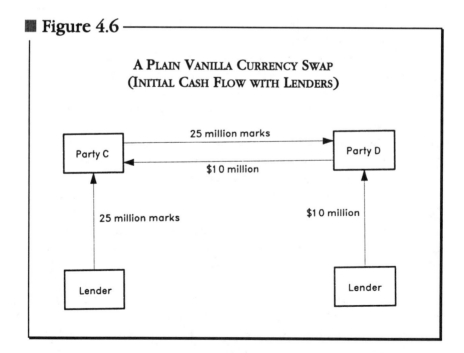

A Plain Vanilla Currency Swap
(Initial Cash Flow with Lenders)

25 million marks

Party C

$10 million

Party D

25 million marks

$10 million

Lender

Lender

interest per year on the 25 million marks it received from Party C. Notice that these rates are the same ones that the two firms could obtain from other sources. However, Figure 4.7 also shows the interest payments that Parties C and D must make on their borrowings. Party C pays 1.75 million marks interest annually, but it receives 2 million marks from Party D. For its part, Party D receives $1 million from Party C, from which it pays interest of $900,000.

Now we can clearly see how the swap benefits both parties. Party C gets the use of $10 million and pays out 1.75 million marks. Had it borrowed dollars on its own, it would have paid a full 10 percent, or $1 million per year. At current exchange rates of 2.5 marks per dollar, Party C is effectively paying $700,000 annual interest on the use of $10 million. This is an effective rate of 7 percent. Party D pays $900,000 interest each year and receives the use of 25 million marks. This is equivalent to paying 2,250,000 marks annual interest ($900,000 times 2.5 marks per dollar) for the use of 25 million marks, or a rate of 9 percent. By using the swap, both parties achieve an effective borrowing rate that is much lower than they could have obtained by borrowing the currency they needed

■ **Figure 4.7**

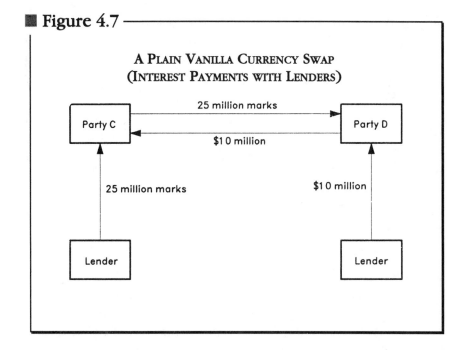

A PLAIN VANILLA CURRENCY SWAP
(INTEREST PAYMENTS WITH LENDERS)

directly. By engaging in the swap, both firms can use the comparative advantage of the other to reduce their borrowing costs. Figure 4.8 shows the termination cash flows for the swap, when both parties repay the principal.

Summary

In this section we have explored two motivations for engaging in swaps: commercial needs and comparative borrowing advantages. The first led to an interest rate swap; the second motivated a currency swap. Both swaps that we have analyzed are plain vanilla swaps. Although swaps can become much more complex, they are generally motivated by the considerations that we have explored in this section.

Swap Facilitators

As we mentioned earlier, a swap facilitator is a third party who assists in the completion of a swap. When a swap facilitator acts

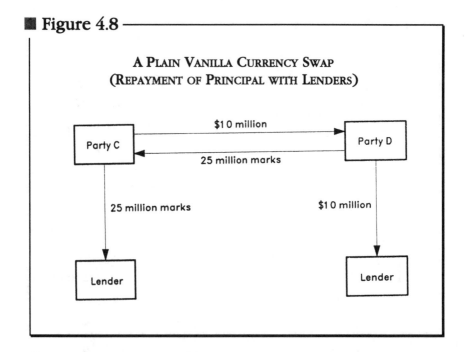

■ **Figure 4.8**

A Plain Vanilla Currency Swap
(Repayment of Principal with Lenders)

strictly as an agent, without taking any financial position in the swap transaction, the facilitator acts as a **swap broker**. In some instances, a swap facilitator may actually transact for its own account to help complete the swap. In this case, the swap facilitator acts as a **swap dealer**. Both swap brokers and swap dealers are known as **swap banks**, so a swap bank is equivalent to a swap facilitator. This section explores the role of swap brokers and dealers.

SWAP BROKERS

For a swap transaction to occur, two counterparties with matching needs must find each other. As we have seen, a firm with a short-term and fairly standard risk exposure might use futures or exchange-traded options to manage that risk. Special risk exposures often lead firms to look beyond futures and exchange-traded options to the swaps market for the management of that special exposure. For example, even with the plain vanilla interest rate and currency swaps examples that we considered, the risks faced by the parties could not be managed completely with futures or exchange-traded options. As the risk exposure goes beyond the plain vanilla variety, futures and exchange-traded options are even less adequate for managing these more complex risks.

For a potential swap participant with a specific need, finding a counterparty can be very difficult. For example, in the previous example of a plain vanilla currency swap, Party C must find another firm that meets a number of conditions. The firm that will act as a counterparty to Party C must have preferential borrowing access to $10 million, a need for German marks, a requirement that matches Party C in size ($10 million versus 25 million marks), a time horizon of seven years, a willingness to transact at the time desired by Party C, and an acceptable credit standing. For Party C to find this potential counterparty is a daunting task.

The difficulty of finding counterparties creates an opportunity for a swap broker. A swap broker has a number of firms in his or her client base and stands ready to search for swap counterparties upon demand. In the example of the plain vanilla currency swap, Party C might approach a swap broker and seek assistance in finding a counterparty. In effect, Party C would rely on the swap broker's specialized knowledge of the swap needs of many firms.

After Party C solicits the assistance of a swap broker, the broker contacts potential counterparties. Generally, a firm like Party C will desire privacy, so the broker will not identify Party C before finding a very likely counterparty. (This is another reason why firms use swap brokers. By having a swap broker conduct the search, Party C in our example can preserve its anonymity.) Once the swap broker finds a suitable counterparty, which turns out to be Party D in our plain vanilla currency swap example, the broker brings the two parties together. The broker then helps to negotiate and complete the swap contract. For his or her services, the swap broker receives a fee from each of the counterparties.

In summary, the swap broker serves as an information intermediary. The broker uses his or her superior knowledge of potential swap participants to find the right counterparty. The broker exercises discretion by protecting the identity of the potential counterparties until the swap partners are found. Notice that the swap broker is not a party to the swap contract. As a broker, the swap facilitator does not bear financial risk, but merely assists the two counterparties in completing the swap transaction.

SWAP DEALERS

A swap dealer fulfills all of the functions of a swap broker. In addition, a swap dealer also takes a risk position in the swap transaction by becoming an actual party to the transaction. Just because the swap dealer may take a risk position to complete a swap transaction does not mean that the swap dealer is a speculator. Instead, the swap dealer accepts a risk position in order to complete the transaction for the initial counterparty. The swap transaction may leave the swap dealer with a risk position, but the swap dealer will then try to offset that risk. The swap dealer functions as a financial intermediary, earning profits by helping to complete swap transactions. If completing a swap results in a risk position for the swap dealer, the dealer will then try to minimize that risk by his or her own further transactions.

To explore the functions served by the swap dealer, we assume that the dealer begins with its optimal set of investments. In other words, the swap dealer has financial assets, but they are invested in a way that the swap dealer finds optimal. Therefore, if the swap dealer takes part in a swap transaction and has his or her financial position altered as a result of that transaction, we assume that the change in the swap dealer's position represents an unwanted risk that the dealer accepted only to help complete the swap transaction and earn profits thereby. Against this background, we return to our example of a plain vanilla interest rate swap to explore the additional role performed by the swap dealer.

In the plain vanilla interest rate swap example, we noted that Party A was a savings and loan association that paid a floating rate of LIBOR + 1 percent to its depositors and made a five-year fixed rate mortgage loan at 12 percent. This initial business position left Party A exposed to rising interest rates, and Party A wanted to avoid this risk by converting the fixed rate it received on its mortgage loan to a floating rate. Party A's ability to complete this swap depended on finding a suitable counterparty with a matching need, such as Party B in our example.

If a firm like Party B cannot be found, Party A is left unable to complete the swap. Often a swap broker will be unable to find a suitable counterparty, or the swap broker can find only a partial match. In many instances, the swap broker may be able to find a potential counterparty that will take only a portion of the swap that the initial counterparty wants to complete or the potential counterparty does not want to transact at the time the initial counterparty desires.

To complete the swap transaction for Party A, the swap dealer may act as a counterparty. Figure 4.9 shows the plain vanilla interest rate swap example as before, except the swap dealer acts as the counterparty to Party A. As a result, we see that the swap gives the swap dealer the same cash flows that Party B had in Figure 4.5.

As a result of this transaction, the swap dealer now has an undesired risk position. Over the next five years the dealer is obligated to pay a floating rate of LIBOR + 3 percent and to receive a fixed rate of 12 percent on a notional amount of $10 million. The swap dealer must believe that he or she can make money by acting as a counterparty to Party A. To do so, the swap dealer wants to offset the risk being undertaken, but needs to offset that risk on better terms than those undertaken as a counterparty to Party A.

Let us assume that the dealer knew of a potential party in the swap market, Party E, that was willing to pay a floating rate of LIBOR + 3.1 percent in exchange for a fixed rate of 12 percent on a notional amount of $10 million. However, Party E is willing to

■ Figure 4.9

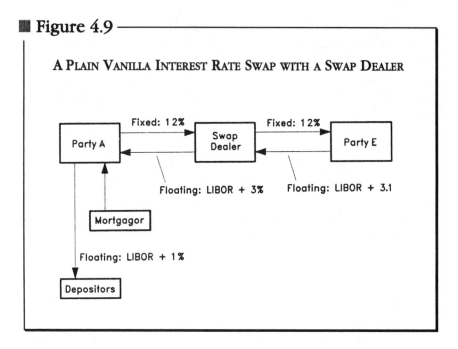

A PLAIN VANILLA INTEREST RATE SWAP WITH A SWAP DEALER

accept a term of only three years, not the five years that Party A desires. Given a knowledge of this client, the swap dealer decides to act as a counterparty to Party A. By also transacting with Party E, the swap dealer is able to offset a substantial portion of the risk accepted by transacting with Party A. Figure 4.10 shows the transactions involving Parties A and E, along with the swap dealer. After completing these transactions, we see that the swap dealer has some profits to show for these efforts. Specifically, the dealer is making 10 basis points on the floating rate side of the transaction because he or she receives LIBOR + 3.1 percent and pays LIBOR + 3 percent. However, the swap dealer still has considerable risk as a result of the transaction.

Table 4.2 shows the swap dealer's cash flows resulting from the swap. The first two columns of Table 4.2 show the cash flows that result from the swap dealer's transactions with Party A. To serve the needs of Party A, the swap dealer has agreed to receive a 12 percent fixed rate payment in exchange for paying LIBOR + 3 percent on a $10 million notional amount. Based on the portion of the transaction with Party A, the swap dealer will receive $1.2 million each year and pay LIBOR + 3 percent on $10 million each year. Which set of cash flows is better is uncertain because the future

■ Figure 4.10

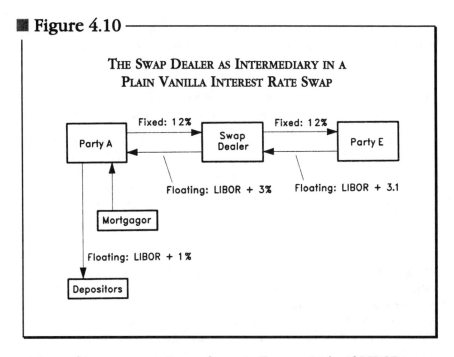

THE SWAP DEALER AS INTERMEDIARY IN A
PLAIN VANILLA INTEREST RATE SWAP

course of interest rates is not known. For example, if LIBOR stays constant at 8 percent over the five years, the swap dealer will profit handsomely, making 1 percent per year for five years on $10 million. However, if LIBOR jumps to 11 percent and remains constant, the swap dealer will be paying 14 percent on $10 million each year. As a result, the swap dealer will receive $1.2 million but must pay $1.4 million each year, for an annual net loss of $200,000. Thus, the riskiness of acting as a counterparty to Party A is clear.

■ Table 4.2

THE SWAP DEALER'S CASH FLOWS

Year	From Party A	To Party A	From Party E	To Party E
1	$1,200,000	LIBOR + 3%	LIBOR + 3.1%	$1,200,000
2	$1,200,000	LIBOR + 3%	LIBOR + 3.1%	$1,200,000
3	$1,200,000	LIBOR + 3%	LIBOR + 3.1%	$1,200,000
4	$1,200,000	LIBOR + 3%	0	0
5	$1,200,000	LIBOR + 3%	0	0

Table 4.2 also shows the swap dealer's cash flows that result from transacting with Party E. For each of the first three years, the dealer will pay a fixed interest rate of 12 percent on $10 million, or $1.2 million. In addition, the dealer will receive a rate of LIBOR + 3.1 percent on a notional amount of $10 million.

The swap dealer's net cash flows are as follows:

Year	Dealer's Net Cash Flow
1	$10,000
2	10,000
3	10,000
4	$1,200,000 – LIBOR + 3%
5	$1,200,000 – LIBOR + 3%

For the first three years, the swap dealer has achieved a perfect match in cash flows, receiving $1.2 million from Party A and paying it to Party E. The dealer has a net zero cash flow on this part of the transaction. During the first three years, the dealer also receives LIBOR + 3.1 percent from Party E and pays LIBOR + 3 percent to Party A, both on notional amounts of $10 million. On this portion of the transaction, the dealer receives a net spread of 10 basis points on a $10 million notional amount. Taking all of the dealer's cash flows during the first three years into account, we see that the dealer has a net cash inflow of $10,000 per year.

Even after transacting with both Parties A and E, the swap dealer has a residual risk that is evident from the total cash flows. In years 4 and 5, the dealer will receive $1.2 million from Party A, but he must pay LIBOR + 3 percent. Whether this will create a profit or loss for the dealer depends on future interest rates. However, in Table 4.2 we can see that the dealer has substantially reduced this risk position by trading with Party E.

SWAP DEALERS AS FINANCIAL INTERMEDIARIES

Table 4.2 also shows that the swap dealer is making a profit as a financial intermediary. Because of superior knowledge of the market, the dealer was able to find Party E. By transacting with Party E, instead of just transacting with Party A, the swap dealer secures a 10 basis point spread on the notional amount for three years. In addition to earning a profit on the spread, the dealer's transaction with Party E offsets a substantial portion of the risk inherent in acting as a counterparty to Party A in the initial swap transaction.

In our example of the swap dealer's transactions, we assumed that the swap dealer had an initial portfolio of assets that met his or her needs in terms of risk and diversification. By acting as a counterparty to Party A, the swap dealer assumed a risk in pursuit of profit. The dealer could have taken this position as a speculation on interest rates. However, the swap dealer preferred to act as a financial intermediary, making a profit by providing informational services. In our example, the swap dealer is able to capture a spread of 10 basis points and reduce risk by transacting with Party C. Ideally, the swap dealer acting as a financial intermediary would also like to avoid the remaining risk exposure in years 4 and 5. Being able to do so requires that the dealer find another swap partner. We explore the ways in which swap dealers manage the risks associated with acting as counterparties later in this chapter.

SUMMARY

In this section we have seen that swap facilitators or swap banks may act as either brokers or dealers. A swap broker facilitates swap transactions by bringing potential counterparties together, but the broker does not take a risk position in the swap. By contrast, a swap dealer acts as a counterparty in the swap, in addition to providing the informational assistance provided by a broker. Notice that the same firm can act as a swap broker in some transactions and as a swap dealer in others. Calling a firm a swap broker or swap dealer refers to the function that the firm fulfills in a particular transaction.

By taking a position in a swap transaction, a swap dealer accepts a risk position. The firm that accepts this risk position could approach the transaction as a speculator or as a swap dealer. Functioning as a swap dealer, the firm accepts the position with the idea of avoiding as much of the risk exposure as possible. Specifically, the firm acting as a financial intermediary will attempt to offset the initial risk and be satisfied to make a profit by acting as a conduit between other swap parties. When the swap dealer acts as a counterparty, the dealer intends to be only a temporary substitute for an unavailable counterparty.

PRICING OF SWAPS

In this section we explore the principles that underlie swap pricing. To simplify the discussion, we focus on plain vanilla interest rate swaps, and we assume that the swap dealer wishes to act as a pure financial intermediary. That is, the swap dealer does not want to assume a risk position with respect to interest rates. The principles apply, however, to swaps of all types.

FACTORS THAT AFFECT SWAP PRICING

The swap dealer must price swaps to reflect a number of factors. These include the creditworthiness of the potential swap partner, the availability of other swap opportunities that will allow the swap dealer to offset the risk of an initial swap, and the term structure of interest rates.[4] We discuss each of these in turn.

Creditworthiness. The swap dealer must appraise the creditworthiness of the swap partner. As we have seen earlier in this chapter, there is no clearinghouse in the swap market to guarantee performance on a contract if one of the counterparties defaults. If one of the counterparties defaults, the dealer must either absorb the loss or institute a lawsuit to seek recovery on the defaulted obligation.

In most swaps, the timing of cash flows between the counterparties is matched fairly closely. For example, in the plain vanilla interest rate swap of Figure 4.10, the fixed and floating cash flows occur at similar times, and we noted that only the net amount is actually exchanged. Thus, default on a swap seldom could involve failure to pay the notional amount or even an entire periodic payment. In this sense, default on a swap is not as critical as default on a corporate bond, in which an investor might lose the entire principal. Instead, a swap default would generally imply a loss of the change in value due to shifting interest rates. Even though this amount can be quite significant, such a default would not be as catastrophic as a bond default in which the entire principal could be lost.

As we saw in Figure 4.10 and as we explore in more detail later in this chapter, the swap dealer seeks to build a swap portfolio in which the risks of individual swaps offset each other. In Figure 4.10, the risks in the swap with Party A are largely offset by the risks in the swap with Party E. When a swap dealer suffers a default, the elaborate structure of offsetting risks can be upset. This leaves the swap dealer in a riskier position, and the dealer must struggle to re-establish the risk control upset by the default.

Because of the potential costs associated with default, the swap dealer will adjust the pricing on swaps to reflect the risk of default. Parties that have a high risk of default are likely to be excluded from the market. For example, airlines under bankruptcy protection probably have very limited access to the swap market. As we noted earlier, the swap market is mainly a market for financial institutions and corporations due to the importance of default considerations and the need for one party to be able to confirm the creditworthiness of a prospective counterparty.

Availability of Additional Counterparties. Because we are assuming that the swap dealer wishes to act only as a financial intermediary, the swap dealer will be very concerned about how the risk involved in a prospective swap can be offset by participating in other swaps. For example, in the dealer's swap of Figure 4.10, the willingness of the swap dealer to enter the transaction with Party A may well depend on the dealer's knowledge of Party E. A dealer who considers transacting with Party A and does not know of Party E may require more favorable terms to transact with Party A. However, the dealer who knows about Parties A and E from the outset may accept less favorable terms because of knowing how to offset some of the risk of acting as Party A's counterparty by engaging in a second swap with Party E.

As we noted, the swap dealer faces the net cash flows in the last column of Table 4.2 after engaging in the two interest rate swaps with Parties A and E. Assume now that another potential swap participant, Party F, is available to swap the cash flows in years 4 and 5. In other words, Party F would be willing to pay a floating rate on a $10 million notional amount for years 4 and 5 and to receive a fixed rate of 12 percent. The swap dealer would find Party F to be a very attractive counterparty. The dealer might be quite willing to swap with Party F on even terms ($1.2 million versus LIBOR + 3 percent) just to offset the risk that remained after swapping with Parties A and E. In sum, the swap dealer will be very pleased to create a structure of swaps that leaves no interest rate risk and still provides a decent profit.

The Term Structure of Interest Rates. The term structure of interest rates is an important feature in bond pricing. Not surprisingly, the market for interest rate swaps must reflect the term structure that prevails in the bond market. If the swaps market did not reflect the term structure, traders would find ready arbitrage opportunities, and they could quickly discipline swap traders to pay attention to the term structure. For example, if the term structure is rising, the swap dealer must charge a higher yield on swaps of longer maturity. The next section illustrates these considerations from the term structure.

THE INDICATION SWAP PRICING SCHEDULE

In the early to middle 1980s, swap banks were often able to charge a **front-end** fee for arranging a swap. As the market has matured, that ability has been competed away. (For some very complicated swaps that require substantial analysis, front-end fees are still charged, however.) Therefore, today generally the total compensation comes from charging a spread between the rates the swap dealer is willing to pay and the rate he or she demands on swap transactions. With a maturing market, this spread has also narrowed. Whereas in the mid-1980s spreads might have been 50 basis points, a 10 basis point spread is much more common today. This tightening spread reflects the increasing liquidity, sophistication, and pricing efficiency of a maturing financial market.

Table 4.3 shows a sample indication pricing schedule for an interest rate swap. The table assumes that the customer of the swap bank will offer LIBOR flat; that is, a rate exactly equal to LIBOR without any yield adjustment. There are two important features of Table 4.3. First, the rate the bank pays or receives increases with the maturity in question. This increase reflects the upward sloping term structure revealed by the column of current T-note yields. Second, the swap bank makes a gross profit that equals the spread between what the bank pays and what it receives. Consequently, the spread ranges from 10 basis points for a 2-year horizon to 22 basis points for a 10-year horizon. This increasing spread for more distant maturities reflects the lower liquidity of longer term instruments.

As an example of how the pricing schedule in Table 4.3 functions, assume that the customer wishes to pay a floating rate and receive a fixed rate for seven years. Based on the pricing schedule

■ **Table 4.3** ―――――――――――――――――――――――――――

SAMPLE SWAP INDICATION PRICING

Maturity (years)	Bank Pays	Bank Receives	T-Note Yields
2	18	28	7.40
3	34	45	7.66
4	52	68	7.84
5	70	89	8.05
7	82	102	8.14
10	88	110	8.20

Source: Adapted from J. Marshall and K. Kapner, *The Swaps Market*, Miami: Kolb Publishing, 1993

of Table 4.3, the customer would pay the LIBOR rate on the notional amount in each period and would receive a fixed rate from the swap bank that equals the seven-year T-note rate of 8.14 percent plus 82 basis points for a total rate of 8.96 percent. By contrast, if the customer wishes to pay a fixed rate for a seven-year horizon, the customer would pay the seven-year T-note rate of 8.14 percent plus 102 basis points for a rate of 9.16 percent. In return, the bank would pay the customer the LIBOR rate in each period.[5]

SWAP PORTFOLIOS

In this section we briefly consider the principal risks that a swap dealer faces in managing a swap portfolio. These risks range from default risk to interest rate risk. We then illustrate how the swap dealer can manage some of these risks.

RISKS IN MANAGING A SWAP PORTFOLIO

In managing a portfolio of many swaps, the swap dealer faces a number of different risks. First, there is the risk that one of its counterparties might default, as we discussed earlier. Second, the bank faces **basis risk** – the risk that the normal relationship between two prices might change. To illustrate this risk, assume that a bank engages in an interest rate swap, agreeing to receive the T-note rate plus some basis points and to pay LIBOR. After this agreement is reached, assume that market disturbances in Europe cause LIBOR to rise relative to the T-note rate. The swap dealer must still pay LIBOR, but this rate is now higher than anticipated when the dealer initiated the swap. Therefore, the swap dealer suffers a loss due to basis risk as the normal relationship between LIBOR and the T-note rate has changed.

The swap dealer also faces mismatch risk. When acting as a counterparty in a swap, the swap dealer accepts a risk position that he or she is anxious to offset by engaging in other swaps. **Mismatch risk** is the risk that the swap dealer will be left in a position that cannot easily be offset through another swap. This arises if there is a mismatch in the needs between the swap dealer and other participants. In Table 4.2, for example, the two swaps with Parties A and E left the swap dealer with a residual risk position, due to the mismatch between the needs of Parties A and E.

One of the most serious risks that the swap dealer faces is interest rate risk. For example, the swap dealer may have promised to pay a floating rate and to receive a fixed rate. If the general level of interest rates rises, the swap dealer's cash outflows will rise as well. However, the dealer continues to receive the stipulated fixed rate. The swap dealer incurs a loss due to a shift in interest rates. In Table 4.2, for example, the swap dealer is left to receive $1.2 million annually and to pay LIBOR + 3 percent on a notional principal of $10 million in years 4 and 5. If rates rise, the payments that the dealer must make will increase, while the cash inflows remain the same. Such a rise in interest rates would generate a loss for the swap dealer, so the dealer faces interest rate risk.

Managing Mismatch and Interest Rate Risk in a Swap

We illustrate how swap dealers can manage mismatch and interest rate risk by considering the swap dealer's transactions with Parties A and E, as shown in Table 4.2. We have already noted that the swap dealer accepts a risk position by acting as a counterparty in a swap. Because we assume that the swap dealer wishes to function strictly as a financial intermediary and not as a speculator, the dealer is anxious to avoid any risk that it might have temporarily undertaken to complete the swap.

In our discussion of Table 4.2, for example, we saw that the dealer participated in a swap with Party A and was able to offset part of the risk by engaging in another swap with Party E. As Table 4.2 shows, however, some residual risk remains. Specifically, the swap bank is still committed to receiving $1.2 million and paying LIBOR + 3 percent on a notional amount of $10 million in years 4 and 5.

This residual risk position reflects both mismatch risk and interest rate risk. The mismatch risk occurs because the dealer was unable to offset the risks associated with the swap with Party A. The transaction with Party E offset most of the risk arising from the swap with Party A, but some risk remains due to the mismatch between the needs of Parties A and E. The transactions of Table 4.2 also reflect a continuing interest rate risk. As we noted, if rates rise, the dealer suffers a loss by having to pay the higher floating rates that result.

As a consequence, the swap dealer will be anxious to avoid these two remaining risks associated with his or her commitments in periods 4 and 5 in Table 4.2. Ideally, the dealer would arrange a third swap, in addition to those with Parties A and E, to offset this risk. For example, the dealer would like to swap to receive a floating rate and pay a fixed rate for years 4 and 5. Such a transaction would avoid both the mismatch and the interest rate risk. However, such swaps are not always immediately available to the dealer. As a consequence, the swap dealer will seek other means to control this risk.

A swap dealer who faces a risk such as that in Table 4.2 can use the futures market as a temporary means of offsetting the risk. For example, the swap dealer might sell Eurodollar futures with a distant expiration. Eurodollar rates are highly correlated with LIBOR. With this transaction, the swap dealer offsets a considerable portion of the risk that remains in Table 4.2. The swap dealer who executes the futures transaction properly will be left only with an obligation to pay a fixed amount.

However, even after this transaction, some risk remains. Eurodollar futures may be a close substitute for the unavailable swap, but they are unlikely to provide a perfect substitute. In our example, the dealer will probably not be able to match the futures expiration with the year 4 and 5 cash flows, there is likely to be some imperfection in setting the quantity of futures to trade, and there is still some basis risk between the LIBOR rate of the cash flows in years 4 and 5 and the rate on the Eurodollars.

Because of these imperfections in substituting for the unavailable swap, the swap dealer will likely continue to seek a swap that meets the risk needs exactly. However, until that is available, the Eurodollar futures position can act as an effective risk-reducing position.

SUMMARY

This chapter introduced the swaps market. From its origins in the late 1970s and early 1980s, the swaps market has grown to enormous proportions, with notionals exceeding $6 trillion. Most of the market is concentrated in interest rate swaps, but there are billions of dollars of foreign currency swaps outstanding as well. Of all swaps, about 40 to 50 percent involve the U.S. dollar.

In contrast with futures and exchange-traded options, we noted that swap agreements are extremely flexible in amount, maturity, and other contract terms. As further points of differentiation between futures and exchange-traded options versus swaps, the swaps market does not utilize an exchange and is virtually free of government regulation.

The chapter also analyzed plain vanilla interest rate and currency swaps. We saw that an interest rate swap essentially involves a commitment by two parties to exchange cash flows tied to some principal, or notional, amount. One party pays a fixed rate, while the second party pays a floating rate. In a foreign currency swap, both parties acquire funds in different currencies and exchange those principal amounts. Each party pays interest to the other in the currency that was acquired, with these interest payments taking place over the term of the swap agreement. To terminate the agreement, the parties again exchange foreign currency. Motivations for swaps arise from a desire to avoid financial risk or a chance to exploit some borrowing advantage.

Swap brokers and dealers are two kinds of swap facilitators. A swap broker helps counterparties complete swaps by providing introduction and guidance in the negotiation of the swap, but the swap broker does not take a risk position in the swap. By contrast, a swap dealer provides the services of the swap broker but will also act as a counterparty in a swap. For the swap dealer, we considered the factors that influence pricing, and we discussed the techniques that swap dealers use to manage the risk associated with their portfolios of swaps.

QUESTIONS AND PROBLEMS

1. Explain the differences between a plain vanilla interest rate swap and a plain vanilla currency swap.

2. What are the two major kinds of swap facilitators? What is the key difference between the roles they play?

3. Assume that you are a financial manager for a large commercial bank and that you expect short-term interest rates to rise more than the yield curve would suggest. Would you rather pay a fixed long-term rate and receive a floating short rate or the other way around? Explain your reasoning.

4. Explain the role that the notional principal plays in understanding swap transactions. Why is this principal amount regarded as only notional? (Hint: What is the dictionary definition of *notional*?)

5. Consider a plain vanilla interest rate swap. Explain how the practice of net payments works.

6. Assume that the yield curve is flat, that the swap market is efficient, and that two equally creditworthy counterparties engage in an interest rate swap. Who should pay the higher rate, the party that pays a floating short-term rate or the party that pays a fixed long-term rate? Explain.

7. In a currency swap, counterparties exchange the same sums at the beginning and the end of the swap period. Explain how this practice relates to the custom of making interest payments during the life of the swap agreement.

8. Explain why a currency swap is also called an *exchange of borrowings*.

9. Assume that LIBOR stands today at 9 percent and the seven-year T-note rate is 10 percent. Establish an indication pricing schedule for a seven-year interest rate swap, assuming that the swap dealer must make a gross spread of 40 basis points.

10. Explain how basis risk affects a swap dealer. Does it affect a swap broker the same way? Explain.

11. Assume a swap dealer attempts to function as a pure financial intermediary avoiding all interest rate risk. Explain how such a dealer may yet come to bear interest rate risk.

SUGGESTED READINGS

Abken, P. A. "Beyond Plain Vanilla: A Taxonomy of Swaps." Federal Reserve Bank of Atlanta *Economic Review* 76, no. 2 (March–April 1991): 12–29.

Apsel, D., J. Cogen, and M. Rabin. "Hedging Long-Term Commodity Swaps with Futures." *The Handbook of Derivative Instruments*, pp. 413–433. Chicago: Probus Publishing Company, 1991.

Brown, K. C., and D. J. Smith. "Forward Swaps, Swap Options, and the Management of Callable Debt." *Journal of Applied Corporate Finance* 2, no. 4 (Winter 1990): 59–71.

Einzig, R., and B. Lange. "Swaps at Transamerica Analysis and Applications." *Journal of Applied Corporate Finance* 2, no. 4 (Winter 1990): 48–58.

Goodman, L. S. "The Use of Interest Rate Swaps in Managing Corporate Liabilities." *Journal of Applied Corporate Finance* 2, no. 4 (Winter 1990): 35–47.

Kapner, K. R., and J. F. Marshall. *The Swaps Handbook: Swaps and Related Risk Management Instruments*. New York: New York Institute of Finance, 1990.

Marshall, J. F., and K. R. Kapner. *The Swaps Market*. Miami: Kolb Publishing, 1993.

Smith, C. W., Jr., C. W. Smithson, and L. M. Wakeman. "The Market for Interest Rate Swaps." *The Handbook of Financial Engineering*, pp. 212–229. New York: Harper Business, 1990.

Venkatesh, R. E. S., V. Venkatesh, and R. E. Dattatreya. "Introduction to Interest Rate Swaps." *The Handbook of Derivative Instruments*, pp. 129–159. Chicago: Probus Publishing Company, 1991.

NOTES

1. This does not mean to imply that exchange trading sacrifices all anonymity. However, traders watch the activities of major institutions. When these institutions initiate major transactions, it is not possible to maintain complete privacy. It is somewhat iron-

ic that individual traders can trade on futures and options markets with a discretion that is not available to multibillion dollar financial institutions.

2. The practice of net payments and not actually exchanging principal also protects each counterparty from default by the other. For example, it would be very unpleasant for Party A if it paid the principal amount of $1 million in our example and Party B failed to make its payment to Party A. Making only net payments greatly reduces the potential impact of default.

3. This discussion of comparative advantage draws on the excellent analysis by K. Kapner and J. Marshall in *The Swaps Handbook* (New York: New York Institute of Finance, 1990).

4. The swap dealer will also consider some other issues in setting final pricing terms. If the swap is very complicated, the swap dealer may charge a higher price than otherwise. Similarly, if the swap is to involve cross-border currency flows, the dealer may be concerned with regulatory constraints that might impede the flow of funds.

5. In actual market practice, the participants must carefully consider the actual way in which yields are calculated on Treasury securities versus the money market computations that govern LIBOR. We abstract from these technicalities.

Chapter 5

Synthesizing and Transforming Securities

OVERVIEW

The three previous chapters, covering futures, options, and swaps, described the building blocks or the raw materials of the derivatives markets. This chapter shows how these building blocks can be combined to create new securities and how these instruments can be combined with traditional securities to transform the risk and return characteristics of an existing securities position.

This chapter has three main purposes. First, it analyzes the relationships among underlying securities, futures, forwards, swaps, and options. As we explore in some detail, each of these building blocks can be simulated by a combination of others. Therefore, we will explore how to create a **synthetic instrument** – a financial structure that has the same value as another identifiable instrument. For example, we will show how investment in options and a risk-free bond can create a synthetic stock position. As another example, we show how to use swaps to change the characteristics of debt instruments. Second, we explore techniques for combining options to generate profit profiles that are not available with positions in single options. These include strategies with rather colorful names: straddles, strangles, bull and bear spreads, and butterfly spreads. Third, we introduce the idea of using derivatives to specifically alter the risk and return characteristics of an existing position, through a technique called portfolio insurance.

SYNTHETIC INSTRUMENTS

In this section, we show how to create synthetic financial instruments. For example, it is possible to create a portfolio of options that will have the same profits and losses as the underlying asset at the expiration date of the options. To understand how to create synthetic instruments, we begin by reviewing the put-call parity relationship first introduced in Chapter 3. We then proceed to illustrate specific synthetic instruments.

PUT-CALL PARITY AND SYNTHETIC INSTRUMENTS

In Chapter 3 we used the principle of put-call parity to find the price of a put option, given knowledge of the price of a call option on the same underlying good. To apply put-call parity, we need a call option with the same striking price and the same term to expiration as the put we are attempting to price. Subject to those conditions, we saw that the put-call parity maintains that

$$P = C - S + \frac{E}{\left(1 + R_f\right)^T} \tag{5.1}$$

where

$$
\begin{aligned}
S &= \text{stock price} \\
P &= \text{put price} \\
C &= \text{call price} \\
E &= \text{common exercise price for the call and put} \\
R_f &= \text{risk-free rate} \\
T &= \text{common term to expiration for the call and put}
\end{aligned}
$$

This put-call relationship provides the basic blueprint for creating synthetic securities. By rearranging equation 5.1 to isolate individual instruments on the left-hand side of the equation, we see what combination of other instruments will simulate a particular instrument of interest. We now show how to create synthetic equity, synthetic puts, synthetic call options, and a synthetic T-bill.

SYNTHETIC EQUITY

Rearranging equation 5.1 to isolate the stock (S), we have

$$S = C - P + \frac{E}{\left(1 + R_f\right)^T}$$ (5.2)

Equation 5.2 shows that a position in the stock is equivalent to a long call plus a short put, coupled with an investment at the risk-free rate. The investment at the risk-free rate is an amount that will pay the common exercise price on the call and the put at the time of expiration. Thus, **synthetic equity** consists of a long call, short put, and an investment of the present value of the exercise price in the risk-free rate.

To illustrate this equivalence, consider the following example. Assume a call and a put have an exercise price of $80 and expire in one year. The risk-free rate of interest is 7 percent per annum. With this interest rate, an investment of $74.77 will pay the exercise price of $80 in one year. Table 5.1 presents several alternative stock prices that might arise in one year, and it shows the value of the call, put, bond, and the synthetic equity as well.

■ Table 5.1

SYNTHETIC EQUITY

Stock Price Expiration	Elements of Synthetic Equity			Synthetic Equity
	Call E=$80	Short Put E=$80	Risk-Free Investment	
$60	$0	-$20	$80	60
65	0	-15	$80	65
70	0	-10	$80	70
75	0	-5	$80	75
80	0	0	$80	80
85	5	0	$80	85
90	10	0	$80	90
95	15	0	$80	95
100	20	0	$80	100

As Table 5.1 shows, the synthetic equity will have the same value as the stock in one year, no matter what the stock price might be. To see this equivalence, consider a stock price in one year of $95. With this stock price, the put will be worthless and the call will be worth $15. The risk-free bond will pay $80, so the synthetic equity position will be worth $95 as well ($15 from the call and $80 from the risk-free bond). Given the purchase of the synthetic equity, it is also possible to convert the synthetic position into the underlying equity, if the trader wishes. For example, the trader could exercise the call option and use the bond proceeds to pay the exercise price.

To complete the example, consider a terminal stock price below $80. If the stock is worth $65 at expiration, for example, then the call expires worthless, and the risk-free bond is worth $80. However, the synthetic equity involves a short position in a put option that can be exercised against the writer. The short put is a liability of $15 for the synthetic equity holder. Considering the long call, the short put, and the bond together, the synthetic equity position is worth $65, the same as the stock itself.

SYNTHETIC PUT OPTIONS

The put-call parity relationship of equation 5.1 shows that a **synthetic put** consists of a long call and short stock position, coupled with investing the present value of the exercise price in a risk-free instrument. Table 5.2 shows the values of an actual put and the synthetic put for alternative stock prices at expiration. The value of the synthetic put equals the sum of a long call, plus a short stock position, plus an investment in the risk-free bond.

SYNTHETIC CALL OPTIONS

As the put-call parity relationship indicates, a **synthetic call** consists of a long position in both the stock and the put option, and a short position in a risk-free bond that will pay the exercise price at the expiration of the option. To create the synthetic call, a trader borrows the present value of the exercise price and uses these funds to help finance the purchase of the put and the stock. Table 5.3 shows the values at expirations for the constituent elements and for a synthetic call. The table also shows that the synthetic call and the actual call have the same values at expiration for every terminal stock price.

■ **Table 5.2**

A SYNTHETIC PUT

Elements of a Synthetic Put

Stock Price Expiration	Put E=$80	Call E=$80	Short Stock	Risk-Free Investment	Synthetic Put
$60	$20	$0	-$60	$80	$20
65	15	0	-65	80	15
70	10	0	-70	80	10
75	5	0	-75	80	5
80	0	0	-80	80	0
85	0	5	-85	80	0
90	0	10	-90	80	0
95	0	15	-95	80	0
100	0	20	-100	80	0

SYNTHETIC T-BILLS

A synthetic T-bill can also be created by the proper combination of a long put, short call, and a long position in the stock. The resulting position is a synthetic T-bill, because the synthetic instrument will pay the exercise price at the expiration date of the options no

■ **Table 5.3**

A SYNTHETIC CALL

Elements of a Synthetic Call

Stock Price Expiration	Call E=$80	Put E=$80	Stock	Risk-Free Investment	Synthetic Call
$60	$0	$20	$60	-$80	0
65	0	15	65	-$80	0
70	0	10	70	-$80	0
75	0	5	75	-$80	0
80	0	0	80	-$80	0
85	5	0	85	-$80	5
90	10	0	90	-$80	10
95	15	0	95	-$80	15
100	20	0	100	-$80	20

matter what the stock price might be. In a sense, it is ironic that "risky" instruments such as a call, put, and stock, can be combined to simulate a T-bill. Table 5.4 shows the value of the constituent elements and the resulting synthetic T-bill.

SYNTHETIC FUTURES AND FORWARDS AND PUT-CALL PARITY

In our discussion of forwards and futures in Chapter 2, we saw that the futures price sometimes conforms to the Cost-of-Carry relationship. This relationship holds almost exactly in some markets, notably the financial futures markets. However, the Cost-of-Carry relationship provides a less complete understanding of markets for traditional commodities, such as foodstuffs. We now consider the special case in which the Cost-of-Carry relationship holds exactly, and we assume that the Cost-of-Carry equals the risk-free rate. Most financial futures closely approximate these assumptions.

Under these assumptions, the futures price will equal the spot price times one plus the Cost of Carry:

$$F = S(1 + R_f) \qquad (5.3)$$

■ Table 5.4 ─────────────────────────────────

A SYNTHETIC T-BILL

| Stock Price at Expiration | Risk-Free Investment | Elements of a Synthetic T-Bill | | | Synthetic T-Bill |
		Short Call E=$80	Put E=$80	Stock	
$60	$80	$0	$20	$60	$80
65	$80	0	15	65	$80
70	$80	0	10	70	$80
75	$80	0	5	75	$80
80	$80	0	0	80	$80
85	$80	-5	0	85	$80
90	$80	-10	0	90	$80
95	$80	-15	0	95	$80
100	$80	-20	0	100	$80

where

F = futures price

S = spot price

R_f = the risk-free rate, assumed to be the Cost-of-Carry for the good

We now want to integrate the Cost-of-Carry model with the put-call parity relationship and with the analysis of synthetic securities. Rearranging the terms of the put-call parity relationship gives

$$C - P = S - \frac{E}{\left(1 + R_f\right)^T}$$

(5.4)

Combining equations 5.3 and 5.4 gives

$$C - P = \frac{F - E}{\left(1 + R_f\right)^T}$$

(5.5)

Equation 5.5 says that the difference between the call and put price equals the present value of the difference between the futures price and the exercise price of the options. For example, if the exercise price is $100, the futures price is $120, the risk-free rate is 10 percent, and the options expire in one year, we have

$$C - P = \frac{F - E}{\left(1 + R_f\right)^T}$$
$$= \frac{\$120 - \$100}{1.10}$$
$$= \$18.18$$

In this example, the call price must exceed the put price by $18.18. Although this equation gives only the relative value of the call and put, we know that the call option must be worth at least $20, because the call is $20 in-the-money. For its part, the put will have relatively little value because it is so far out-of-the-money.

For the special case in which the current futures price equals the exercise price, then the quantity $F - E$ equals zero. This implies that $C - P$ also equals zero, which means that the call and put must have the same price. If the futures price is less than the exercise price, the quantity $F - E$ is negative. This implies that the put will be more valuable than the call. For the same instruments of the example in the last paragraph, if the futures price is $90, the quantity $F - E = -\$10$, and the value of $C - P$ must be $-\$9.09$.

THE SWAP AS A PORTFOLIO OF FORWARDS

In this section, we show how swaps are related to forward and futures contracts. We present the analysis in terms of forwards to avoid the complications with margin cash flows on futures. However, if we ignore the daily settlement cash flows characteristic of futures, the analysis holds equally well for both futures and forwards. We illustrate that a swap agreement may be analyzed as a portfolio of forward contracts by focusing on an interest rate swap. However, the principle holds for any kind of swap. This equivalence means that we may regard an interest rate swap as a synthetic portfolio of forward contracts. Equivalently, a portfolio of forward or futures positions can be used to synthetically create a swap agreement.

In an interest rate swap, two parties agree to make interest payments on the same underlying principal or notional amount over a specified period. One party agrees to pay a fixed interest rate, while the second party promises to pay a floating rate. Upon contracting, the fixed payor knows exactly the cash flows that it is obligated to make, but the floating payor's cash flows depend on the course of interest rates during the life of the agreement. For example, an interest rate swap might have a notional amount of $1 million and the fixed rate payor might promise to pay 10 percent annually for 10 years. Thus, the fixed payor promises to make 10 annual payments of $100,000. For its part, the floating rate payor might promise to pay LIBOR plus 2 percent. If LIBOR is 8 percent at the time a particular payment is made, the floating rate payor will also pay 10 percent of $1 million or $100,000. If LIBOR is less than 8 percent, the floating rate payor will pay less than it receives; if LIBOR exceeds 8 percent, the floating rate payor will pay more than it receives. (Generally, only the difference is paid on any particular payment date.)

Let us consider just one of the 10 payments in this example of an interest rate swap. The fixed rate payor has promised to pay $100,000 in return for a payment that depends on LIBOR. We may analyze this payment as a forward contract to pay $100,000 at a future date in return for a value that is to be determined by the value of LIBOR on that future date. In essence, this forward contract has the same structure as any interest rate forward or futures contract.

We can see this equivalence by considering a T-bill futures contract. The purchaser of a futures contract promises to pay a certain amount on a future date in return for a 90-day T-bill to be delivered at that time. At the time of contracting, the buyer of the futures knows what payment it will be required to make, but it does not know the value of the T-bill it will receive. The value of the bill depends upon future interest rates. Similarly, in the swap agreement, the fixed rate payor knows what payment it will make on a future date, but it does not know what payment it will receive.

An interest rate swap generally includes a series of payments. In our example, the swap had 10 annual payments. We saw that each of these payments can be analyzed as an interest rate forward contract. Because the swap agreement includes a sequence of 10 such arrangements, the swap is a portfolio of forward contracts.[1] Consider a forward contract on an interest rate instrument that calls for the purchaser to receive delivery of a three-month money market instrument on the expiration date in exchange for a payment determined when the forward contract is negotiated. The purchaser of the forward contract will gain from the transaction when the yield implied by the forward contract is lower than the yield prevailing on three-month instruments at the expiration of the forward contract. In effect, the forward contract requires the exchange of a fixed payment for a floating payment, with the gain or loss being realized at the expiration date.

To make this example more concrete, assume that today is December 15, 1994, and a party buys a forward contract to mature on December 15, 1995, that calls for the purchase of $1 million face value of three-month Eurodollar deposits at a yield of 9 percent. This contract essentially establishes the payment of a fixed rate of 9 percent for these instruments. If the actual yield on these instruments at the expiration date is lower than 9 percent, say 8 percent, then the purchaser of the forward contract has a gain. For a three-month zero coupon instrument and typical money market yield conventions, this 1 percent interest rate differential would be worth $2,500, reflecting a $25 per basis point value.

In essence, this forward contract is similar to one of the payments in an interest rate swap agreement. An interest rate swap agreement is a portfolio of such payments. Therefore, we may analyze an interest rate swap as a portfolio of forward contracts with successive expiration dates.

As we learned in Chapter 2, futures contracts are a type of forward contract with specific additional institutional features. A futures is distinguished from other forward contracts by the margining and daily resettlement feature along with the presence of exchange trading and clearinghouse guarantees. Aside from these institutional considerations, an interest rate futures contract is essentially like an interest rate forward contract. Therefore, an interest rate swap can be viewed as a portfolio of successively maturing interest rate futures contracts. In terms of our earlier example, we might think of an interest rate swap as being similar to a strip of interest rate futures contracts. A **strip** is a sequence of futures contracts with successive expirations. Because interest rate swap agreements so often use LIBOR as the floating rate in the contract, a strip of Eurodollar futures contracts is highly analogous to an interest rate swap agreement.

One of the main reasons for the development of the swaps market was the need for custom-tailored instruments with a tenor that exceeded the maturities available in the futures market. Typically, futures contract maturities do not extend for more than two years or so, but swap agreements can have a considerably longer tenor. Further, most futures contracts have very limited volume and open interest in the more distant maturities. As we have seen in Chapter 4, a swap dealer who participates in an interest rate swap may be left with a risk position that is undesired. As we saw in our earlier discussion, the swap dealer accepts this risk position to complete the swap agreement and earn a fee, but the dealer would typically like to avoid this risk.

If a strip of futures contracts could be regarded as a substitute for an interest rate swap, the swap dealer might be able to use Eurodollar strips to hedge unwanted interest rate risk that arises in the swap business. However, such a strategy would require an active market in distant Eurodollar maturities. In the earlier days of the swaps market, the Eurodollar futures contract certainly did not possess the depth or liquidity to allow Eurodollar strips to serve this role. For example, at the end of 1986, total open interest in all Eurodollar contract expirations was 214,000 and the most distant listed Eurodollar futures was the December 1988 contract, which was only two years distant. Figure 5.1 shows recent quotations for the Eurodollar contract with an extremely high level of open interest and with contract expirations extending for many years. This extended maturity range and deep liquidity is unparalleled for any other futures contract of any type. The main reason for these special features is the interest of swap dealers in using Eurodollar strips to offset risk inherent in the interest rate swap positions that they undertake.

■ **Figure 5.1**

QUOTATIONS FOR EURODOLLAR FUTURES

EURODOLLAR (CME) – $1 million; pts of 100%

	Open	High	Low	Settle	Chg	Yield Settle	Chg	Open Interest
June	93.62	93.62	93.53	93.54	− .07	6.64 +	.07	520,191
Sept	93.44	93.44	93.30	93.32	− .11	6.68 +	.11	332,735
Dec	93.23	93.24	93.07	93.09	− .14	6.91 +	.14	253,467
Mr96	93.23	93.23	93.07	93.09	− .14	6.91 +	.14	203,746
June	93.13	93.13	92.98	92.99	− .14	7.01 +	.14	166,450
Sept	93.06	93.06	92.91	92.92	− .14	7.08 +	.14	139,461
Dec	92.96	92.96	92.79	92.82	− .14	7.18 +	.14	110,886
Mr97	92.95	92.95	92.80	92.83	− .14	7.17 +	.14	93,107
June	92.90	92.90	92.76	92.78	− .13	7.22 +	.13	81,814
Sept	92.85	92.85	02.72	92.74	− .12	7.26 +	.12	67,845
Dec	92.76	92.77	92.66	92.67	− .11	7.33 +	.11	59,319
Mr98	92.77	92.77	92.65	92.68	− .10	8.32 +	.10	54,715
June	92.72	92.72	92.62	92.63	− .09	7.37 +	.09	48,823
Sept	92.67	92.67	92.57	92.58	− .09	7.42 +	.09	38,676
Dec	92.59	92.59	92.49	92.50	− .09	7.50 +	.09	34,342
Mr99	92.60	92.60	92.50	92.51	− .09	7.49 +	.09	27,253
June	92.54	92.54	92.46	92.46	− .08	7.54 +	.08	22,201
Sept	92.49	92.49	92.41	92.41	− .08	7.59 +	.08	14,208
Dec	92.41	92.41	92.33	92.33	− .08	7.67 +	.08	12,973
Mr00	92.41	92.42	92.33	92.34	− .07	7.66 +	.07	9,546
June	92.28	92.35	92.27	92.28	− .06	7.72 +	.06	7,597
Sept	92.22	92.23	92.21	92.21	− .06	7.79 +	.06	7,689
Dec	92.13	92.20	92.13	92.13	− .06	7.87 +	.06	6,093
Mr01	92.15	92.16	92.13	92.14	− .06	7.86 +	.06	5,988
June	92.10	92.13	92.06	92.06	− .06	7.94 +	.06	6,910
Sept	92.04	92.07	92.00	92.00	− .06	8.00 +	.06	6,881
Dec	91.95	91.95	91.91	91.91	− .06	8.09 +	.06	7,013
Mr02	92.02	92.02	91.95	91.94	− .06	8.06 +	.06	4,321
June	91.90	91.93	91.90	91.90	− .06	8.10 +	.06	3,904
Sept	91.90	91.90	91.83	91.83	− .06	8.17 +	.06	2,492
Dec	91.75	91.75	91.75	91.76	− .05	8.24 +	.05	1,553
Mr03	91.77	91.77	91.77	91.78	− .05	8.22 +	.05	2,260
June	....	....	....	91.71	− .05	8.29 +	.05	1,847
Sept	....	....	....	91.65	− .05	8.35 +	.05	1,748
Dec	91.55	91.55	91.55	91.56	− .05	8.44 +	.05	1,692
Mr04	91.58	91.58	91.58	91.59	− .05	8.41 +	.05	1,955
June	....	....	....	91.51	− .05	8.49 +	.05	672
Sept	91.44	91.44	91.44	91.45	− .05	8.55 +	.05	904
Dec	....	....	....	91.38	− .05	8.62 +	.05	800

Est vol 391,116; vol Mon 225,239; open int 2,364,074, +12,080.

Source: *The Wall Street Journal*, March 29, 1995.

CREATING SYNTHETIC SECURITIES WITH SWAPS

Earlier in this chapter, we saw that certain securities could be synthesized from combinations of derivatives, such as through the put-call parity relationship. We saw that any three of four instruments (a put, a call, the underlying good, a risk-free bond) can synthesize the fourth instrument. In this section, we explore some similar relationships using swaps. This idea is already familiar, as we have just seen in the preceding section that a swap is, in effect, a portfolio of forward contracts.

SYNTHETIC FIXED RATE DEBT

Consider a firm, with an existing floating rate debt obligation, that wishes to eliminate the uncertainty inherent in floating debt. A firm in this position could create a synthetic fixed rate debt instrument by combining its existing floating rate obligation with an interest rate swap. Assume a firm has an outstanding issue of $50 million on which it pays a floating rate annual coupon and that the debt matures in six years. The firm wishes to transform this obligation into a fixed rate instrument with the same maturity.

Figure 5.2 shows the firm's existing obligation in the upper time line. To transform this existing obligation into a fixed rate instrument, the firm can engage in a swap agreement to receive a floating rate and pay a fixed rate, with a tenor and payment timing to match its existing debt, as shown in the bottom time line of Figure 5.2. The combination of the existing debt and the pay fixed/receive floating interest rate swap gives the firm a synthetic fixed rate obligation instead of its current floating rate debt.

SYNTHETIC FLOATING RATE DEBT

An existing fixed rate obligation can be transformed into floating rate debt by reversing the technique used to create synthetic fixed rate debt. Assume a firm has an existing fixed rate debt obligation with a maturity of six years that requires annual interest rate payments. The upper time line of Figure 5.3 shows the cash flows associated with this obligation. (This example parallels that of Figure 5.2, except the initial obligation has fixed rate coupons.)

■ Figure 5.2

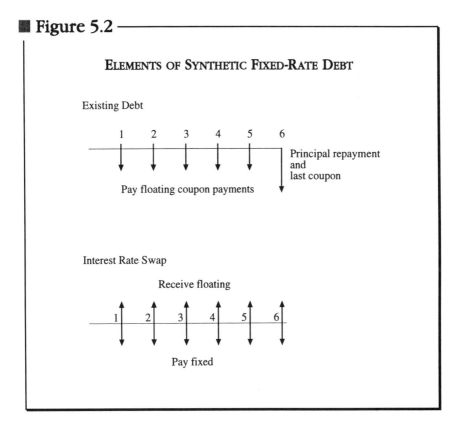

ELEMENTS OF SYNTHETIC FIXED-RATE DEBT

Existing Debt

Pay floating coupon payments

Principal repayment
and
last coupon

Interest Rate Swap

Receive floating

Pay fixed

By combining this fixed rate obligation with an interest rate swap to pay a fixed rate and receive a floating rate, the instrument can be transformed from a fixed rate to a synthetic floating rate obligation. The lower time line of Figure 5.3 shows the cash flows on an interest rate swap to pay the fixed rate and receive the floating rate. By combining this swap with the existing obligation, the firm transforms its existing fixed rate obligation into a synthetic floating rate debt with the same maturity.

SYNTHETIC CALLABLE DEBT

Consider a firm with an outstanding fixed rate obligation that possesses no call feature. The issuing firm would like to be able to call this debt in three years, but does not want the obligation to retire

■ Figure 5.3

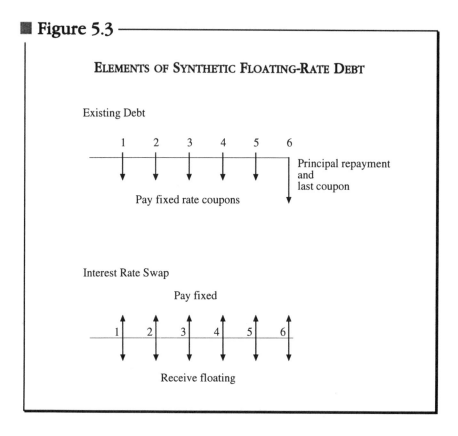

ELEMENTS OF SYNTHETIC FLOATING-RATE DEBT

Existing Debt

Pay fixed rate coupons

Principal repayment and last coupon

Interest Rate Swap

Pay fixed

Receive floating

the issue. In essence, the firm wishes that the existing noncallable debt had a call provision allowing a call in three years.

When a firm calls an existing debt instrument, it repays the debt. We may view that repayment as creating a new financing need that the firm will meet from floating rate obligations. After all, in calling the debt, it retired the existing fixed rate obligation. From this perspective we may see that the decision to call an existing fixed rate obligation is like creating a synthetic floating rate debt obligation using a call. As we have just seen, a fixed rate debt obligation, combined with an interest rate swap to receive fixed payments and pay floating ones transforms the fixed rate instrument into a floating rate obligation.

However, in the present instance, the issuer wishes to have the option, but not the obligation, to make this transformation. Therefore, the firm can create a synthetic callable bond by using a

swaption – an option on a swap.[2] Because the firm wants to possess the call option, we know that the firm must purchase a swaption, because only buying an option gives that flexibility. The swap must allow the firm to receive a fixed rate and pay a floating rate; therefore, the firm needs the option to sell a swap. (Recall that purchasing a swap means to pay a fixed rate and receive a floating rate.) Consequently, the firm needs to purchase a put swaption with a maturity of three years. The exercise price on the put swaption will play the role of the call price on a callable bond. Thus, by combining a noncallable fixed rate debt obligation with the purchase of a put swaption, the firm can transform its initial obligation into a callable bond.

SYNTHETIC NONCALLABLE DEBT

A firm with outstanding callable debt can use interest rate swaps to eliminate the call feature. When it issued the callable debt, the firm essentially purchased a call option from the bondholders. If the firm is sure that it will not wish to call the debt, it may wish to recapture the value represented by that call option.

If the issuance of callable debt involves the sale of a call option to the bondholders, this can be "unwound" by now selling a call swaption with the correct characteristics – the same characteristics possessed by the option that the firm purchased from its bondholders. Specifically, the call swaption that the firm now decides to sell should have maturity and exercise incentives that match those inherent in the original callable debt. Measured from the expiration date of the swaption, the swap should have a tenor that matches the remaining life of the bond from that date.

Once it sells the call swaption, two outcomes are possible. The option can expire worthless or the option can be exercised against the issuing firm. If the option is never exercised, the firm merely continues to pay the fixed rate of interest for the full life of the bond and the original call feature on the bond never comes into play. The first line of Table 5.5 shows the firm's position if the swaption is never exercised. If the swaption is not exercised against the firm, the firm will simply not exercise the call provision in the bonds it has issued and the firm will have a straight debt obligation in effect.

■ **Table 5.5**

TRANSFORMING CALLABLE INTO NON-CALLABLE DEBT

Call Date Scenario	Swap	Issuer	Result
Interest rates higher.	Swaption not exercised	Does not call the bond	Issuer has fixed rate financing.
Interest rates lower.	Swaption exercised. Issuer pays fixed and receives floating for remainder of bond's life.	Calls the bond and funds floating for remainder of bond's life.	Issuer has fixed rate financing

Source: Adapted from L.S. Goodman, "Capital Market Applications of Interest Rate Swaps," Chapter 7 of C.R. Beidleman, *Interest Rate Swaps,* Homewood, IL: Business One Irwin, 1991.

If interest rates fall sufficiently, the owners of the call swaption will exercise that option against the firm. However, the firm will then exercise the call provision of the bond it has issued. In effect, when the firm suffers the exercise, it passes that exercise through to its own bondholders, and the firm remains unaffected by the exercise of the call against it. As the second line of Table 5.5 indicates, the issuer continues to enjoy a position that is effectively like having issued noncallable straight debt initially.

SYNTHETIC DUAL CURRENCY DEBT[3]

A **dual currency bond** has principal payments denominated in one currency, with coupon payments denominated in a second currency. For example, a firm might borrow dollars and pay coupon payments on the instrument in German marks. When the bond expires, the firm would repay its principal obligation in dollars. This dual currency bond can be synthesized from a regular single currency bond with all payments in dollars (a dollar-pay bond) combined with a fixed-for-fixed currency swap.

The upper time line in Figure 5.4 shows the cash flows from

owning a typical dollar-pay bond from the point of view of the bond owner. The purchaser of the bond invests at the outset and then receives coupon inflows and the return of principal upon maturity. Thus the down arrows indicate outflows, and the up arrows represent cash inflows. The second time line in Figure 5.4 shows the cash flows for a fixed-for-fixed foreign currency swap in which the party receives fixed German mark inflows and pays fixed dollar amounts. Notice that there is no exchange of borrowings in this swap. The amount of the cash flows in the currency swap are constructed to equal the coupon payments.

Figure 5.5 shows the effect of combining the dollar-pay bond with the foreign currency swap. The dollar coupon payments on the dollar-pay bond and the dollar payments on the fixed-for-fixed currency swap perfectly offset each other. This leaves German mark inflows from the swap, which take the place of the coupon payments. As Figure 5.5 shows, the principal payment and repayment are in dollars; all of the coupon cash flows are in German marks. Thus, a dollar-pay bond combined with the appropriate fixed-for-fixed currency swap with no exchange of borrowings produce a dual-currency bond.

TRANSFORMING THE MATURITY OF AN INVESTMENT

In the previous section, we saw how to use swaps to change the characteristics of debt instruments, such as transforming fixed to floating debt. In this section, we show how to use futures contracts to change the effective maturity of a debt instrument. Many investors find themselves with an existing portfolio that may have undesirable maturity characteristics. For example, a firm might hold a six-month T-bill and realize that it will have a need for funds in three months. By the same token, another investor might hold the same six-month T-bill and fear that those funds might have to face lower reinvestment rates upon maturity in six months. This investor might prefer a one-year maturity. Both the firm and the investor could sell the six-month bill and invest for the preferred maturity. However, spot market transactions costs are relatively high, and many investors prefer to alter the maturities of investment by trading futures. The two examples that follow show how to use futures to accomplish both a shortening and lengthening of maturities.

Figure 5.4

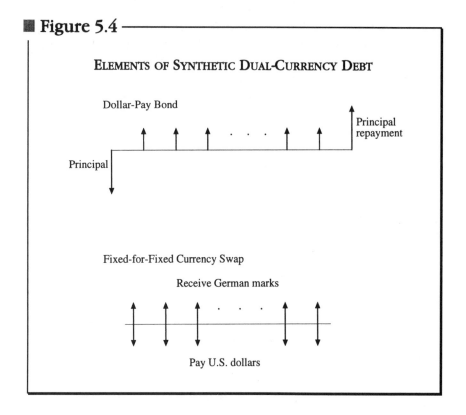

ELEMENTS OF SYNTHETIC DUAL-CURRENCY DEBT

Dollar-Pay Bond

Principal repayment

Principal

Fixed-for-Fixed Currency Swap

Receive German marks

Pay U.S. dollars

Figure 5.5

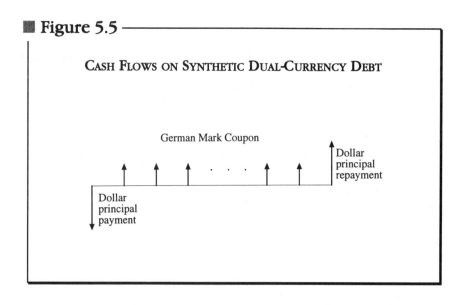

CASH FLOWS ON SYNTHETIC DUAL-CURRENCY DEBT

German Mark Coupon

Dollar principal repayment

Dollar principal payment

SHORTENING THE MATURITY OF A T-BILL INVESTMENT

Consider a firm that has invested in a T-bill. Now, on March 20, the T-bill has a maturity of 180 days, but the firm learns of a need for cash in 90 days. Therefore, it would like to shorten the maturity so it can have access to its funds in 90 days, around mid-September.

For simplicity, we assume that the short-term yield curve is flat with all rates at 10 percent on March 20. For convenience, we assume a 360-day year to match the pricing conventions for T-bills. The face value of the firm's T-bill is $10 million. With 180 days to maturity and a 10 percent discount yield, the price of the bill is

$$P = FV - [DY(FV)(DTM)]/360$$

where:

P=bill price
FV=face value
DY=discount yield
DTM=days until maturity

Therefore, the 180-day bill is worth $9.5 million. If the yield curve is flat at 10 percent, the futures yield must also be 10 percent, and the T-bill futures price must be $975,000 per contract. Starting from an initial position of a six-month T-bill, the firm of our example can shorten the maturity by selling T-bill futures for expiration in three months, as Table 5.6 shows. On March 20, there was no cash flow, because the firm merely sold futures. On June 20, the six-month bill is now a three-month bill and can be delivered against the futures. In Table 5.6, the firm delivers the bills and receives the futures invoice amount of $9.75 million. (Although we have assumed the futures price did not change, this does not limit the applicability of our results. No matter how the futures price changed from March to June, the firm would still receive a total of $9.75 million. We assume that this occurs in June instead of over the period.) The firm has effectively shortened the maturity from six months to three months.

LENGTHENING THE MATURITY OF AN INVESTMENT

Consider now, on August 21, a firm holds a $100 million face value T-bill that matures in 30 days on September 20. The firm plans to

■ Table 5.6 ─────────────────────────

TRANSACTIONS TO SHORTEN MATURITIES

Date	Cash Market	Futures Market
March 20	Holds six-month T-bill with a face value of $100,000,000, worth $9,500,000. Wishes a three month maturity.	Sell 10 JUN T-bill futures contracts at 90.00, reflecting the 10% discount yield.
June 20		Deliver cash market T-bills agains futures; receive $9,750,000.

reinvest for another three months after the T-bill matures. However, it fears that interest rates might fall unexpectedly. If so, it would be forced to reinvest at a lower rate than is now reflected in the yield curve. The SEP T-bill futures yield is 9.8 percent, as is the rate on the current investment. The firm finds this rate attractive and would like to lengthen the maturity of the T-bill investment. The firm can lengthen the maturity by buying a September futures contract and taking delivery. It will then hold the delivered bills until maturity in December.

With a 9.8 percent discount futures yield, the value of the delivery unit is $975,500. With $100 million coming available on September 20, the firm knows it will have enough funds to take delivery of ($100,000,000/$975,500) = 102.51 futures contracts. Therefore, it initiates the strategy presented in Table 5.7.

On August 21, the firm held a bill worth $99,183,333, assuming a yield of 9.8 percent. With the transactions of Table 5.7, it had no cash flow on August 21. With the maturity of the T-bill in September, the firm received $100 million and used almost all of it to pay for the futures delivery. It also received $499,000, which we assume was invested at 9.8 percent for three months. In December, this investment would be worth $499,000 + $499,000(.098)(90/360) = $511,226. With the T-bills maturing in December, the total proceeds will be $102,511,226, from an investment that was worth $99,183,333 on August 21. This gives the firm

■ **Table 5.7**

TRANSACTIONS TO SHORTEN MATURITIES

Date	Cash Market	Futures Market
Aug. 21	Holds 30-day T-bill with a face value of $100,000,000. Wishes to extend the maturity for 90 days.	Buy 102 SEP T-bill futures contracts, with a yeild of 9.8%
Sept. 20	30-day T-bill matures and investor receives $100,000,000. Invest $499,000 in money market fund	Accept delivery on 102 SEP futures, paying $99,501,000.
Dec. 19	T-bills received on SEP futures mature for $102,000,000.	

a discount yield of 9.8 percent over the four-month horizon from August to December.

Notice that this transaction "locked in" the 9.8 percent on the futures contract. In the example, this happens to match the spot rate of interest. However, the important point to recognize is that lengthening the maturity involves locking into the futures yield, no matter what that yield may be. Thus, for the period covered by the T-bill delivered on the futures contract, the investment will earn the futures yield at the time of contracting.

OPTION COMBINATIONS

The reader of the popular financial press would almost surely receive the impression that options are very risky instruments. This is partially correct, because option positions can be extremely risky. However, options are complex instruments. By combining options in certain ways, it is possible to create a position that has almost any desired level of risk exposure. In this section, we explore techniques for combining options to create new payoff profiles.

STRADDLES

A **straddle** is an option position involving a put and a call option on the same stock. To buy a straddle, an investor will buy both a put and a call that have the same expiration and the same striking price. To sell a straddle, a trader sells both the call and the put. Consider a put and a call option and assume that both have an exercise price of $100. Assume further that the call sells for $10 and that the put trades at $7. Table 5.8 shows the profits and losses for the call, the put, and the straddle as a function of the stock price at expiration. If the stock price equals the exercise price at expiration, both the put and the call expire worthless, and the loss on the straddle is $17, the entire premium paid for the position.

Any movement in the stock price away from $100 at expiration

■ Table 5.8 ————————————————

PROFITS AND LOSSES FOR A CALL, PUT AND STRADDLE

Stock Price Expiration	Elements of a Straddle		Straddle P=$17
	Call E=$100, P = $10	Put E=$100, P = $7	
$50	-$10	$43	$33
80	-10	13	3
83	-10	10	0
85	-10	8	-2
90	-10	3	-7
95	-10	-2	-12
100	-10	-7	-17
105	-5	-7	-12
110	0	-7	-7
115	5	-7	-2
117	7	-7	0
120	10	-7	3
150	40	-7	33

gives a better result. In fact, the value of the straddle increases $1 for every $1 movement in the stock price at expiration away from $100. The straddle position breaks even if the stock price either rises to $117 or falls to $83. In other words, a $17 price movement away from the exercise price at expiration will cover the initial investment of $17. If the price of the stock differs greatly from the exercise price, there is an opportunity for substantial profit. These possible results are shown graphically in Figure 5.6, which shows the profit and losses for the long and short straddle positions.

The graph shows the profits and losses for buying the straddle position with a solid line. As this graph makes clear, the purchaser of a straddle is betting that the price of the stock will move dramatically away from the exercise price of $100. The owner of the straddle will profit if the stock price goes above $117 or below $83. Figure 5.6 shows the profit-and-loss position for the seller of a straddle with the dotted lines. The seller of the straddle will profit if the stock price at expiration lies between $83 and $117.

▪ Figure 5.6

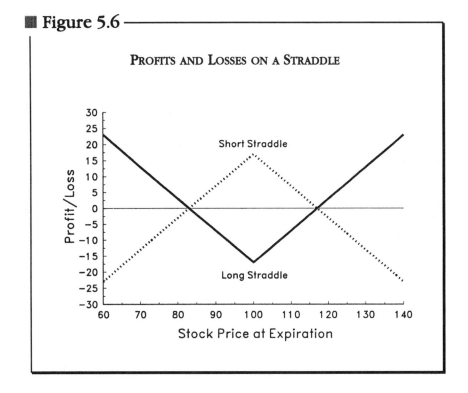

PROFITS AND LOSSES ON A STRADDLE

Obviously, the purchaser of this straddle would be making a bet on a large movement in the stock price in some direction, while the seller of a straddle would be betting that the stock price remains reasonably close to the exercise price of $100.

STRANGLES

A strangle is similar to a straddle. As we have seen, buying a straddle involves buying a call and buying a put option with the same striking price and the same term to expiration. A long position in a **strangle** consists of a long position in a call and a long position in a put on the same underlying good with the same term to expiration, with the call having a higher exercise price than the put. For example, consider the same put option of the previous example, which had an exercise price of $100 and a premium of $7. A call option on the same good with the same term to expiration has a striking price of $110 and sells for $3.

■ **Table 5.9**

PROFITS AND LOSSES FOR A CALL, PUT, AND STRANGLE

Elements of a Strangle

Stock Price Expiration	Call E=$110, P = $3	Put E=$100, P = $7	Straddle P=$10
$50	-$3	$43	$40
80	-3	13	10
83	-3	10	7
85	-3	8	5
90	-3	3	0
95	-3	-2	-5
100	-3	-7	-10
105	-3	-7	-10
110	-3	-7	-10
115	2	-7	-5
117	5	-7	2
120	7	-7	0
125	12	-7	5
150	37	-7	30

■ Figure 5.7

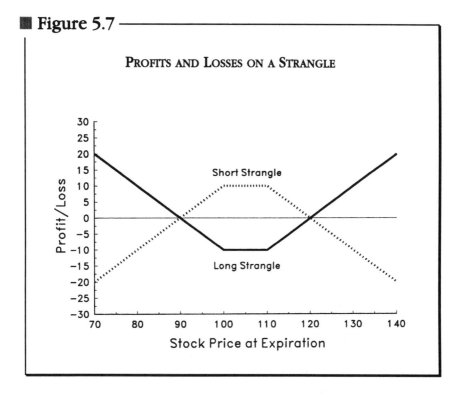

PROFITS AND LOSSES ON A STRANGLE

To buy a strangle with these options, a trader buys both the put and the call, for a total outlay of $10. Table 5.9 shows the profits and losses at expiration for the call and put individually and on the strangle position as well. Figure 5.7 shows the profit profile for the long and short strangle. As the table and figure show, the put and the call cannot both have value at expiration. If the stock price rises above $110, the call has a value, whereas a stock price below $100 allows the put to finish in-the-money. For the long strangle to show a profit, the call or the put must be worth more than the $10 total cost of the strangle. This means that the stock price must exceed $120 or fall below $90 for the strangle to show a net profit.

The figure shows that a wide range of stock prices will give a loss, even a total loss of the $10 investment for some prices. For example, if the stock price is between $100 and $110 at expiration, both the put and the call will expire worthless, giving a net loss of $10.

BULL AND BEAR SPREADS

A **bull spread** in the options market is a combination of call options designed to profit if the price of the underlying good rises.[4] Both calls in a bull spread have the same expiration, but they have different exercise prices. The buyer of a bull spread buys a call with an exercise price below the stock price and sells a call option with an exercise price above the stock price. The spread is a "bull" spread because the trader hopes to profit from a price rise in the stock. The trade is a "spread" because it involves buying one option and selling a related option. Compared to buying the stock itself, the bull spread with call options limits the trader's risk. However, it also limits the profit potential compared to the stock itself.

To illustrate this spread, assume that the stock trades at $100. One call option has an exercise price of $95 and costs $7. The other call has an exercise price of $105 and costs $3. To buy the bull spread, the trader buys the call with the $95 exercise price and sells the other. The total outlay for the bull spread is $4. Figure 5.8 graphs the profits and losses for the two call positions individually. The long position profits if the stock price moves above $102. The short position profits if the stock price does not exceed $108. As the graph shows, low stock prices result in an overall loss on the position, because the cost of the long position outweighs the amount received from the short position. It is also interesting to consider prices at $105 and above. For every dollar by which the stock price exceeds $105, the long position has an extra dollar of profit. However, at prices above $105, the short position starts to lose money. Thus, for stock prices above $105, the additional gains on the long position match the losses on the short position. Therefore, no matter how high the stock price goes, the bull spread can never give a greater profit than it does for a stock price of $105.

Figure 5.9 graphs the bull spread as the solid line. For any stock price at expiration of $95 or below, the bull spread loses $4. This $4 is the difference between the cash inflow for selling one call and buying the other. The bull spread breaks even for a stock price of $99. The highest possible profit on the bull spread comes when the stock sells for $105. Then the bull spread gives a $6 profit. For any stock price above $105, the profit on the bull spread remains at $6. Therefore, the trader of a bull spread bets that the stock price goes up, but hedges this bet. We can see that the bull spread protects the trader from losing any more than $4. However, the trader

■ **Figure 5.8**

THE TWO CALL OPTIONS FOR A BULL SPREAD

Short Call: E = $105; C = $3

Long Call: E = $95; Price = $7

■ **Figure 5.9**

PROFITS AND LOSSES ON BULL AND BEAR SPREADS

Bull Spread

Bear Spread

cannot make more than a $6 profit. We can compare the bull spread with a position in the stock itself in Figure 5.9. Comparing the bull spread and the stock, we find that the stock offers the chance for bigger profits, but it also has greater risk of a serious loss.

Figure 5.9 also shows the profit and loss profile for a bear spread with the same options. A bear spread is a combination of options designed to profit from a drop in the stock price. In our example, the bear spread is just the short positions that match the bull spread. In other words, the short position in the bull spread is a bear spread. The dotted line shows how profit and losses vary if a trader sells the call with the $95 strike price and buys the call with the $105 strike price. This position exactly mirrors the bull spread we have considered. In a bear spread, the trader bets that the stock price will fall. However, the bear spread also limits the profit opportunity and the risk of loss compared to a short position in the stock itself. We can compare the profit and loss profiles of the bear spread in Figure 5.9 with the short position in the stock.

BUTTERFLY SPREADS

To buy a **butterfly spread**, a trader buys one call with a low exercise price and buys one call with a high exercise price, while selling two calls with a medium exercise price. The spread profits most when the stock price is near the medium exercise price at expiration. In essence, the butterfly spread gives a payoff pattern similar to a straddle. Compared to a straddle, however, a butterfly spread offers lower risk at the expense of reduced profit potential.

As an example of a butterfly spread, assume that a stock trades at $100 and a trader buys a spread by trading options with the following prices. As the following table shows, the buyer of a butterfly spread sells two calls with a striking price near the stock price and buys one each of the calls above and below the stock price.

	Exercise Price	Option Premium
Long 1 Call	$105	$3
Short 2 Calls	$100	$4
Long 1 Call	$95	$7

Figure 5.10 graphs the profits and losses from each of these three option positions. (This is the most complicated option posi-

■ Figure 5.10

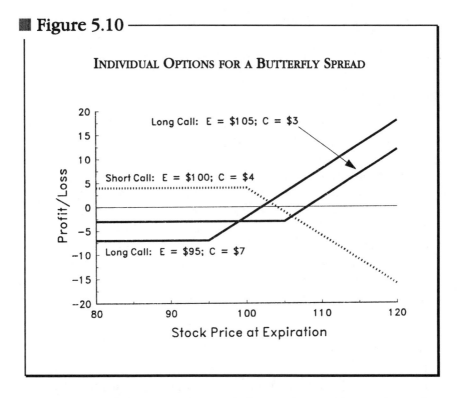

INDIVIDUAL OPTIONS FOR A BUTTERFLY SPREAD

tion we consider.) To understand the profits and losses from the butterfly spread, we need to combine these profits and losses, remembering that the spread involves selling two options and buying two.

Let us consider a few critical stock prices to see how the butterfly spread profits respond. The critical stock prices always include the exercise prices for the options. First, if the stock price is $95, the call with an exercise price of $95 is worth zero and a long position in this call loses $7. The long call with the $105 exercise price also cannot be exercised, so it is worthless, giving a loss of the $3 purchase price. The short call position gives a profit of $4 per option and the spread trader sold two of these options, for an $8 profit. Adding these values gives a net loss on the spread of $2, if the stock price is $95. Second, if the stock price is $100, the long call with a striking price of $95 loses $2 (the $5 stock profit minus the $7 purchase price). The long call with an exercise price of $105 loses its full purchase price of $3. Together, the long calls lose $5. The short call still shows a profit of $4 per option, for a profit of $8 on the two options. This gives a net profit of $3 if the stock price is $100. Third, if the stock price is $105 at expiration, the long call with an exercise price of $95 has a profit of $3. The long call with an exercise price of $105 loses $3. Also, the short call position loses $1 per option for a loss on two positions of $2. This gives a net loss on the butterfly spread of $2. In summary, we have a $2 loss for a $95 stock price, a $3 profit for a $100 stock price, and a $2 loss for a $105 stock price.

Figure 5.11 shows the entire profit and loss graph for the butterfly spread. At a stock price of $100, we noted a profit of $3. This is the highest profit available from the spread. At stock prices of $95 and $105, the spread loses $2. For stock prices below $95 or above $105, the loss is still $2. As the graph shows, the butterfly spread has a zero profit for stock prices of $97 and $103. The buyer of the butterfly spread essentially bets that stock prices will hover near $100. Any large move away from $100 gives a loss on the butterfly spread. However, the loss can never exceed $2. Comparing

■ Figure 5.11 —

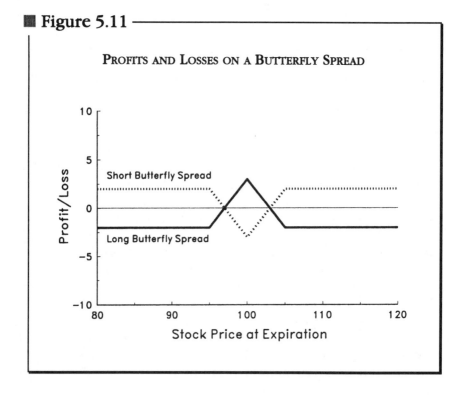

PROFITS AND LOSSES ON A BUTTERFLY SPREAD

the butterfly spread with the straddle in Figure 5.6, we see that the butterfly spread resembles a short position in the straddle. Compared to the straddle, the butterfly spread reduces the risk of a very large loss. However, the reduction in risk necessarily comes at the expense of a chance for a big profit.

SUMMARY

In this section, we saw how to combine options to create new payoff profiles. Although options are typically regarded as very risky instruments, we saw that it is possible to create option positions that have substantially lower risk than an outright position in an option.

If we compare the payoff profiles for a straddle and a strangle, we see that a straddle is a riskier position than a strangle, other factors being equal. The straddle offers a speculation with a more varied outcome. It has a chance of losing all of the investment, but it also holds a promise of substantial reward if prices move radically away from the striking price.

Compared to a straddle, a strangle has a bigger chance of incurring some loss. However, the maximum possible loss will usually be lower with a strangle than with a straddle. Of course, the likely payoffs are also smaller for a strangle. For a butterfly spread, there is a higher probability of some loss, but it will likely be a small one, if it occurs. The maximum loss on a butterfly spread is relatively low because the position involves purchasing and selling some calls. The receipts from selling calls helps to finance the purchase of the other calls.

PORTFOLIO INSURANCE

In **portfolio insurance**, a trader transacts to ensure that the value of a portfolio cannot fall below a given amount. By combining a long position in a put option with a long position in the underlying good, a trader ensures that the value of the combined portfolio cannot fall below a given level. An outright investment in a portfolio can be transformed into an investment with a completely different risk profile through this technique. This section begins by explaining the rationale and strategy of portfolio insurance through a detailed case analysis. Portfolio insurance can also be implemented by using futures contracts in a strategy called dynamic hedging, and the next section explores this second method of insuring a portfolio.

CASE ANALYSIS

In this section, we consider how to use options on the physical or options on futures to tailor the risk of an investment. For convenience, we focus on payoffs at option expirations, so we can ignore the difference between American and European options. Because the analysis focuses on European options, the conclusions we reach apply to both futures options and options on the physical.

We present the case analysis for a stock index, although the conclusions we reach apply to many different instruments. Consider a stock index that is currently at $100. Stocks in the index pay no dividends, and the expected return on the index is 10 percent, with a standard deviation of 20 percent. A put option on the index with an exercise price of $100 is available and costs $4. We consider three investment strategies:

Portfolio A: Buy the index; total investment $100.
Portfolio B: Buy the index and one-half of a put; total investment $102.
Portfolio C: Buy the index and one put; total investment $104.

At expiration in one year, the profits and losses associated with these three portfolios depend entirely on the value of the index, because the value of the put at expiration also depends strictly on the index value. For the put, the value at expiration equals the maximum of either zero or the exercise price minus the index value.

At expiration, the three portfolios will have profits and losses computed according to the following equations:

Portfolio A: Index Value – $100
Portfolio B: Index Value + .5 MAX{0, $100 – Index Value} – $102
Portfolio C: Index Value + MAX{0, $100 – Index Value} – $104

The value of Portfolio A at expiration is just the index value, and the profit or loss is the value of the portfolio at expiration less the

■ Figure 5.12

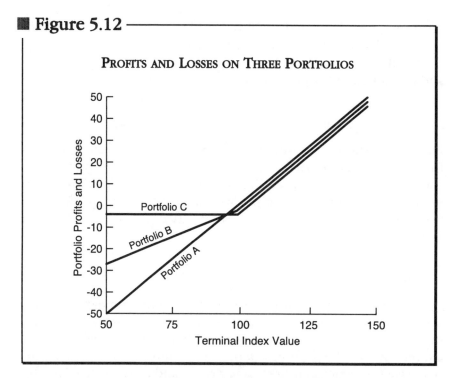

PROFITS AND LOSSES ON THREE PORTFOLIOS

investment of $100. The terminal value of Portfolio C is the index value plus the value of the put. The profit or loss is the terminal value less the investment of $104. Portfolio B consists of the index plus one-half of a put. This gives a total investment of $102, and the terminal value of Portfolio B consists of the index value plus the value of the half put. Figure 5.12 graphs the profits and losses of these three portfolios for different terminal index values.

Of particular interest in Figure 5.12 is the profit and loss graph for Portfolio C, consisting of the index plus a put on the index. The worst possible loss on Portfolio C is $4. This loss occurs if the terminal index value is $100 or below. With a terminal index value of $100, the portfolio is worth $100, because the put expires worthless. This is the worst possible loss, however. For instance, if the terminal index value is $95, the put is worth $5 and the index investment is worth $95, for a total of $100. Portfolio C must always be worth at least $100.

Portfolio C is an insured portfolio, whose value cannot fall below $100. Further, this example is the classic case of portfolio insurance: buying a good at a given price and buying a put on the same good with an exercise price equal to the purchase price of the good. To create Portfolio C, a trader bought the index at $100 and bought an index put with an exercise price of $100.

SYNTHETIC PORTFOLIO INSURANCE AND PUT-CALL PARITY

Figure 5.12 shows that the insured portfolio's profit and loss profile is exactly the profile for a call option on the stock index. This should not be surprising. Earlier we saw that a long position in the underlying good plus a long put would have the same profits and losses as a call. Applying the put-call parity equation to our index example, we have

$$C = \text{INDEX} + P - \frac{E}{\left(1 + R_f\right)^T} \qquad (5.6)$$

The put-call parity equation shows that an instrument with the same value and profits and losses as a call can be created by holding a long put, long index, and borrowing the present value of the exercise price. The portfolio on the right-hand side of equation 5.6 will have the same value and same profits and losses as the call. By contrast, the long index plus long put merely has the same profits and losses as the call. At expiration, the value of the put plus the index will exceed the value of the call.

Therefore, we now see that an insured portfolio is the long put/long index position that has the same profits and losses as a call. From put-call parity, there is another way to create a portfolio that exactly mimics the insured portfolio's value at expiration. We can hold a long call plus invest the present value of the exercise price in the risk-free asset. From the put-call parity relationship, we see

$$C + \frac{E}{\tau} = P + \text{INDEX} \qquad (5.7)$$

The long call plus investment in the risk-free asset creates the same insured portfolio as the long index plus long put. Both positions have the same value and the same profits and losses at expiration.

This also shows why the put plus index portfolio that has the same profits and losses as a call does not have the same value as the call. The put plus index portfolio requires considerable investment to purchase the underlying index.

TAILORING RISK AND RETURN CHARACTERISTICS WITH FUTURES AND OPTIONS

To this point we have not explicitly considered Portfolio B as defined previously. Portfolio B consists of buying the index and buying one-half put. In essence, Portfolio B is half-insured. Expressed differently, Portfolio B consists of two equal portions: $50 in an insured portfolio, plus $50 in an outright position in the index. As Figure 5.12 shows, Portfolio B has profits and losses that fall between the totally insured and completely uninsured portfolios.

The partially insured Portfolio B has less risk than the uninsured Portfolio A, but it has more risk than the fully insured Portfolio C. Figure 5.12 shows this intermediate risk position by showing that the losses for the half-insured Portfolio B are less than the losses for the uninsured Portfolio A, but more than the losses for the fully insured Portfolio C. This example suggests that traders can use futures and options to tailor the risk characteristics of the portfolio to individual taste. With the variety of futures and option instruments available, the financial engineer can create almost any feasible combination of risk and return.

One of the dominant lessons of modern finance concerns the risk/expected return tradeoff. In well-functioning markets, finding the chance for higher returns always means accepting higher risk. In comparing the fully and partially insured portfolios with the uninsured portfolio, we have seen that portfolio insurance reduces risk. However, there must be a reduction in expected return that accompanies the reduction in risk.

RISK AND RETURN IN INSURED PORTFOLIOS

We now explore the risk and expected return characteristics for Portfolios A–C. The portfolios have different probabilities of achieving given terminal values that depend on the price of the index at expiration. Likewise, the probability of achieving a given return on the portfolios depends on the index value at expiration. We explore these issues by assuming that returns on the index follow a normal distribution with a mean of 10 percent and a standard deviation of 20 percent.

TERMINAL VALUES FOR PORTFOLIOS A–C

The portfolio values at expiration depend on the price of the index at expiration. For each, the terminal value is

Portfolio A = Index
Portfolio B = Index + MAX{0, .5(100.00 – Index)}
Portfolio C = Index + MAX{0, 100.00 – Index}

We can now answer questions such as, What is the probability that Portfolio C will have a terminal value equal to or less than $100? Portfolio C will have a terminal value of at least $100 no matter what the value of the underlying index. In fact, there is a 30.85 percent probability that Portfolio C will have a terminal value of exactly $100. Portfolio C is worth $100 at expiration if the index is

■ Table 5.10

PROBABILITY THAT THE TERMINAL PORTFOLIO VALUE WILL BE
EQUAL TO OR LESS THAN A SPECIFIED VALUE

Terminal Portfolio Value	Probabilities		
	Uninsured Portfolio A	Half-Insured Portfolio B	Fully Insured Portfolio C
50.00	0.0014	0.0000	0.0000
60.00	0.0062	0.0000	0.0000
70.00	0.0228	0.0002	0.0000
80.00	0.0668	0.0062	0.0000
90.00	0.1587	0.0668	0.0000
100.00	0.3085	0.3085	0.3085
110.00	0.5000	0.5000	0.5000
120.00	0.6915	0.6915	0.6915
130.00	0.8413	0.8413	0.8413
140.00	0.9332	0.9332	0.9332
150.00	0.9773	0.9773	0.9773
160.00	0.9938	0.9938	0.9938
170.00	0.9987	0.9987	0.9987

$100 or less at expiration, and there is a 30.85 percent chance that the index value will be $100 or less. What is the probability that Portfolio A will have a terminal value less than $90? The probability that the terminal value of Portfolio A will lie below $90 is the probability that the terminal index value will fall more than 1.0 standard deviation below its expected value. Because we assume the returns on the index are normally distributed, there is a 15.87 percent chance that Portfolio A's value will be less than $90 at expiration. Table 5.10 shows some portfolio values and the probabilities that each portfolio will be equal to or less than the given terminal value at the expiration date.

In Table 5.10, the uninsured Portfolio A has the largest chance of an extremely low terminal value. For example, the chance that Portfolio A will be worth $80 or less is 6.68 percent. For Portfolio B, the chance of such an unhappy outcome is less than 1 percent, and there is no chance that Portfolio C could be worth $80 or less. (We already know that Portfolio C has to be worth at least $100.) It

■ Figure 5.13

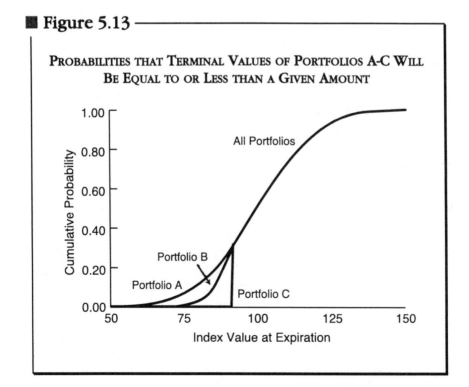

PROBABILITIES THAT TERMINAL VALUES OF PORTFOLIOS A-C WILL BE EQUAL TO OR LESS THAN A GIVEN AMOUNT

is interesting to note in Table 5.10 that the chance of each portfolio being worth $100 or less is the same – 30.85 percent. Likewise, there is a 50 percent chance for each portfolio that the portfolio's value will be $110 or less. In fact, for terminal portfolio values at or above $100, the three portfolios have exactly the same probabilities. This makes sense, because if the terminal index value is $100 or more, the put option has zero value, and the remaining portion of each portfolio is the same.

Figure 5.13 graphs terminal portfolio values from $50 to $170 and shows the probability for each portfolio that the terminal portfolio value will be below or equal to the given amount. The three probability graphs differ for terminal portfolio values below $100. However, for all terminal portfolio values at or above $100, the graphs are identical. This matches the values we already saw in Table 5.10.

Concentrating on only terminal values, and neglecting the different investments required to obtain each portfolio, Figure 5.13 shows that the fully insured portfolio is the most desirable, followed by the half-insured portfolio, and then the uninsured portfolio. If we could choose one of these three portfolios as a gift, the fully insured portfolio is the clear choice. No matter what the terminal index value is, the fully insured Portfolio C will pay at least as much as either Portfolio A or B. If the terminal index value is less than $100, the insured portfolio still pays $100, which is more than either Portfolio A or B. However, this conclusion neglects the different investment costs. Portfolio A costs only $100, while Portfolio B costs $102, and Portfolio C costs $104. We now consider the returns on each portfolio.

RETURNS ON PORTFOLIOS A–C

Because Portfolios A–C have different costs, we need to compare the returns on each portfolio to make them more directly comparable. As we saw, Portfolio C is preferable to Portfolios A or B if we neglect cost. Once we consider cost, the answer is much less clear. Instead of having a clear choice, the investor faces the risk/expected return tradeoff in portfolio insurance.

For each portfolio, we can evaluate the chance of a given return. For example, the lowest possible terminal value for the fully insured portfolio is $100, which implies a return of $(100/104) - 1$

▇ Table 5.11

PROBABILITY OF ACHIEVING A RETURN EQUAL TO OR GREATER
THAN A SPECIFIED RETURN

Portfolio Return	Probabilities		
	Uninsured Portfolio A	Half-Insured Portfolio B	Fully Insured Portfolio C
-0.5000	0.9987	1.0000	1.0000
-0.4000	0.9938	1.0000	1.0000
-0.3000	0.9773	0.9996	1.0000
-0.2000	0.9332	0.9904	1.0000
-0.1000	0.8413	0.9066	1.0000
0.0000	0.6915	0.6554	0.6179
0.1000	0.5000	0.4562	0.4129
0.2000	0.3085	0.2676	0.2297
0.3000	0.1587	0.1292	0.1038
0.4000	0.0668	0.0505	0.0375
0.5000	0.0228	0.0158	0.0107

= −0.0385. The chance of a return on Portfolio C below −0.0385 is zero. However, the chance of Portfolio C having a return of exactly -0.0385 is 30.85 percent, the chance that Portfolio C is worth $100 at expiration.

Table 5.11 shows the probability that each portfolio will achieve a return greater than a specified return. For example, there is an 84.13 percent probability that the uninsured Portfolio A will do better than -10 percent. The half-insured Portfolio B has a 90.66 percent chance of returning at least − 10 percent. For fully insured Portfolio C, there is no chance the return could be as bad as -10 percent.

So far, everything still looks good for the insured portfolios. The greater the level of insurance, it seems, the better the portfolio performs. However, we must now consider other possible returns. For example, what is the probability of no gain or a loss? For the uninsured Portfolio A, there is a 30.85 percent chance of a loss. The fully insured Portfolio C, however, stands a 38.21 percent chance of a zero gain or a loss. Similarly, let us consider the chances of gaining more than 10 percent. The uninsured Portfolio A has a 50 percent chance, because there is a 50 percent chance the terminal index value will exceed the expected value of $110. The insured portfolio has only a 41.29 percent chance of beating a 10 percent return.

Now we can see the risk/expected return tradeoff implied by portfolio insurance strategies. Portfolio insurance protects against large losses by sacrificing the chance for large gains. Thus, portfolio insurance is aptly named. With any insurance contract, the insured pays the insurance premium to insure against some unpleasant event. By paying the insurance, the insured knows that the expected return on the portfolio will be less than it would be without insurance, but the insured hopes to avoid the extreme loss.

Figure 5.14 graphs the probabilities for each portfolio for the range of returns from –50 percent to 50 percent. Each point in the graph shows the probability that a portfolio will have returns greater than the return specified on the x-axis. For example, consider the returns in the range of -15 percent. There is a 100 percent

■ **Figure 5.14**

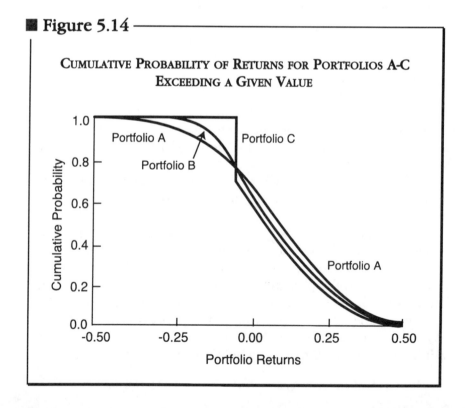

CUMULATIVE PROBABILITY OF RETURNS FOR PORTFOLIOS A-C
EXCEEDING A GIVEN VALUE

chance that the fully insured Portfolio C will beat a -15 percent return. Also, Portfolio C has a 100 percent chance of beating any return up to -3.846 percent. The chance of doing better than -3.846 percent, however, is only 61.15 percent. Similarly, the half-insured Portfolio B has a very good chance of beating -15 percent. Portfolio A has the lowest chance of beating -15 percent.

As we noted from Table 5.11, however, the fortunes of the portfolios turn when we consider the probability of particularly favorable outcomes. For instance, the probability of exceeding a 20 percent return is 30.85 percent for Portfolio A, but only 26.76 percent for Portfolio B and only 22.97 percent for Portfolio C. Thus, the uninsured Portfolio A has the biggest chance of big gains and big losses. By comparison, the fully insured Portfolio C gives up the chance for big gains to avoid the chance of large losses. The half-insured Portfolio B occupies the middle ground.

SUMMARY

In this section we have seen that holding a stock index in conjunction with a put option creates an insured portfolio. By increasing the degree of insurance, the trader can avoid more and more risk. However, this risk avoidance has a price – the sacrifice of the chance for high returns. Thus, the concepts of portfolio insurance constitute one more example of the perennial tradeoff between risk and expected return.

PORTFOLIO INSURANCE AND DYNAMIC HEDGING

As we have seen, traders can tailor the risk of a stock portfolio by trading stock index futures. For a given well-diversified portfolio, selling stock index futures can create a combined stock and futures portfolio with reduced risk. Holding a stock portfolio and buying stock index futures results in a portfolio with greater risk and expected return than the initial portfolio.

Portfolio insurance refers to a collection of techniques for managing the risk of an underlying portfolio. With most portfolio insurance strategies, the goal is to manage the risk of a portfolio to ensure that the value of the portfolio does not drop below a specified level, while at the same time allowing for the portfolio's value to increase. Portfolio insurance strategies are often implemented using options, as we have seen. However, stock index futures are equally important tools for portfolio insurance. Implementing portfolio insurance strategies using futures is called **dynamic hedging**. Although the mathematics of dynamic hedging are too complex for full treatment here, we can understand the basic idea behind portfolio insurance with stock index futures.

A DYNAMIC HEDGING EXAMPLE

Consider a fully diversified stock portfolio worth $100 million. The value of this portfolio can range from zero to infinity. Many investors would like to put a floor beneath the value of the portfolio. For example, it would be very desirable to ensure that the portfolio's value never falls below $90 million. Portfolio insurance offers a way to control the downside risk of a portfolio. However, in a financial market there is no free lunch, so it is possible to limit the risk of a large price fall only by sacrificing some of the potential for a gain. Portfolio insurance, like life insurance, is not free, but it may be desirable for some traders.

We have seen that a risk-minimizing hedge converts a stock portfolio to a synthetic T-bill. By fully hedging our example stock portfolio, we can keep the portfolio's value above $100 million. A fully hedged portfolio will increase in value at the risk-free rate, although full hedging eliminates all of the potential gain in the portfolio beyond the risk-free rate. In dynamic hedging, however,

■ **Table 5.12** ─────────────────────────────

PORTFOLIO INSURANCE TRANSACTIONS AND RESULTS

Time	Gain/Loss $million		Total Value	Futures Position	Portion Hedged
	Stocks	Futures			
0	0.00	0.00	100.00	-50	.50
1	-2.00	1.00	99.00	-55	.56
2	-2.00	1.11	98.11	-60	.61
3	-2.00	1.22	97.33	-70	.72
4	-4.00	2.88	96.21	-80	.83
5	-36.86	30.65	90.00	-90	1.00
6	-10.00	10.00	90.00	-90	1.00

the trader holds the stock portfolio and sells some futures contracts. The more insurance the trader wants, the more futures he or she will sell.

Let us assume that a stock index futures contract has an underlying value of $100 million and a trader sells futures contracts to cover $50 million of the value of the portfolio. Thus, in the initial position, the trader is long $100 million in stock and short $50 million in futures, so 50 percent of the portfolio is hedged. Table 5.12 shows this initial position in the time zero row. At $t = 0$, there has been no gain or loss on either the stock or futures. In the first period, we assume that the value of the stock portfolio falls by $2 million. The 50 futures contracts cover half of that loss with a gain of $1 million. Therefore, at $t = 1$, the combined stock and futures portfolio is worth $99 million. Now the manager increases the coverage in the futures market by selling five more contracts. This gives a total of 55 short positions and coverage for 56 percent (55/99) of the total portfolio. In the second period, the stock portfolio loses another $2 million, but with 55 futures contracts, the futures gain is (55/99)$2 million = $1.11 million. This gives a total portfolio value of $98.11 million.

By $t = 4$, the stock portfolio has fallen $10 million, but the futures profits have been $6.21 million. This gives a total portfolio value of $96.21 million. Also, the manager has increased the futures position in response to each drop in stock prices. At $t = 4$, the trader is short 80 contracts, hedging 83 percent of the stock market portfolio. At $t = 5$, the stock price drops dramatically, losing $35.86 million. The futures profit covers $30.65 million. This leaves a total portfolio value of $90 million. However, this is the floor amount of the portfolio, so the trader must now move to a fully hedged position. If the stock portfolio is only partially hedged, the next drop in prices can take the value of the entire portfolio below the floor amount of $90 million. At $t = 6$, the price of the stocks drops $10 million, but the futures position fully covers the loss. Therefore, the combined portfolio maintains its floor value of $90 million.

Table 5.12 shows the basic strategy of portfolio insurance with dynamic hedging. Initially, the portfolio is partially hedged. If stock prices fall, the trader increases the portion of the portfolio that is insured. Had the stock portfolio risen in value, the futures position would have lost money. However, the loss on the futures position would have been less than the gain on the stocks, because the portfolio was only partially hedged. As the stock prices rose, the manager would have bought futures, thereby hedging less and less of the portfolio. Less hedging would be needed if the stock price rose, because there would be little chance of the portfolio's total value falling below $90 million.

IMPLEMENTING PORTFOLIO INSURANCE VIA DYNAMIC HEDGING

By design, Table 5.12 is highly simplistic. First, it does not show how the starting futures position was determined. Second, it does not show how the adjustments in the futures position were determined. Third, it considers only large changes in the value of the stock portfolio. For instance, the smallest change in the table is 2 percent of the stock portfolio's value. The exact answer to these questions is highly mathematical. However, we can explore these issues in an intuitive way.

Choosing the initial futures position depends on several factors. First, it depends on the floor that is chosen relative to the initial value of the portfolio. For example, if the lowest acceptable value of the portfolio is $100 million, then the manager must hedge 100 percent at $t = 0$. Thus, the lower the floor relative to the portfolio value, the lower the percentage of the portfolio the manager will need to hedge. Second, the purpose of the insurance strategy is to guarantee a minimum terminal portfolio value while allowing for more favorable results. As a consequence, the futures position must take into account the volatility of the stock portfolio. The higher the estimated volatility of the stock portfolio, the greater is the chance of a large drop in value that will send the total portfolio value below the floor. Therefore, the portion of the portfolio that is to be hedged depends critically on the estimated volatility of the stock portfolio. Of course, this will differ both across time and for portfolios of different risk.

Adjustments in the futures position depend upon the same kinds of considerations that determine the initial position. First, the value of the portfolio relative to the floor is critical. Second, new information about the volatility of the stock portfolio also affects the futures position. In Table 5.12, the volatility of the stock portfolio accelerates. Each percentage drop is larger than the previous one. Therefore, this increasing volatility will lead to a larger short futures position than would otherwise be necessary.

In Table 5.12, the drops in the stock portfolio's values are large. In actual practice, dynamic hedging works by continually monitoring the value of the portfolio. Small changes in the portfolio can trigger small adjustments in the futures position. For many portfolios, monitoring and updating can occur many times a month. This is the reason it is called dynamic hedging – the hedge is monitored and updated continuously, often with computerized trading programs. Table 5.12 does not show that continual monitoring. Instead, we might take the different rows in the table as snapshots of the portfolio's value at different times.

Table 5.12 abstracts from some of the cash flow issues that dynamic hedging will raise. For example, it does not explicitly consider the cash flows that come from daily settlement of the futures position. There are a host of technical issues such as these that actual dynamic hedging must face.[5]

SUMMARY

In this chapter we have seen how the financial engineer can use single instruments as building blocks to create new financial structures with new risk and return characteristics. First, we saw how options can be combined to create positions with risk and return profiles that differ markedly from the position attainable with a single option. For example, we saw that a butterfly spread can be created that has very limited potential for large gains or losses.

We also used the put-call parity relationship to explore the creation of synthetic securities. If we consider an underlying instrument, a call, a put, and an investment in a risk-free instrument, we saw that any of the four could be created synthetically by a combination of the other three instruments. We also analyzed an interest rate swap as a portfolio of interest rate forward contracts.

As the last topic, we considered portfolio insurance. There we saw that the financial engineer could take an existing stock portfolio and purchase accompanying put options to make the stock plus put portfolio behave like a call option. We went on to show how slightly different commitments to the put option could dramatically affect the risk and return profile of the resulting stock plus put portfolio.

QUESTIONS AND PROBLEMS

1. Is a call option a synthetic instrument? Explain what makes a financial instrument synthetic.

2. Explain the difference between a straddle and a strangle.

3. A stock trades at $100 per share. A call option on the stock has an exercise price of $100, costs $16, and expires in six months. A put on the stock also has an exercise price of $100, costs $10, and expires in six months as well. The six-month risk-free rate of interest is 10 percent. State exactly what instruments to buy and sell to create a synthetic equity position in the stock.

4. For the preceding question, make a table showing the profits and losses from the option portion of the synthetic equity as a function of the stock price in six months.

5. A stock trades for $40 and a call on the stock with an expiration date in three months and a $40 strike price sells for $5. The risk-free rate of interest is 12 percent. State exactly how you would trade to create a synthetic put with a strike price of $40. Make a table showing the terminal values of your synthetic put and the actual put at expiration as a function of the stock price.

6. A stock sells for $75 and a call with an exercise price of $75 sells for $7 and expires in six months. The risk-free rate of interest is 10 percent. What is the price of a put with a striking price of $75 and the same term to expiration?

7. How much would you pay for a portfolio consisting of a short stock, a short put, and a long call? Assume that the options have a striking price equal to the current price of the stock and that both options expire in one year.

8. For the same underlying stock, a call and put both expire in one year, and their exercise price equals the current market price of the stock. Assume that you sell the stock short and can use 100 percent of the proceeds. You buy the call option and sell the put. You invest all remaining funds in the risk-free asset for one year. How much will this entire portfolio (stock, put, call, and bond) be worth in one year? Explain.

Use this information for the remaining questions. Assume a stock portfolio manager believes that his or her portfolio has an expected return of 12 percent and a standard deviation of 20 percent. Also, assume that the portfolio mimics an index on which call and put options trade. Assume that the index value is now 100 and the portfolio is worth $100. The risk-free rate of interest is 8 percent. Calls and puts on the index trade with a $100 strike price and are one year away from expiration. The call costs $11.40. The focus is on the value of the portfolio in one year.

9. How much should the put cost? Explain.

10. The manager asks you to devise a strategy to keep the value of the portfolio no less than $92. How would you transact? Explain.

11. The manager asks you to devise a strategy that will provide a terminal portfolio value of $112. How would you transact? Explain.

12. The manager asks you to devise a strategy that will dramatically increase the expected return on the portfolio. Give a qualitative description of how you would transact to achieve this goal.

13. The manager is determined not to trade any stocks to avoid transaction costs. Nonetheless, he or she desires a risk-free portfolio. How would you transact to meet her wishes? Explain.

SUGGESTED READINGS

Bullen, H. G., R. C. Wilkins, and C. C. Woods III, "The Fundamental Financial Instrument Approach: Identifying the Building Blocks." *The Handbook of Financial Engineering*, pp. 579–586. New York: Harper Business, 1990.

Finnerty, J. D. "The Case for Issuing Synthetic Convertible Bonds." *The Handbook of Financial Engineering*, pp. 461–477. New York: Harper Business, 1990.

Finnerty, J. D. "Financial Engineering in Corporate Finance: An Overview." *The Handbook of Financial Engineering*, pp. 69–108. New York: Harper Business, 1990.

Markese, J. "Asset Allocation Strategies: Portfolio Balancing Acts." *American Association of Individual Investors* 12, no. 6 (July 1990): 31–34.

Marshall, J. F., and V. K. Bansal. *Financial Engineering: A Complete Guide to Financial Innovation*. New York: New York Institute of Finance, 1992.

O'Brien, T. J. "How Option Replicating Portfolio Insurance Works: Expanded Details." *Monograph Series in Finance and Economics* 4 (1988).

Rubinstein, M. "Derivative Assets Analysis." *Journal of Economic Perspectives* 1, no. 2 (Fall 1987): 73–93.

Smith, C. W., Jr., and C. W. Smithson. "Financial Engineering: An Overview." *The Handbook of Financial Engineering*, pp. 3–29. New York: Harper Business, 1990.

Smith, C. W., Jr., C. W. Smithson, and D. S. Wilford. *Managing Financial Risk*. New York: Harper and Row, Ballinger Division, 1990.

Smith, D. J. "The Arithmetic of Financial Engineering." *Journal of Applied Corporate Finance* 1, no. 4 (Winter 1989): 49–58.

NOTES

1. See I. G. Kawaller, "Interest Rate Swaps versus Eurodollar Strips," *Financial Analysts Journal* (September–October 1989), for a discussion of the relationship between swaps and strips.

2. Chapter 6 discusses swaptions in more detail.

3. This example is adapted from John F. Marshall and Kenneth R. Kapner, *The Swaps Market*, 2d ed. (Miami: Kolb Publishing, 1993), pp. 143–146.

4. The reader should note that the use of terms such as **bear spread** and **bull spread** is not standardized. Although this book uses these terms in familiar ways, other traders may use them differently.

5. The following articles introduce various aspects of portfolio insurance. For the most part, they are not highly mathematical. M. Rubinstein, "Alternative Paths to Portfolio Insurance," *Financial Analysts Journal* 41, no. 4 (July–August 1985): 42–52; F. Black and R. Jones, "Simplifying Portfolio Insurance," *Journal of Portfolio Management* 14, no. 1 (Fall 1987): 48–51; T. O'Brien, "The Mechanics of Portfolio Insurance," *Journal of Portfolio Management* 14, no. 3 (Spring 1988): 40–47; P. Abken, "An Introduction to Portfolio Insurance," Federal Reserve Bank of Atlanta, *Economic Review* 72, no. 6 (November–December 1987): 2–25; H. Bierman, "Defining and Evaluating Portfolio Insurance Strategies," *Financial Analysts Journal* 44, no. 3 (May–June 1988): 84–87. The following articles are somewhat more technical or specialized, but of considerable interest: F. Gould, "Stock Index Futures: The Arbitrage Cycle and Portfolio Insurance," *Financial Analysts Journal* 44, no. 1

(January–February 1988): 48–62; J. Merrick, "Portfolio Insurance with Stock Index Futures," *The Journal of Futures Markets* 8, no. 4 (1988): 441–455; R. Bookstaber and J. Langsam, "Portfolio Insurance Trading Rules," *The Journal of Futures Markets* 8, no. 1 (1988): 15–31; Y. Zhu and R. Kavee, "Performance of Portfolio Insurance Strategies," *Journal of Portfolio Management* 14, no. 3 (Spring 1988): 48–54; J. Singleton and R. Grieves, "Synthetic Puts and Portfolio Insurance Strategies," *Journal of Portfolio Management* 10, no. 3 (Spring 1984): 63–69; M. Kritzman, "What's Wrong with Portfolio Insurance?" *Journal of Portfolio Management* 13, no. 1 (Fall 1986): 13–17. Finally, Donald L. Luskin, *Portfolio Insurance: A Guide to Dynamic Hedging* (New York: Wiley, 1988), contains a collection of interesting articles on portfolio insurance.

■ Chapter 6

Risk Management and Financial Engineering

OVERVIEW

This chapter presents examples of how to use financial derivatives to take, avoid, and shape risks. The chapter begins by showing how to use futures to hedge financial risk, with examples being drawn from foreign currencies, stock index futures, and interest rate futures. The chapter then turns to a consideration of index arbitrage and program trading, techniques by which sophisticated traders exploit pricing discrepancies between prices of stocks and stock index futures. These applications are fairly straightforward and use exchange-traded instruments.

As we have seen in Chapter 5, the financial engineer can use simple instruments as building blocks to create synthetic securities and transform one security into another. In this chapter, we follow the techniques of the financial engineer in the creation of more complicated instruments and in the development of solutions tailored to unique business risks. As examples of how financial engineers create new products, we explore more complex instruments such as forward contracts on swaps, and options on swaps. These techniques of customization have given rise to the creation of entirely new instruments. As examples of newly created financial products, we consider equity-linked certificates of deposit, preferred equity redemption cumulative stocks, and structured notes. In addition to creating new products that can be widely disseminated, special purpose solutions can be engineered. As examples, we consider a real-world swap that was constructed for Northwestern Bell Telephone, and we explore a specially engineered solution to the financial problems of Sonatrach, an Algerian oil company.

Although financial derivatives are a powerful tool for managing risk and taking calculated risks, their use can sometimes go awry. Disasters can arise from ignorance, hubris, and even dishonesty. As examples of problems with derivatives we consider the bankruptcy of Orange County, California, and the problems involving Bankers' Trust, Procter & Gamble, and Gibson Greetings. Finally, we consider the risk inherent in a portfolio of derivatives and new initiatives for measuring and controlling the risk of a derivatives portfolio.

HEDGING WITH FUTURES

Hedging with futures provides one of the most useful, yet simple, applications of financial derivatives for managing risk. In this section, we consider hedging techniques using a variety of financial futures: foreign exchange futures, stock index futures, and interest rate futures. We begin with a simple example of using foreign exchange futures to hedge the foreign exchange risk inherent in a typical import-export firm. We then show how to manage the risk of a stock portfolio by trading stock index futures. As this chapter also illustrates, it is possible to use stock index futures to change the beta of an existing stock portfolio. This section concludes by exploring two more complicated hedging techniques using interest rate futures.

HEDGING IMPORT-EXPORT TRANSACTIONS

Consider a small import-export firm that is negotiating a large purchase of Japanese watches from a firm in Japan. The Japanese firm, being a very tough negotiator, has demanded that payment be made in yen upon delivery of the watches. (If the contract had called for payment in dollars, rather than yen, the Japanese firm would bear the exchange risk.) Delivery will take place in seven months, but the price of the watches is agreed today to be Yen 2,850 per watch for 15,000 watches. This means that the purchaser will have to pay Yen 42,750,000 in about seven months. Table 6.1 shows the current exchange rates on April 11. With the current spot rate of .004173 dollars per yen, the purchase price for the 15,000 watches would be $178,396. If the futures prices on April 11 are treated as a forecast of future exchange rates, it seems that the dollar is expected to lose ground against the yen. With the DEC futures trading at .004265, the actual dollar cost might be closer to $182,329. If delivery and payment are to occur in December, the importer might reasonably estimate the actual dollar outlay to be about $182,000 instead of $178,000.

To avoid any worsening of the exchange position, the importer decides to hedge the transaction by trading foreign exchange futures. Delivery is expected in November, so the importer decides to trade the DEC futures. By selecting this expiration, the hedger avoids having to roll over a nearby contract, thereby reducing transaction costs. Also, the DEC contract has the advantage of being the first contract to mature after the hedge horizon, so the DEC futures exchange rate should be close to the spot exchange rate prevailing in November, when the yen are needed.

The importer's next difficulty stems from the fact that the futures contract is written for Yen 12.5 million. If he trades three contracts, the transaction will be for Yen 37.5 million. If he trades four contracts, however, trading would be Yen 50 million, when coverage really is needed for only Yen 42.75 million. No matter which way he trades, the importer will be left with some unhedged exchange risk. Finally, he decides to trade three contracts. Table 6.2 shows these transactions. On April 11 he anticipates that he will need Yen 42.75 million, with a current dollar value of $178,396 and an expected future value of $182,329, where

▮ Table 6.1 ——————————————————————

$/YEN FOREIGN EXCHANGE RATES, APRIL 11	
Spot	.004173
JUN Futures	.004200
SEP Futures	.004237
DEC Futures	.004265

■ **Table 6.2**

THE IMPORTER'S HEDGE

Date	Cash Market	Futures Market
April 11	The importer anticipates a need for Yen 42,750,000 in November, the current value of which is $178,396, and which have an expected value in November of $182,329	The importer buys 3 DEC yen futures contracts at .004265 for a total commitment of $159,938.
Nov 1	Receives watches; buys Yen 42,750,000 at the spot market rate of .004273 for a total of $182,671.	Sells 3 DEC yen futures contracts at .0042-70 for a total value of $160,125.

Spot Market Results:		Futures Market Results:
Anticipated Cost	$182,329	Profit = $187
− Actual Cost	-182,671	
	-$342	
Net Loss:	- $155	

the expected future worth of the yen is measured by the DEC futures price. This expected future price is the most relevant price for measuring the success of the hedge. In the futures market, the importer buys three DEC yen contracts at .004265 dollars per yen.

On November 18, the watches arrive, and the importer purchases the yen on the spot market at .004273. Relative to the anticipated cost of yen, he pays $342 more than expected. Having acquired the yen, the importer offsets his futures position. Because the futures has moved only .000005, the futures profit is only $187. This gives a total loss on the entire transaction of $155. Had there been no hedge, the loss would have been the full change of the price in the cash market, or $342. This hedge was only partially effective for two reasons. First, the futures price did not move as much as the cash price. The cash price changed by .000008 dollars per yen, but the futures price changed by only .000005 dollars per yen. Second, the importer was not able to fully hedge his position, due to the fact that his need for yen fell between two contract amounts. Having a need for Yen 42.75 million and trading futures for only Yen 37.5 million, the importer was left with an unhedged exposure of Yen 5.25 million.

HEDGING WITH STOCK INDEX FUTURES

In this section we analyze stock index futures hedging. We begin by finding the futures position to establish a combined stock and futures portfolio with the lowest possible risk. We illustrate this hedging technique with actual market data. It is also possible to use futures to alter the beta of an existing portfolio. For example, if a stock portfolio has a beta of 0.8 and the desired beta is 0.9, it is possible to trade stock index futures to make the combined stock and futures portfolio behave like a stock portfolio with a beta of 0.9.

THE MINIMUM RISK HEDGE RATIO

For any two asset portfolio, composed of assets A and B, the risk of the portfolio is given by

$$\sigma_P^2 = W_A^2\sigma_A^2 + W_B^2\sigma_B^2 - 2\rho_{A,B}W_A\sigma_A W_B\sigma_B \tag{6.1}$$

where

σ_A^2 = variance of the portfolio

σ_B^2 = variance of the portfolio

σ_{AB} = variance of the portfolio

σ_A = variance of the portfolio

σ_B = variance of the portfolio

We can use this basic result from portfolio theory to guide a hedging strategy. Let us assume that we have a cash market stock portfolio C that is fixed. Thus, we assume that the commitment of funds to this portfolio is 1.0, so that WC = 1.0. We can use futures to hedge the risk associated with this portfolio by adding the right amount of futures to create a two asset stock and futures portfolio.

Denoting the futures position by F, and letting the weight given to the futures be denoted as W_F, the variance of the stock and futures portfolio is

$$\sigma_P^2 = \sigma_C^2 + W_F^2 \sigma_F^2 - 2W_F \rho_{CF} \sigma_C \sigma_F$$

We can minimize the risk of the stock and futures portfolio by choosing W_F to make the variance as small as possible. Denoting the minimum risk hedge ratio as HR, it can be proven that[1]

$$\text{HR} = \frac{\rho_{CF} \sigma_C \sigma_F}{\sigma_F^2} = \frac{\text{COV}_{CF}}{\sigma_F^2} \tag{6.2}$$

where: COV_{CF} = the covariance between C and F

As a practical matter, the easiest way to find the risk-minimizing hedge ratio is to estimate the following regression:

$$C_t = \alpha + \beta_{RM} F_t + \varepsilon_t \tag{6.3}$$

where

C_t = the returns on the cash market position in period t
F_t = the returns on the futures contract in period t 2
α = the constant regression parameter
β_{RM} = the slope regression parameter for the risk-minimizing hedge
ε = an error term with zero mean and standard deviation of 1.0

The estimated beta from this regression is the risk-minimizing hedge ratio, because the estimated β_{RM} equals the sample covariance between the independent (F) and dependent © variables divided by the sample variance of the independent variable. The R^2 from this regression shows the percentage of risk in the cash position that is eliminated by holding the futures position.

Having found the risk-minimizing hedge ratio, β_{RM}, we need to compute the number of contracts to trade. Notice that the regression of equation 6.3 uses the returns on the portfolio and the futures contract, so it does not reflect differences in the size of the portfolio and the futures contract. To find the right number of futures contracts to trade, we need to adjust for the relative sizes of the portfolio and the futures contract. Therefore, the risk-minimizing number of futures contracts is

$$\left(\frac{V_P}{V_F}\right)\beta_{RM} = \text{number of contracts} \qquad (6.4)$$

A MINIMUM RISK HEDGING EXAMPLE

In this section we consider an example of a minimum risk hedge in stock index futures using actual market data. Let us assume a trader has a portfolio worth $10 million on November 28. The portfolio is invested in the 20 stocks in the MMI. The portfolio manager will hedge this cash market portfolio using the S&P 500 JUN futures contract. We consider each step that the portfolio manager follows to compute the hedge ratio and to implement the hedge.

Organize Data and Compute Returns. The manager plans to hedge according to equation 9.6. Therefore, she needs to find the beta for the hedge ratio. Accordingly, she collects data for her portfolio value for 101 days from July 6 through yesterday, November 27. She also finds the price of the S&P 500 JUN futures for each day. There is nothing magic about using 101 days, but these data are available and she believes that this procedure will provide a sufficient sample to estimate the hedging beta. From the 101 days of prices, she computes the daily percentage change in the value of the cash market portfolio and the futures price. This gives 100 paired observations of daily returns data.

Estimate Hedging Beta. With the data in place, the portfolio manager regresses the cash market returns on the returns from the futures contract as shown in equation 10.1. From this regression the estimated beta is .8801, so β_{RM} = .8801. This indicates that each dollar of the cash market position should be hedged with $.8801 dollars in the futures position. The R^2 from the regression is .9263, and this high R^2 encourages the belief that the hedge is likely to perform well. Again, for emphasis, the estimated beta from regressing the portfolio's returns on the stock index futures returns is not the same as the portfolio's Capital Asset Pricing model (CAPM) beta; β_P does not equal β_{RM}[3]

Compute Futures Position. The portfolio manager wants to hedge a $10 million cash portfolio with the S&P JUN futures contract. Having found the risk-minimizing hedge ratio, she needs to translate the hedge ratio into the correct futures position that takes account of the size of the futures contract. On November 27, the S&P futures closed at 354.75. The futures contract value is for the index times $500. Therefore, applying equation 9.6, she computes the number of contracts as

$$\left(\frac{V_P}{V_F}\right)\beta_{RM} = \left(\frac{\$10,000,000}{(354.75)(\$500)}\right).8801 = 49.6180$$

The estimated risk-minimizing futures position is 49.62 contracts, so the portfolio manager decides to sell 50 contracts.

Evaluate Hedging Results   Figure 6.1 shows the value of the unhedged and hedged portfolio for the next 60 days until February 22 of next year, when our trader decides to terminate the hedge. The unhedged portfolio's ending value is $9,656,090. The settlement price for the futures on February 22 is 330.60. Therefore, the futures profit is 50($500)(354.75 - 330.60) = $603,750. The futures profit results from trading 50 contracts with each index point being worth $500 and the index having fallen 24.15 points. The value of the hedged portfolio consists of the cash market portfolio plus the futures profit, so the hedged portfolio's terminal value is $10,259,840. In this example, the hedge protected the portfolio against a substantial loss.

Altering the Beta of a Portfolio

Portfolio managers often adjust the CAPM betas of their portfolios in anticipation of bull and bear markets. A manager who expects a bull market might increase the beta of the portfolio to take advantage of the expected rise in stock prices. Similarly, if a bear market seems imminent, the manager might reduce the beta of a stock portfolio as a defensive maneuver. If the manager trades only in the stock market itself, changing the beta of the portfolio involves selling some stocks and buying others. For example, to reduce the beta of the portfolio, the manager would sell high beta stocks and use the funds to buy low beta stocks. With transaction costs in the stock market being relatively high, this procedure can be expensive.

The portfolio manager has an alternative. Stock index futures can be used to create a combined stock and futures portfolio with the desired response to the market condition. In this section we consider techniques for changing the risk of a portfolio using

■ Figure 6.1

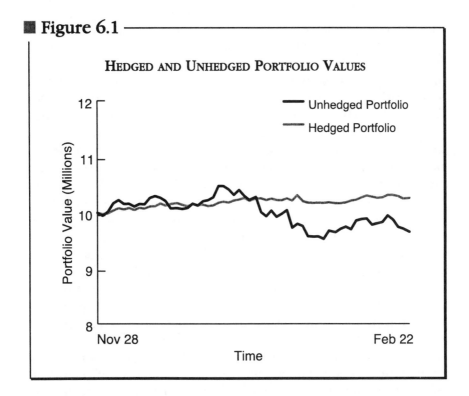

HEDGED AND UNHEDGED PORTFOLIO VALUES

stock index futures.

In the Capital Asset Pricing model, all risk is either systematic or unsystematic. **Systematic risk** is associated with general movements in the market and affects all investments. By contrast, **unsystematic risk** is peculiar to a certain investment or a certain range of investments. Diversification can almost completely eliminate unsystematic risk from a portfolio. The remaining systematic risk is unavoidable. Studies show that a random selection of 20 stocks will create a portfolio with very little unsystematic risk. Therefore, in this section we restrict our attention to portfolios that are well diversified and consequently have no unsystematic risk.

Starting with a stock portfolio that has systematic risk only and combining it with a risk-minimizing short position in stock index futures creates a combined stock and futures portfolio with zero systematic risk. According to the Capital Asset Pricing model, a portfolio with zero systematic risk should earn the risk-free rate of interest. Instead of eliminating all systematic risk by hedging, it is possible to hedge only a portion of the systematic risk to reduce, but not eliminate, the systematic risk inherent in the portfolio. Similarly, a portfolio manager can use stock index futures to increase the systematic risk of a portfolio.

A risk-minimizing hedge matches a long position in stock with a short position in stock index futures in an attempt to create a portfolio whose value will not change with fluctuations in the stock market. To reduce, but not eliminate, the systematic risk, a portfolio manager could sell some futures, but fewer than the risk-minimizing amount. For example, to eliminate half of the systematic risk, the portfolio manager could sell half of the number of contracts stipulated by the risk-minimizing hedge. The combined stock and futures position would then have a level of systematic risk equal to half of the stock portfolio's systematic risk.

It is also possible to trade stock index futures to increase the systematic risk of a stock portfolio. A trader who buys stock index futures increases his or her systematic risk. Therefore, if a portfolio manager holds a stock portfolio and buys stock index futures, the resulting stock and futures position has more systematic risk than the stock portfolio alone. For example, assume a portfolio manager buys, instead of sells, the risk-minimizing number of stock index futures. Instead of eliminating the systematic risk, the resulting stock and long futures position should have twice the systematic risk of the original portfolio.

We can illustrate this principle by considering the same data we used to illustrate the risk-minimizing hedge. In that example, the risk-minimizing futures position was to sell 50 contracts. Selling 50 contracts created a stock and futures position with zero systematic risk. By selling just 25 contracts, the portfolio manager could cut the systematic risk of the original portfolio in half. Similarly, by buying 50 contracts, the resulting stock and futures position would have twice the systematic risk of the original futures position.

Figure 6.2 shows the price paths of two portfolios over the 60-day hedging period from November 28 to February 22. First, the graph shows the unhedged portfolio. Its value begins at $10 million and terminates at $9,656,090, as we have seen. Over this period, the unhedged portfolio lost about $350,000. The graph also shows the portfolio created by holding the stocks and buying 50 futures contracts. In our analysis of the risk-minimizing hedge, we found that the trader could minimize risk by selling 50 futures contracts. Buying 50 contracts doubles the systematic risk. The new

■ Figure 6.2

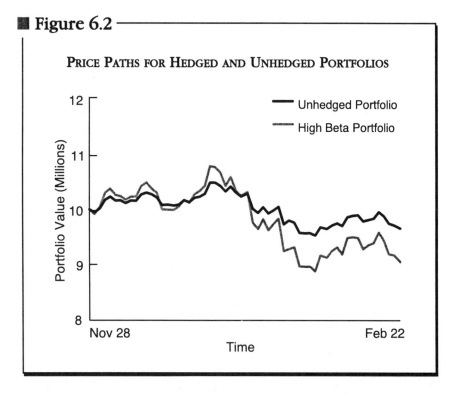

PRICE PATHS FOR HEDGED AND UNHEDGED PORTFOLIOS

— Unhedged Portfolio
— High Beta Portfolio

Portfolio Value (Millions)

Time
Nov 28   Feb 22

portfolio of stock plus a long position of 50 contracts increases the sensitivity of the portfolio to swings in the stock market. In effect, holding the stock portfolio and buying stock index futures simulates more than 100 percent investment in the stock index. Stock prices in general fell during this 60-day period. For example, the all stock portfolio lost 3.44 percent of its value over this period.

By buying stock index futures, the portfolio manager would increase the overall sensitivity of the portfolio to changes in the stock market. Not surprisingly, then, the stock and long futures portfolio lost more than the pure stock portfolio. As Figure 6.2 shows, every move of the stock and long futures portfolio exaggerates the movement of the all stock portfolio. For the portfolio of stock plus a long position of 50 index futures, the terminal value is $9,052,340. This portfolio lost 9.48 percent of its value. However, as Figure 6.2 shows, for periods when the stock prices advanced from their initial level, the stock and long futures position rose even more. This is just what we expect, because buying futures increases the systematic risk of the existing stock portfolio.

HEDGING WITH T-BOND FUTURES

Often the need arises to hedge an instrument very different from those underlying the futures contract. The effectiveness of a hedge depends on the gain or loss on both the spot and futures sides of the transaction. But the change in the price of any bond depends on the shifts in the level of interest rates, changes in the shape of the yield curve, the maturity of the bond, and its coupon rate. For example, a long maturity, low coupon bond will be much more sensitive to a given change in interest rates than a short maturity, high coupon bond.

To illustrate the effect of the maturity and coupon rate on hedging performance, consider the following example. A portfolio manager learns on March 1 that he will receive $5 million on June 1 to invest in AAA corporate bonds paying an annual coupon of 5 percent and having 10 years to maturity. The yield curve is flat and is assumed to remain so over the period from March 1 to June 1. The current yield on AAA bonds is 9.5 percent. Fearing a drop in rates, he decides to hedge in the futures market to lock in the rate of 9.5 percent. The manager decides to hedge with T-bond futures, and we assume that the deliverable T-bond is a 20 year, 8 percent coupon bond.

Assuming the manager implements the hedge using $5 million face value of T-bond futures, Table 6.3 presents the transactions and results, assuming that yields fall by 42 basis points on both instruments. For the cash instrument, the loss is $150,739, and the futures gain is $193,750. This more than offsets the loss in the cash market and generates a net wealth change of +$43,011.

If the goal of the hedge is to secure a net wealth change of zero, a gain is appropriately viewed as no better than a loss. If rates had risen, the loss on the futures would have exceeded the gain on the cash instrument. This discrepancy arose even though the yield curve was flat and rates on both instruments changed in the same direction and by the same amount. Because the coupon and maturity of the hedged and hedging instruments do not match, prices changed by different amounts on the two instruments. Therefore, a simple hedge of $1 in the futures market per $1 in the cash market is unlikely to produce satisfactory results.

For satisfactory hedging results, it is necessary to adjust the futures position so it has the same interest rate sensitivity as the cash market position being hedged. Two typical techniques for

■ Table 6.3 ────────────────────────────────

A CROSS HEDGE BETWEEN CORPORATE BONDS AND T-BOND FUTURES

Date	Cash Market	Futures Market
March 1	A portfolio learns he will receive $5 million to invest in 5%, 10-year AAA bonds in 3 months, with an expected yield of 9.5% and a price of $717.45. The manager expectes to buy 6,969 bonds.	The portfolio manager buys $5 million face value of T-bond futures (50 contracts) to mature on June 1 with a futures yield of 8.5% and a futures price, per contract, of $96,875.
June 1	AAA yields have fallen to 9.08%, causing the price of the bonds to be $739.08. This represents a loss, per bond, of $21.63. Since the plan was to buy 6,969 bonds, the total loss is (6,969 X $21.63) = -$150,739.	The T-bond futures yield has fallen to 8.08%, so the futures price = spot price = $100,750 per contract, or a profit of $3,875 per contract. Since 50 contracts were traded, the total profit is $193,750.
	Loss = -$150,739	Gain = $193,750

Net wealth change = +$43,011

making this adjustment are the basis point model and the price sensitivity model. A common intuition underlies both approaches.

Basis Point Model The Basis Point (BP) model focuses on the price effect of a one basis point change in yields on the cash market instrument and on the futures market hedging instrument. The futures market position necessary to hedge a given cash market risk position depends on the ratio of the dollar price change for the cash market instrument to the futures instrument for a common interest rate change of one basis point. Therefore, the hedge ratio is given by equation 6.5:

$$HR = -\frac{BPC_C}{BPC_F} \tag{6.5}$$

where

BPC_C = dollar price change for a 1 basis point change in the cash instrument

BPC_F = dollar price change for a 1 basis point change in the futures instrument

The ratio BPC_0/BPC_F indicates the relative number of contracts to trade.

Price Sensitivity Model. The Price Sensitivity (PS) model has been designed explicitly for interest rate hedging.[4] The PS Model assumes that the goal of hedging is to eliminate unexpected wealth changes at the hedging horizon, as defined in equation 8.9:

$$dP_i + dP_F(N) = 0 \qquad (6.6)$$

where

dPi = unexpected change in the price of the cash market instrument

dP_F = unexpected change in the price of the futures instrument

N = number of futures to hedge a single unit of the cash market asset

Equation 6.6 expresses the goal that the unexpected change in the value of the spot instrument, denoted by i, and the futures position, denoted by F, should together equal zero. If this is achieved, the wealth change, or hedging error, is zero. Like the basis point model, the PS model uses a hedge ratio that reflects the relative price sensitivities of the cash and futures market instruments.

The problem for the hedger is to choose the correct number of contracts, denoted by N in equation 6.6, to achieve a zero hedging error. Equation 6.7 gives the correct number of contracts to trade (N) per spot market bond:

$$N = -\left(\frac{R_F P_i D_i}{R_i FP_F D_F} \right) RV \qquad (6.7)$$

where

R_F = 1 + the expected futures yield

R_i = 1 + the expected yield to maturity on asset i

FP_F = the futures contract price

P_i = the price of asset i expected to prevail at the hedging horizon

D_i = the duration of asset i expected to prevail at the hedging horizon

D_F = the duration of the asset underlying futures contract F expected to prevail at the hedging horizon[5]

RV = the volatility of the cash market asset's yield relative to the volatility of the futures instrument's yield

In nontechnical terms, Equation 6.7 says that the number of futures contracts to trade for each cash market instrument to be hedged is the number that should give a perfect hedge, assuming that yields on the cash and futures instrument change by the same amount. To explore the meaning and application of this technique, consider again the AAA bond hedge of Table 6.3. The large hedging errors resulted from the different price sensitivities of the futures instruments and the AAA bonds.

Table 6.4 presents the data needed to calculate the hedge ratios for hedging the AAA bonds with T-bill or T-bond futures. Here we assume that the cash and futures market assets have the same volatilities, so RV = 1.0. For the T-bill hedge,

$$N = -\frac{(1.08)(-\$717.45)(7.709)}{(1.095)(\$980,944)(.25)} = .022244$$

The hedger should buy .022244 T-bill futures per AAA bond to be hedged. Because the portfolio manager plans to buy 6,969 bonds, he should hedge this commitment by trading 155 (actually, 155.02) T-bill futures. For the T-bond hedge,

■ **Table 6.4**

DATA FOR THE PRICE SENSITIVITY HEDGE

Cash Instrument		T-Bill Futures		T-Bond Futures	
P_i	$717.45	FP_i	$980,944	FP_F	$96,875
D_i	7.709	D_F	.25	D_F	10.143
R_i	1.095	R_F	1.08	R_F	1.085
		N	.022244	N	.005577
		Number of Contracts to trade	155	Number of Contracts to trade	39

$$N = -\frac{(1.085)(-\$717.45)(7.709)}{(1.095)(\$96,875)(10.143)} = .005577$$

With 6,969 bonds to hedge, the portfolio manager should buy 39 (actually, 38.8667) T-bond futures.

With either of these hedges, the same shift in yields on the AAA bonds and the futures instrument should give a perfect hedge. Table 6.5 presents the performance of these two hedges for the same 42 basis point drop in rates used in Table 6.3.

With the given hedges and the same drop in yields, the T-bill hedge gave a futures gain of $148,203 to offset the loss on the AAA bonds of $150,742. The futures gain on the T-bond hedge is $150,608. The next line of Table 6.5 shows the size of the hedging error for the T-bill and T-bond hedges, and the final line gives the percentage of the cash market loss that was hedged. The T-bill hedge was 98.32 percent effective, while the T-bond hedge was 99.91 percent effective. Both hedges were almost perfect. The slight errors were due to rounding error and to the large change in interest rates. In these examples, the PS model worked very effectively. In actual hedging situations, one could not hope for such nearly perfect results, because yields need not change by the same amount on all instruments all of the time. The most widely used technique for hedging with interest rate futures is some version of the basis point or price sensitivity models.

REAL WORLD PROGRAM TRADING AND INDEX ARBITRAGE

Chapter 2 explained the basic idea of index arbitrage through pro-

■ **Table 6.5** ———

PERFORMANCE ANALYSIS OF PRICE SENSITIVITY FUTURE HEDGE

	Cash Market	T-Bill Hedge	T-Bond Hedge
Gain/Loss	-$150,742	+$148,203	+$150,608
Hedging Error	-$150,742	$2,539	$134
Percentage of Cash Market Loss Hedged		98.32%	99.91%

gram trading. There we considered an imaginary two stock index and showed how to engage in cash-and-carry and reverse cash-and-carry strategies to exploit mispricing of the index versus the index futures. To provide a more realistic feel for real world program trade in stock index futures, this section begins with a historical example of an actual program trade. We then consider the risks inherent in program trading that make the enterprise much more perilous than our historical example would seem to indicate.

REAL WORLD PROGRAM TRADING: AN EXAMPLE

This section discusses a historical example of a cash-and-carry program trading transaction.[6] The trader buys the stocks and carries them forward while selling the futures to profit from the spot being underpriced relative to the futures. Table 6.6 shows the actual prices for the MMI stocks on February 26, 1986, when the trade began. The table also shows the MMI stock prices at the end of the trade on March 21, 1986, and the dividends that the various stocks paid between the two dates.

Faced with the prices shown for February 26, 1986, in Table 6.7, the trader bought 2,000 shares of each of 20 stocks, with a total purchase price of $2,749,100. The trader used $1,374,500, or 50 percent, of his own funds and borrowed the same amount at 8.5 percent. At the same time, he sold 35 MAR 1986 MMI futures at 313.55. This value implies an underlying stock value of $2,743,563 (313.55 index value × $250 multiplier × 35 contracts). (At this time the MMI multiplier was $250. It is now $500.) Trading this number of contracts gives the spot and futures positions very similar dollar values, which is exactly the desired relationship to profit on the relative mispricing.

RISKS IN INDEX ARBITRAGE AND PROGRAM TRADING

The index arbitrage transactions on February 26 in Table 6.7 ensure a profit, subject to a few minor risks. Because the stock index contracts are settled in cash, the spot and futures values at the close of trading for the contract must converge. For the MAR 1986 MMI, trading ended on March 21. Table 6.7 shows the transactions involved in this arbitrage. All of the values in Table 6.7 are actual market prices. Notice that the purchase of shares in Table 6.7 used 50 percent debt and 50 percent investable funds. This is

■ Table 6.6

DATA FOR INDEX ARBITRAGE

	Price Feb. 26	Price Mar. 21	Dividends $/Share
American Express	64.000	65.625	
AT&T	22.500	22.875	
Chevron	37.875	37.375	
Coca-Cola	92.000	100.375	.78
Dow Chemical	48.750	52.375	
DuPont	70.500	72.500	
Kodak	55.000	59.750	
Exxon	54.875	54.750	
General Electric	75.500	75.750	.58
General Motors	78.250	83.250	
IBM	158.125	148.500	
International Paper	57.000	60.000	
Johnson & Johnson	48.375	54.000	
Merck	150.750	161.250	.90
3M	97.25	104.000	
Mobil Oil	30.125	29.500	
Philip Morris	101.125	119.250	1.15
Procter & Gamble	67.000	73.500	
Sears	42.875	46.125	
U.S. Steel	22.675	22.750	
MMI Index	311.740	328.070	
MAR 86 MMI Futures	313.550	328.070	

necessary because of Federal Reserve Board requirements that no more than 50 percent of the purchase price of stocks can be borrowed. Table 6.7 reflects the opportunity cost of those invested funds by assuming that they could have earned the 8.5 percent interest rate that was paid to borrow money.

In computing the cash flows in Table 6.7, we consider all interest, dividends, and out-of-pocket transaction costs. The dividends totaled $3.41 from Table 6.6. With 2,000 shares of each firm, the total dividends received were $6,820. Total transaction costs were $1,100. This is about $.014 per share to buy and the same amount to sell, including the futures contracts. Notice, however, that the analysis does not reflect the daily resettlement cash flows that may have been incurred between February 26 and March 21, nor do we consider interest that might have been earned on the dividends

■ Table 6.7 ——————————————————

PROGRAM TRADING TRANSACTION

February 26, 1986

Sell 35 MMI MAR 1986 futures at 313.55

Use $1,374,500 of investable funds; borrow another $1,374,500 at 8.5% and use these funds to buy 2,000 shares of each of the 20 stocks comprising the MMI at a total cost of $2,749,000.

March 21, 1986

Buy 35 MMI MAR 1986 futures at 328.07

Sell all stocks purchased on February 26, receiving $2,887,000.

Pay interest of $8,438 on borrowed $1,374,500

Charge opportunity cost of woen $1,374,500 that was invested at appropriate cost of funds of 8.5% for a total of $8,438.

Pay transaction costs: -$1,100.

Dividends received while stocks were owned: +$6,820.

Net Cash Flows:

February 26	None because we will charge an opportunity cost for the portion of funds that were invested	
March 21	Futures	-$127,050
	Stocks	144,000
	Transaction Costs	-1,100
	Dividends	6,820
	Interest on Actual Loan	-8,438
	Opportunity Cost on Invested Funds	-8,438
	Arbitrage Profit	$5,794

received. In addition, the cash flow computation does not reflect the cost of searching for this opportunity.[7]

This kind of transaction has certain elements of risk stemming from three sources. First, there is execution risk, because the trader must successfully enter and close the entire position. To establish the position, the trader must buy 2,000 shares of 20 stocks and sell 35 futures contracts. Imagine that the trader finds the opportunity and sells futures. Then the trader starts buying shares of the 20 stocks. During this time, assume that three of the stocks increase in price by $1.00 each. Because the trader has sold the futures contracts, the price of that side of the position is fixed. With three stocks increasing in price by $1.00, the long position in the stocks will cost a total of $6,000 more than anticipated. If this happens, the trader pays $6,000 more than anticipated for the stocks, and the arbitrage profit turns to an arbitrage loss.[8]

The second part of the execution risk exposure occurs on March 21, when the position must be closed. The profit or loss on the futures contract depends on the index value at the close of trading on March 21. However, the risk arbitrage strategy calls for the stocks to be sold at the end of trading on the same day. If the stocks are held until the next day, there will be considerable risk, because any kind of news could be received after the close of trading on March 21. Because of this risk, it is customary to close out such stock positions at the close of trading on the futures expiration day. To close the position, the trader enters a market on close order to sell these stocks. A **market on close order** instructs the broker to sell these shares for the market price at the close of trading. The obvious goal is to sell the shares at the settlement price of the day's trading, because that will be the share price that figures into the index, and the index value on that day determines the futures profit or loss. If the trader could be certain that the shares would be sold at the day's closing price, this element of risk would be eliminated. However, it is difficult to trade in the last 15–30 seconds to get execution at the day's final price. Therefore, there is risk involved in closing the position as well as opening the position.

In addition to execution risk, there is some risk that the dividends will not be paid as the trader anticipates. In this example, if the firms cancel their dividend payments, the trader does not receive $6,820 and the transactions will generate a loss. Such a rash of dividend cancellations is unlikely but at least remotely possible. The final source of risk is financing risk. The trader might not be able to secure financing for the entire period at the same rate. If the stocks are financed with overnight obligations and interest rates suddenly jump, financing costs could be higher than anticipated. In summary, the index arbitrage transaction faces execution risk, dividend risk, and interest rate risk. Of these, execution risk is the most important. Nonetheless, once the transactions of February 26 are put in place, there is very little real danger of a loss.[9]

More Sophisticated Swap and Option Structures

In this section, we consider more sophisticated swap and option structures, including instruments that combine features of options and swaps. We begin by analyzing an equity swap, in which payments between counterparties depend on the performance of a stock index. We go on to consider forward swaps and extension swaps, which allow for the changing of the payment streams obligated in the swap agreements. We also consider swaptions, which are options on a swap.

Equity Swaps

In an **equity swap**, the counterparties exchange payments based on a notional principal specified as a stock portfolio. Like a commodity swap, the equity swap is quite similar to an interest rate swap, because there is an underlying notional principal, a fixed tenor, and one party paying a fixed rate while the other pays a floating rate.

Consider an institutional investor with a $100 million portfolio of stocks invested in an index fund that tracks the S&P 500. If the manager of this portfolio becomes bearish, she has several choices for avoiding the risk of a stock market decline. She could sell the stocks in the portfolio, hedge the stock market risk in the futures market, or hedge the risk by using index options. She could also use an equity swap.

For her situation, the portfolio manager could enter an equity swap agreement in which she pays the S&P 500 return each period and receives a fixed percentage payment, with both payments being based on the $100 million notional principal of her portfolio. For example, each quarter the portfolio manager might pay the total return earned by the S&P 500 and receive a quarterly payment of 2.5 percent, both payments being based on the $100 million notional principal. Figure 6.3 illustrates these cash flows. This arrangement would insulate the value of the portfolio against any drop in the stock market and guarantee the portfolio manager a quarterly return of 2.5 percent.

For example, if the S&P 500 enjoyed a return of 3 percent in a given quarter, her undisturbed portfolio would rise in value by 3 percent and she would pay this to the counterparty, so this would leave the portfolio value unchanged. However, the portfolio man-

■ **Figure 6.3**

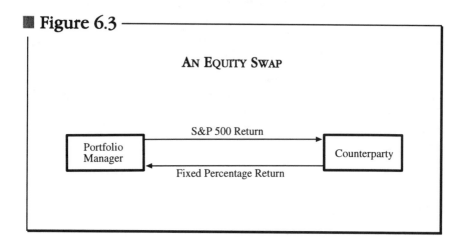

AN EQUITY SWAP

ager would also receive a payment of 2.5 percent. If the S&P 500 had a return of –5 percent, the portfolio manager would make no payment and would receive a payment of 7.5 percent. This inflow of 7.5 percent, combined with the drop in the value of the portfolio of 5 percent, would still give a net return on the portfolio of 2.5 percent.

As with the other swap structures we have considered in this chapter, the equity swap can be elaborated by allowing variations in the notional principal or the periodic payment. For example, one variant of the equity swap might be for one counterparty to pay the S&P 500 return and receive the Russell 2000 return, creating a swap agreement to speculate on the differential return between large and small stocks.

Forward and Extension Swaps[10]

A **forward swap** is a swap agreement in which the parties agree that the cash flows will begin at a date in the future and that they may be interest rate, currency, commodity, or equity swaps. For example, two counterparties might agree to exchange LIBOR for a fixed rate beginning in two years, with the tenor of the swap being five years from that date. If the contractual rates are based on the forward rate for the two instruments at the planned initiation date, there should be no exchange of cash at the initiation of the agreement. If the rates specified do not conform to the forward rates for the planned inception of the cash flows, then the swap is an off-market swap and one party will be obligated to pay the other.

An **extension swap** is a swap agreement designed to extend the tenor of an existing swap. As such, an extension swap is a special type of forward swap. For example, in the middle of the tenor of an interest rate swap in which one party pays LIBOR plus 50 basis points and receives the two-year T-note rate, the parties might agree to extend the tenor of the swap by an additional three years. If the agreement is initiated based on the forward rates for the date of inception (i.e., at the termination of the current swap agreement), there should be no payment at the time the agreement is made.

SWAPTIONS

A **swaption** is an option on a swap. Like all options, there are call swaptions and put swaptions. These options may be either American or European in form. The owner of a call swaption has the right to buy a swap by paying the exercise price, but the seller of a call swaption is obligated to sell a swap for the exercise price. (The buyer of an interest rate swap pays a fixed rate of interest and receives a floating rate.) The owner of a put swaption has the right to sell a swap at the exercise price, but the seller of a put swaption is obligated to sell a swap at the exercise price. For all of these options, there is some stated expiration date.

To understand these features more clearly, consider a call swaption. The purchaser of the call will pay an agreed premium to the seller at the inception of the transaction. Usually the premium is stated as some number of basis points on the notional principal of the swap underlying the option. It is typical for this premium to lie in the range of 20–40 basis points, but the premium depends upon the exercise price, the time to expiration, and the volatility of the underlying rates.[11] The exercise price of the swaption is a fixed rate specified in the swaption agreement. Assuming the swaption is European, the owner will exercise the call swaption if the contractual fixed rate (the exercise price) is lower than the fixed rate prevailing in the open market for swaps with the same tenor as that underlying the swaption.

As an example, consider a European call swaption on a five-year swap with annual payments and a notional principal of $10 million. Let us assume that the fixed rate specified in the swap agreement is 8 percent and the floating rate is LIBOR plus 50 basis points. For such a call swaption, the premium might be 30 basis points. With a principal of $10 million, the premium would then be $30,000. Six months after contracting, at the expiration date of the option, the owner of the call swaption can either exercise it or let the option expire worthless. The owner will exercise it if the market rate for the fixed payor on this type of option is less than 8 percent. The benefit for the call holder is the present value of the cash flows due to the difference between the contractual rate of 8 percent and the fixed rate available in the open market, say 7.60 percent. The call holder benefits if the market rate for fixed payments is less than 8 percent, because by exercising the option, the call owner will secure a swap agreement in which he or she receives a fixed payment of 8 percent over the tenor of the swap. Without the call swaption, the trader would receive only the currently available fixed rate of 7.60 percent. In virtue of the swaption, the trader receives an additional 40 basis points over the tenor of the swap.

Swaptions offer the same kinds of speculative and hedging opportunities of all other options, as we have studied in previous chapters. As an example, consider a firm that has issued a callable bond. We may analyze a bond with a call provision as consisting of a noncallable bond plus the purchase of a call option on the bond. From the issuing firm's point of view, the firm has paid for the option by promising a higher coupon rate for the callable bond than the rate necessary for a noncallable bond.

Now assume that the firm has determined that it will not wish to call the bond. Having made this determination, the call feature on the bond has no value to the firm, yet the option still has value in the marketplace. The bond issuing firm could then sell a call swaption with terms that match the call feature of the bond. In effect, this transaction would unwind the call feature inherent in the original bond. In effect, the firm bought a call swaption from the bondholders with its original issuance, and by selling a call swaption, it recaptures the remaining value in the call feature that the firm no longer desires.

If rates do not fall sufficiently to engender exercise of the call swaption against the firm, the firm merely keeps the option premium, and this cash inflow offsets the value of the call feature inherent in the callable bond. On the other hand, if the owner of the call swaption exercises it against the firm, that owner will have done so because fixed rates are below the currently available fixed rate on a swap. If this exercise is reasonable, the issuer of the callable bond now has an incentive to exercise its call option against its own bondholders, and it should not lose on the exercise.

ENGINEERING NEW PRODUCTS

In this section, we consider examples of new financial products that have been created and marketed in the United States. As new products, these are intended to be securities that trade in an active market, as opposed to custom solutions that might be designed for the particular needs of a given investor. As a first example, we consider preferred equity redemption cumulative stock (PERCS). PERCS are a type of preferred stock that will necessarily be converted into the common shares of the issuing firm. As we will see, the main advantage of PERCS stems from an exploitation of market imperfections. Second, we consider equity-linked certificates of deposit. For these equity-linked CDs, the investor accepts a low or zero rate of interest in return for a payoff that depends on the performance of a stock index. Third, we consider structured notes. In a structured note, the rate of return depends on the performance of some other security. These versatile instruments can be tied to the performance of various debt instruments, equities, or commodities.

PERCS

A PERCS is a preferred equity redemption cumulative stock. The PERCS is a hybrid security invented by Morgan Stanley, and the first PERCS was issued by Avon in 1988. After Avon, 15 other mostly blue chip firms also issued PERCS, including General Motors, Kmart, Sears, Texas Instruments, and Citicorp. Through mid-year 1994, total volume exceeded $8 billion.[12] As the name indicates, a PERCS is a type of preferred stock. Like other preferred stocks, a PERCS pays a fixed dividend, but these dividends are significantly higher than the dividend of the firm's common stock. In contrast to conventional preferred shares, PERCS must be converted into shares of common stock, typically about three years after issuance. The conversion price, or "cap," is typically about 30–45 percent above the price of the common share when the PERCS is issued.

The PERCS must be converted at the maturity date, but it may be converted earlier. If the PERCS is converted at maturity, each PERCS will be converted into a share of stock. If the PERCS is converted prior to maturity, the PERCS will be converted to a full share if the share price is less than the cap. If the share price exceeds the cap, the PERCS will be converted to a fractional share equal to the cap divided by the share price at conversion.

We noted that the dividend rate on a PERCS exceeds that of the underlying common share. If the PERCS paid the same dividend as the common stock, a PERCS would be equivalent to a covered call – a long position in the common share plus a short position in a call option on the share with an expiration date equal to the maturity of the PERCS. Because the PERCS pays a dividend above the common share, we may, following Chen, Kensinger, and Pu, analyze a PERCS as consisting of a covered call plus an annuity. The annuity is the present value of the difference between the dividend stream of the PERCS and the dividend stream of the common stock.

From the description thus far, it seems that a PERCS is not a truly new security or at least not a unique security. If we could completely replicate a PERCS by buying the stock, selling a call, and buying an annuity, there would be little reason for a PERCS to exist. The true importance of PERCS comes from the imperfect market factors of transaction costs and taxes. First, because a PERCS is a single security, trading PERCS may be cheaper than trading a covered call plus annuity. Second, a PERCS effectively translates the call premium realized on a covered call into a higher dividend investment. This could be particularly valuable to an institutional investor that pays taxes on only 70 percent of dividends. Third, corporations might like to issue PERCS because they provide an alternative means of raising equity. When the PERCS is converted to a common share, a new share is issued. Compared to issuing straight equity, a PERCS may have a lower agency cost to the firm because of the built-in short position in a call option that the purchaser of the PERCS receives.

Ignoring market imperfections, a PERCS is equivalent to a long stock, short call, long annuity portfolio; and the price of the PERCS can be measured against that replicating portfolio. Such a study would, of course, not fully consider any benefits of creating PERCS due to the market imperfections mentioned previously. If PERCS constitute a valuable security innovation, the value of a PERCS should exceed the value of the replicating portfolio, due to the savings on transaction costs and agency costs.

For each of the eight PERCS examined, Chen, Kensinger, and Pu found that the PERCS was worth more than the replicating portfolio. The excess value of the PERCS ranged from zero to almost 11 percent of the value of the replicating portfolio. Therefore, the PERCS must provide some additional value over its replicating portfolio. Chen, Kensinger, and Pu also find that the price differential is not large enough to make arbitrage between the PERCS and its replicating portfolio profitable due to transaction costs. As an illustration, Figure 6.4 shows the difference in value between the PERCS and the equivalent portfolio for Kmart. Apparently, the excess value of the PERCS is due to the market imperfections already discussed. The creation of the PERCS helps to economize on the costs represented by market imperfections.

EQUITY-LINKED CERTIFICATES OF DEPOSITS[13]

An equity-linked certificate of deposit, or an equity-linked CD, pays little or no interest. However, these CDs promise a minimum maturity value plus a return based on the performance of a stock market index. For example, Citicorp issued a five-year CD that guarantees a return of principal, plus twice the average increase in the S&P 500 over that period. Merrill Lynch issued a 5.5-year note that guaranteed a return of 100 percent of the principal, plus 115 percent of the appreciation in the S&P 500 index.

As an example, consider an investment instrument of $1 million in an equity-linked CD for a five-year horizon when the CD rate is 8 percent compounded annually and the S&P index stands at 500.00. The equity-linked CD guarantees the return of principal and pays 115 percent of the appreciation in the S&P 500 index over the five-year period. The following table shows the payoff at maturity for various levels of the S&P index at the maturity date. The breakeven level of the S&P index is 704.0557, the level of the index that leads to an 8 percent return over the horizon. By contrast, if the S&P index is 600 at maturity, the realized rate of return is only 4.23 percent, and if the index reaches 800, the annualized return is 11.07 percent.

■ **Figure 6.4**

THE VALUE OF THE KMART PERCS AND ITS
EQUIVALENT PORTFOLIO

Price of PERCS   Value of Equivalent Pkg.

Source: Andrew H. Chen, John Kensinger, and Hansong Pu, "An Analysis of PERCS," *The Journal of Finanacial Engineering*, 3:2, June 1994, p. 100.

S & P Terminal Value	Payoff on CD	Annual Percentage Return on CD
400	$1,000,000	0.00%
450	$1,000,000	0.00%
500	$1,000,000	0.00%
550	$1,115,000 = $1,000,000 +1.15($1,000,000)(50/500)	2.20%
600	$1,230,000 = $1,000,000 +1.15($1,000,000)(100/500)	4.23%
700	$1,460,000 = $1,000,000 +1.15($1,000,000)(200/500)	7.86%
704.0557	$1,469,327.08 = $1,000,000 +1.15($1,000,000)(204.0557/500)	8.00%
800	$1,690,000 = $1,000,000 +1.15($1,000,000)(300/500)	11.07%

■ **Figure 6.5**

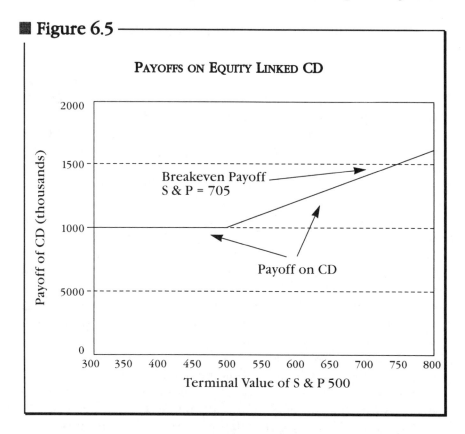

PAYOFFS ON EQUITY LINKED CD

Figure 6.5 shows the payoffs on this equity-linked CD graphically. The payoff is $1 million for any S&P index value of 500.00 or less. For higher S&P values, the payoff on the CD rises dramatically. If the index value is 704.0557, the payoff is $1,469,372.08, which exactly equals an 8 percent return on the investment. The payoffs graphed in Figure 6.5 have exactly the characteristic shape of a call option, as explored in Chapter 3. Notice, however, that the minimum value of the CD is $1 million. This contrasts with a regular call option in which the minimum value is zero.

Figure 6.5 suggests that we might be able to analyze the equity-linked CD of the example as embodying a combination of a call option and some other security. In essence, the investor in the equity-linked CD of our example buys a call option on the S&P 500 index. The cost of the option is the foregone interest, which is sacrificed to gain the payoff that is contingent on the index. Therefore, the cost of the option is

$$\$1,000,000(1.08)^5 - \$1,000,000 = \$469,328.08$$

The exercise price of the option component is an index value of 500.00, because it is at this level that the option starts to pay. At expiration, the payoff on the option is 115 percent of the amount by which the index exceeds the exercise price of 500.00. Therefore, the payoff on the option component is

$$MAX\{0, 1.15(\text{Terminal Index Value} - 500.00)\}$$

Thus, this equity-linked CD may be viewed as the combination of a zero interest CD plus a call option on the S&P 500 index. Equivalently, we may view this equity-linked CD as a combination of a CD plus the purchase of a call option with a premium equal to the interest on the CD.

If this equity-linked CD is merely a combination of a normal CD with the purchase of a call option on the S&P 500 index, we might well wonder why this instrument is of any interest. After all, CDs exist, as do options on the S&P 500 index. One important feature of this type of equity-linked CD is the deposit insurance provided by the Federal Deposit Insurance Corporation. This feature can make these instruments more attractive than otherwise. In essence, the ability to capture deposit insurance represents a market imperfection that the creation of an equity-linked CD can capture to the mutual benefit of the issuing bank and the investor. These instruments are fairly new, and their future is uncertain. However, they have attracted considerable investor interest, and some observers believe that they may be positioned for considerable growth.

STRUCTURED NOTES

A **structured note** is a debt instrument combined with some type of derivative instrument. The payoffs on a structured note depend on interest earnings and the performance of the derivative that is embodied in the structure of the note. The equity-linked CDS of the previous section qualify as a type of structured note, because their payoffs depend on the performance of the S&P 500 index. According to some estimates, the annual issuance of structured notes is approaching $100 billion, so these new instruments represent a potent force in today's capital markets.[14]

Structured notes embrace a rich variety of instruments, because new types of structured debt can be created by tying the payoff on the note to a new index or instrument. As examples, consider the following types of structured notes:

Floating Rate Note: The rate of return on a structured note might depend on the floating rate of interest on another instrument. For example, a multiyear debt obligation might pay LIBOR plus a spread.

Inverse Floating Rate Note: The rate of return on a structured not might depend on the inverse of a floating rate of instrument. For example, a multiyear debt obligation might pay 15 percent per year minus LIBOR. This type of instrument is called an **inverse floater**.

Yield Curve Notes: The rate of return on a structured note might depend on the spread between 2-year and 30-year Treasury yields. For example, the yield on the structured note might depend on the difference between a 30-year and 2-year constant maturity Treasury (CMT) index.. Such a note would be advantageous if the yield curve became steeper.

Relative Rate Differential Notes: The rate of return on a structured note might depend on the spread between yields on two different kinds of debt instruments. For example, the yield on a structured note might depend on the yield differential between the prime rate and LIBOR.

Foreign Rate Structured Notes: The rate of return on a structured note might depend on the yield differential between LIBOR for German marks and Swiss francs.

Equity Performance Structured Notes: The rate of return on a structured note might depend on the performance of a stock market index. The equity-linked CDs considered earlier are a type of equity performance structured note.

Commodity Performance Structured Notes: The rate of return on a structured note might depend on the price change in a physical commodity, such as the price of a barrel of crude oil.

We now consider some more detailed examples of structured notes, such as an inverse floating rate note, a constant maturity indexed note, and a yield curve note.

Inverse Floating Rate Note.[15] Consider an investor who believes that six-month LIBOR will fall over the next three years from its present level of 4.75 percent. The investor buys a note paying 13 percent minus six-month LIBOR, which yields 8.25 percent at the outset. If LIBOR rises, the return on the inverse floater falls. If

LIBOR reaches 13 percent in a given period, the note pays zero interest for that period; if LIBOR falls to 3 percent, the note would pay 10 percent. (This kind of note might have a floor of zero percent interest, specifying that if LIBOR exceeds 13 percent, the interest rate remains at zero, rather than becoming negative.)

The typical issuer for such a structured note would be an investment bank. The investment bank might prefer a fixed rate obligation, even though it issues the inverse floater to accommodate the investor. To avoid the floating obligation, the investment bank could enter a swap agreement to change its floating obligation to a fixed obligation. In this example, the issuing investment bank might enter a swap in which it pays the lesser of LIBOR or 13 percent and receives a fixed rate of 6.6 percent paid semiannually. Figure 6.6 shows the transactions involved, both for the investor and the issuing investment bank. As the figure shows, the investor buys a note that pays 13.00 percent minus LIBOR. For its part, the investment bank pays 13.00 percent minus LIBOR on the structured note, pays LIBOR in the swap agreement, and receives a fixed swap rate of 6.6 percent. For the investment bank, the net obligation is a fixed rate obligation of 6.4 percent:

$$-(13 \text{ percent} - \text{LIBOR}) - \text{LIBOR} + 6.6 \text{ percent} = 6.4 \text{ percent}$$

■ Figure 6.6

CASH FLOWS FOR AN INVERSE FLOATER

Source: Adapted from "Anatomy of the Structured Note Market," *Journal of Applied Corporate Finance*, 7:3, Fall 1994, pp 85-98.

The investor who purchases the inverse floater is essentially making a bet about the future course of interest rates, effectively betting that LIBOR will be less than the forward rates predicted by the Eurodollar yield curve. To see the bet implicit in this inverse floater, we assume that the instruments are fairly priced, so that the price of the structured note equals the present value of the anticipated payments discounted at the forward rates implicit in the Eurodollar yield curve. Assume that the forward rate for two years in the future is 7 percent. If this forward rate correctly predicts the future rate, the structured note will pay 6 percent for that period (13 percent minus LIBOR for that period of 7 percent). If LIBOR in that period is less than the forward rate of 7 percent, say 5 percent, then the investor in the inverse floater will receive 8 percent for that period (13 percent minus the LIBOR of 5 percent).

Constant Maturity Treasury Indexed Note In a constant maturity Treasury (CMT) indexed note, the payoff on the note is tied to changes in the yield on a constant maturity Treasury rate. For example, an investor might buy a 2-year note that pays the 10-year CMT rate minus 3 percent. At each period, the yield on the structured note will vary with the CMT rate. The yield on such a note must reflect the prevailing rate on a two-year floating rate note. The investor will profit if the CMT rises enough so that the realized yield exceeds the available two-year floating rate yield. The issuer of the structured note undertakes a floating rate obligation, which it can translate into a fixed rate obligation through a swap transaction.

Yield Curve Note An investor can use a yield curve note to express a view about future changes in the yield curve. An investor who believes that the yield curve will steepen necessarily expects the difference between 10-year and 2-year CMTs to increase. Such an investor might buy a floating rate note that pays a rate of interest depending on the difference between the 10-year and 2-year CMT index rates.

ENGINEERING TAILORED SOLUTIONS

In contrast with the new products discussed in the previous section, this section considers two examples of custom solutions to the needs of a particular customer. Both the creation of new products and the development of custom tailored solutions illustrate the techniques of the financial engineer. In this section, we first examine a swap agreement developed for Northwestern Bell Telephone designed to economize on taxes. We then consider an inverse oil-indexed bond developed for an Algerian government agency. This oil-indexed bond is a type of structured note.

NORTHWESTERN BELL TELEPHONE DEBT-FOR-DEBT SWAP[16]

Northwestern Bell Telephone (NWB) is a subsidiary of U.S. West, one of the Baby Bell telephone companies. On May 2, 1990, NWB extinguished $42.7 million of several debt issues with coupons ranging from 4.875 to 9.5 percent having maturities of 8–26 years. To extinguish this debt, NWB issued a new security paying 7.75 percent and maturing in May 2030. Morgan Stanley & Co. assisted in this transaction.

Morgan Stanley purchased $42.675 million of NWB's debt for about $34.5 million through open market and privately negotiated transactions. NWB gave to Morgan Stanley a cash payment of $408,000 and $42.883 million face value of its newly issued 7.75 bonds due in 2030 in exchange for the $42.675 million of NWB bonds that Morgan Stanley had acquired in the open market. Figure 6.7 shows the transactions involved. In these transactions, Morgan did not act as the agent of NWB. If Morgan acted as NWB's agent, buying the old bonds for NWB's account, the difference between the basis and the market value of each bond would have been treated as taxable income to NWB. At the time of the transaction, the tax law allowed for a tax-free exchange if the principal amount of the new issue was about the same as the principal amount retired. Because the transaction was structured as an exchange, NWB avoided any unfortunate tax implications.

The advantage of this transaction stemmed from the difference between the corporate tax rate and the marginal investor's tax rate. By creating a transaction that avoided taxation on the book gain from extinguishing the old debt, NWB was able to profit by repurchasing the old discount bonds and simultaneously issuing par bonds. Constructing this swap as an exchange was necessary to make the deal profitable. Table 6.8 shows the profits from the NWB transaction. The total present value gain was $1.125 million; the cost of the exchange was $248,000, leaving a profit of $877,000.

■ **Figure 6.7**

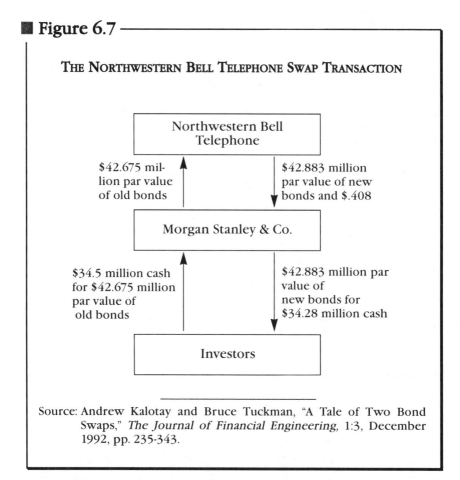

THE NORTHWESTERN BELL TELEPHONE SWAP TRANSACTION

Northwestern Bell Telephone

$42.675 million par value of old bonds

$42.883 million par value of new bonds and $.408

Morgan Stanley & Co.

$34.5 million cash for $42.675 million par value of old bonds

$42.883 million par value of new bonds for $34.28 million cash

Investors

Source: Andrew Kalotay and Bruce Tuckman, "A Tale of Two Bond Swaps," *The Journal of Financial Engineering*, 1:3, December 1992, pp. 235-343.

SONATRACH'S INVERSE OIL-INDEXED BONDS[17]

Sonatrach is the state-owned hydrocarbon producer of Algeria. In late 1989, Sonatrach was faced with financial difficulty in meeting payments to a banking syndicate on its borrowings through a floating rate note (FRN). Sonatrach was paying LIBOR plus a large spread of several full percentage points. To resolve this financial embarrassment, Chase Manhattan Bank helped Sonatrach retire its existing FRNs by issuing a series of inverse oil-indexed bonds. The new debt structure substantially reduced the cash flows due from Sonatrach in each period, thereby reducing the likelihood of financial difficulty.

■ Table 6.8 —————————————

PROFITS FROM THE NORTHWESTERN BELL TELEPHONE
SWAP TRANSACTION

Coupon	Maturity	Market Yield	Market Price	Corporate Value	Principal Retired	PV Gain
4.875	6/01/98	9.30	75.23	81.60	9.590	.611
7.50	4/01/05	9.42	84.77	87.79	4.000	.121
6.25	1/01/07	9.45	73.39	78.29	10.300	.506
7.00	1/01/09	9.54	78.03	81.73	7.185	.266
7.875	1/01/11	9.53	85.14	87.45	4.600	.106
9.5	8/15/96	9.78	97.34	97.66	7.000	.023
7.75	5/01/30	9.80	79.54	80.72	42.833	-.508

Total present value gain:	$1.125 million
Costs of doing the exchange:	.248
Net gain	$.877 million

Source: Andrew Kalotay and Bruce Tuckman, "A Tale of Two Bond Swaps," *The Journal of Financial Engineering*, 1:3, December 1992, pp. 235-343.

The Sonatrach transaction was organized as follows. First, Sonatrach issued new FRNs paying LIBOR plus 100 basis points to a group of syndicate banks. Second, Sonatrach wrote two-year call options on oil with a striking price of $23 to Chase. Third, Chase wrote seven-year calls on oil with a striking price of $22 to the syndicate banks. Fourth, Chase wrote seven-year puts on oil with a striking price of $16 to the syndicate banks. Fifth, the banks extinguished the previously existing FRNs, accepting the new FRN from Sonatrach and the calls and puts from Chase as a substitute. Figure 6.8 summarizes the transaction.

After the transaction, Sonatrach was obligated to pay a lower annual sum on the FRN. Before the transaction, Sonatrach was paying LIBOR plus approximately 300 basis points; after the transaction Sonatrach's interest payment was LIBOR plus 100 basis points. This change greatly reduced the financial pressure on Sonatrach. However, Sonatrach was also obligated to make additional payments if the price of oil rose above $23. If this were to occur, Sonatrach would be enjoying substantially larger income from the sale of its oil production and would be able to afford the addition-

■ Figure 6.8

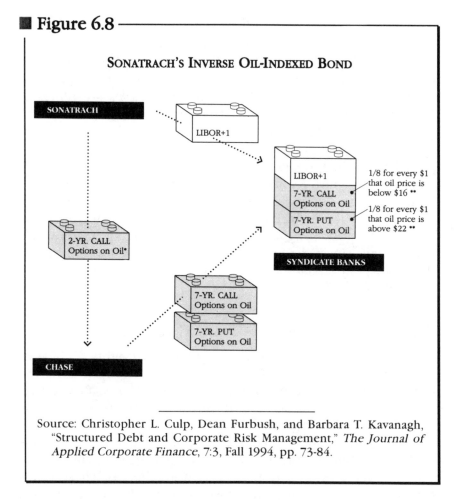

SONATRACH'S INVERSE OIL-INDEXED BOND

Source: Christopher L. Culp, Dean Furbush, and Barbara T. Kavanagh, "Structured Debt and Corporate Risk Management," *The Journal of Applied Corporate Finance*, 7:3, Fall 1994, pp. 73-84.

al payments without incurring financial distress. The banks in the syndicate accepted a lower interest payment in exchange for the chance to profit from oil price volatility. In the new arrangement, the syndicate banks held a strangle on oil with exercise prices of $16 and $22. In effect, Sonatrach relinquished a portion of its upside potential from rising oil prices to escape high interest payments that were generating financial distress. Chase received a two-year call option from Sonatrach and wrote a strangle on oil prices to the banks in the syndicate. The difference in value between the call option Chase received and the strangle Chase wrote was the compensation to Chase for arranging the transaction. By this restructuring of debt, and the issuance of the inverse oil-indexed structured note, all three parties received a benefit.

DEBACLES

To this point, we have concentrated on the techniques for using derivatives. This is appropriate, as the proper use of derivatives provides substantial benefits to transactors and to the economy as a whole. We must also recognize that derivatives are powerful instruments that can be misused by ignorant or malicious economic agents. In this section, we consider some recent notorious financial debacles in which the abuse of financial derivatives has played a role. First, we consider the bankruptcy of Orange County, California, in which a mistaken bet on interest rates lost about $2 billion of public funds. Second, we consider misfortunes that have beset Bankers Trust, an investment banking firm that has been a leader in financial engineering and the marketing of derivative instruments. Finally, we analyze the demise of Barings Bank, a firm that lost its entire net worth in a few months, apparently through the actions of a single trader.

THE BANKRUPTCY OF ORANGE COUNTY, CALIFORNIA

In December 1994, the government of Orange County, California, shocked the financial world as well as its citizens by declaring bankruptcy. The sole cause of this disaster was losses of more than $2 billion in the investment portfolio of the county managed by the treasurer of the county, Robert Citron.

The investment pool consisted of about $7 billion, with funds being contributed from many government agencies in Orange County, such as school districts and water boards. These funds from other government agencies were effectively on deposit with the county for investment management, with the idea that the funds would be readily available to meet the financial needs of the government entities, such as payrolls. In most similar situations, the funds would be invested in very safe, very short maturity, money market instruments.

In the sharply upward sloping yield curve environment of the early to mid-1990s, Citron followed a strategy of investing the funds of the county in longer maturity instruments. This decision alone could not account for the stupendous losses incurred in Orange County, however. Orange County used its $7 billion of capital as a foundation upon which it borrowed additional funds through reverse repurchase agreements, or reverse repos. By using the principal of the fund as collateral, Citron borrowed about $13 billion in additional funds on a short-term basis. Having assembled a war chest of about $20 billion, Citron invested the vast bulk of these funds in long maturity instruments. Thus, Orange County was attempting to capture the large yield differential between short-term and long-term securities. As long as the yield curve maintained a steep upward slope, Orange County was effectively borrowing at a low rate of interest and investing at a substantially higher rate. However, this strategy involved considerable risk. The value of longer maturity debt instruments can change dramatically if interest rates change, so a rise in the long-term rates could create a substantial capital loss on the invested funds.

This yield curve play, combined with substantial leverage, was the essence of the Orange County strategy. It was a high risk strategy that worked well for several years, but one with inherent dangers that finally came to dominate. As such, derivatives did not play a key role in the decision to use leverage and make the yield curve bet. However, derivatives did play an important role in allowing Citron to increase leverage and in effectively lengthening the average maturity of the investments in the portfolio. The full story of the Orange County disaster will emerge only over the next few years, and will undoubtedly involve considerable litigation. However, we can explore one way in which derivatives figured into the management of the portfolio.

The principal derivative strategy used by Orange County focused on structured notes, with the portfolio including as much as $8 billion in structured notes.[18] One of the Orange County structured notes was an inverse floater that pays interest according to the following formula:[19]

Principal × (10.5 percent – six-month LIBOR)

The principal for this particular note was $50 million with a maturity of September 24, 1997. At the time of the bankruptcy, this note had a market value of $43.3 million. Compared with a normal floating rate note, this structured note had approximately twice the sensitivity to changes in interest rates. For example, a 1 percent increase in rates on this note would result in a loss of about $2 million, or about 4.67 percent of the value of the note. This greater sensitivity in the investment, combined with 300 percent leverage, is the kind of transaction creating the dramatic risk exposure that destroyed Orange County.

In 1994, not only did interest rates rise in general, but the yield curve also flattened. This meant that the differential long and short rates that Orange County was trying to captured narrowed at the same time that the rising short-term rates increased the county's borrowing cost. The rise in long-term rates also generated considerable capital losses on the long-term instruments in the portfolio.

In the aftermath, Orange County is trying to restructure its obligations. The bankruptcy has led to major layoff of government workers and will probably require tax increases at some point. Merrill Lynch acted as Orange County's principal broker for many of these transactions and had received fees of $37 million in recent years. Orange County has filed suit against Merrill Lynch, accusing Merrill of a variety of offenses. The county treasurer, Robert Citron, was fired. The rupture with Merrill and the dismissal of Citron left the county with an enormously complex portfolio that still involved considerable interest rate risk. Therefore, the county moved swiftly to dispose of the more complex instruments and deleverage the portfolio. As this sad story shows, derivatives are powerful instruments that can be used to greatly increase risk as well as to manage risk.

BANKERS TRUST

Bankers Trust (BT) has been a major player in the development of derivatives markets. BT both creates and markets instruments for sale to a wider public and develops custom-tailored derivative solutions for individual corporate customers. Two of these recent customers are Gibson Greetings and Procter & Gamble. To say that these customers were dissatisfied would be a major understatement. Bankers Trust executed interest rate swaps for both Gibson Greetings and P&G. The transactions with Gibson Greetings have led to a consent decree being signed by BT with the Securities and Exchange Commission and the Commodities Futures Trading Commission. Of the Gibson Greetings matter, Mary Schapiro, chairperson of the Commodities Futures Trading Commission said, "This case stands on the fact that you cannot lie to the customer."[20] In the consent agreement, BT agreed to pay a fine of $100 million without admitting any guilt. In essence, the charges against BT in the Gibson Greeting case turn on misrepresentations made to Gibson. A taped conversation of a BT managing director and his supervisor includes the passage: "From the very beginning, [Gibson] just, you know, really put themselves in our hands like 96 percent. . . . And we have known that from day one . . . these guys have done some pretty wild stuff. And you know, they probably did not understand it quite as well as they should. I think that they have a pretty good understanding of it, but not perfect. And that's like perfect for us."[21]

Procter & Gamble is suing over its similar experience with BT. P&G accuses BT of misleading statements about the terms and consequences of an interest rate swap in which P&G lost $157 million. In its swap with BT, BT would pay a fixed plain vanilla swap rate. P&G would pay a floating rate equal to the commercial paper rate minus 75 basis points plus a spread.[22] The spread depended on the yield of the 5-year and 30-year U.S. Treasuries. In this swap, P&G effectively borrowed at 75 basis points below the commercial paper rate, but to capture this very attractive rate, P&G accepted some risk. The notional amount of the swap was $200 million with a five year tenor, and the agreement was consummated on November 2, 1993. The swap agreement also included some very complicated option features designed to allow P&G to lock in a favorable interest rate, even if interest rates rose.

By February 22, 1994, interest rates had risen significantly, and BT informed P&G that it would have to pay an additional $44 million in interest over the remaining 4.5 years of the swap. In the next few weeks, rates continued to rise. By March 29, 1994, P&G found it was obligated to pay interest to BT at the commercial paper rate plus 14.12 percent, giving a total loss of more than $150 million.

The pricing of the deal was from a proprietary model of **Bankers Trust**. P&G had placed itself in a position in which it had to rely on the computations of BT, without understanding how the results were reached. In large part, this was due to the complex option provisions of the swap. P&G says that it relied on BT to correctly assess and convey the exact terms of the provision for locking in a favorable rate. Instead, P&G claims, it was the victim of a financial fraud, a charge that BT strongly contests. However this case is ultimately resolved, it shows that derivatives customers must fully, completely, and objectively understand the exact terms of their derivatives contracts. If the deal is too complicated for the customer to understand, the deal should not be done.

THE DEMISE OF BARINGS BANK

In previous chapters, we have considered the strategy of index arbitrage. Theoretically, index arbitrage is risk free, and properly executed index arbitrage transactions involve very low levels of actual risk. The risk is limited, because of the close relationship between a stock index futures contract and the underlying stock index itself. Thus, as we have seen, index arbitrage is a low risk strategy that seeks to capture small and temporary pricing discrepancies between stocks and stock index futures.

Nicholas Leeson, a trader for Barings Bank stationed in Singapore, was supposed to be conducting index arbitrage between Japanese stocks and futures contracts on the Japanese index. Such trading involves taking equal and offsetting positions in stocks and futures, which were traded in both Japan and Singapore. Although the details remain somewhat unclear, it seems apparent that Leeson did exactly the opposite in late 1994 and early 1995. Through the futures markets, Leeson made very large one-sided bets that Japanese stocks would rise. The Kobe earthquake, however, rocked the entire Japanese economy and led to a dramatic drop in the Japanese stock market. The highly leveraged bets on a rising Japanese market turned out to be giant losers. In a short period, Leeson's trades lost about $1 billion. These losses completely exhausted the net worth of Barings, which declared bankruptcy and was acquired by a Dutch investment bank.

Early reports suggested that Leeson was a rogue trader who acted alone, and further investigation seems to indicate a considerable awareness of his activities on the part of senior management. Shortly after the losses became public, Leeson was arrested in Germany and was being held in a German jail, as Singapore pressed its extradition request. As with most cases, the full truth will probably emerge only after lengthy litigation. It is clear, however, that these losses destroyed Barings, one of the oldest and most respected merchant banks in the world.

SUMMARY

In this chapter, we have considered techniques for managing risk, and we have launched a preliminary exploration of financial engineering. We began our analysis of risk management by considering how financial futures can be used to hedge foreign exchange, equity, and interest rate risk. We turned to a real-world example of program trading in the support of index arbitrage. We then considered more complex swap transactions, such as equity swaps, forward swaps, and extension swaps. As we noted, options can be combined with swaps to create swaptions, which are options on swaps. As we move from simple risk management techniques, such as hedging with futures, to index arbitrage, to more complicated swap structures, we enter the world of the financial engineer.

The chapter analyzed several types of products that have been created in recent years by financial engineers. First, we considered PERCS – preferred equity redemption cumulative stock. There we noted that a PERCS can be analyzed as a share of stock, plus a long call, plus an annuity. Compared to this portfolio, a PERCS gives added value due to its ability to exploit market imperfections. We also saw that an equity-linked certificate of deposit is a financial product engineered to exploit market imperfections as well. As a third general class of engineered products, we considered structured notes, instruments that embrace a wide range of specialized debt structures with complicated payoffs.

In addition to engineered products, we considered some examples of more custom engineered products designed to meet the need of a particular customer. We explored the terms of Northwestern Bell Telephone's debt-for-debt swap, which was designed to realize tax savings. As a quite different example, we saw how Sonatrach's inverse oil-indexed bond helped maintain that firm's solvency.

The chapter concluded with a brief overview of some recent derivatives debacles. We saw that massive leverage with a huge term structure bet helped bring Orange County, California, to bankruptcy, and we noted that structured notes helped Orange County get enough leverage to ruin itself. We considered the dubious business practices of Bankers Trust and reviewed some of the transactions that brought Bankers Trust into disrepute and into litigation with some of its customers. This example highlighted the need for the customer to understand its derivatives positions completely. Finally, we saw that Barings Bank went bust through massive losses incurred in a supposedly safe index arbitrage program. For Barings, the problem was not a flawed trading strategy, but a serious lack of control and oversight. These poor controls created a situation in which trading directed by a single individual bankrupted a merchant bank that had been in business for more than 200 years.

QUESTIONS AND PROBLEMS

1. You expect a steepening yield curve over the next few months, but you are not sure whether the level of rates will increase or decrease. Explain two different ways you can trade to profit if you are correct.

2. The Iraqi invasion of Alaska has financial markets in turmoil. You expect the crisis to worsen more than other traders suspect. How could you trade short-term interest rate futures to profit if you are correct? Explain.

3. You believe that the yield curve is strongly upward sloping and that yields are at very high levels. How would you use interest rate futures to hedge a prospective investment of funds that you will receive in nine months? If you faced a major borrowing in nine months, how would you use futures?

4. Explain the risks inherent in a reverse cash-and-carry strategy in the T-bond futures market.

5. Assume you hold a T-bill that matures in 90 days, when the T-bill futures expires. Explain how you could transact to effectively lengthen the maturity of the bill.

6. Assume that you will borrow on a short-term loan in six months, but you do not know whether you will be offered a fixed rate or a floating rate loan. Explain how you can use futures to convert a fixed to a floating rate loan and to convert a floating rate to a fixed rate loan.

7. Assume you hold a well-diversified portfolio with a beta of 0.85. How would you trade futures to raise the beta of the portfolio?

8. An index fund is a mutual fund that attempts to replicate the returns on a stock index, such as the S&P 500. Assume you are

the manager of such a fund and that you are fully invested in stocks. Measured against the S&P 500 index, your portfolio has a beta of 1.0. How could you transform this portfolio into one with a zero beta without trading stocks?

9. You hold a portfolio consisting of only T-bills. Explain how to trade futures to create a portfolio that behaves like the S&P 500 stock index.

10. For the most part, the price of oil is denominated in dollars. Assume that you are a French firm that expects to import 420,000 barrels of crude oil in six months. What risks do you face in this transaction? Explain how you could transact to hedge the currency portion of those risks.

11. A financial comptroller for a U.S. firm is reviewing the earnings from a German subsidiary. This sub earns DM 1 million every year with exactitude, and it reinvests those earnings in its own German operations. This plan will continue. The earnings, however, are translated into U.S. dollars to prepare the U.S. parent's financial statements. Explain the nature of the foreign exchange risk from the point of view of the U.S. parent. Explain what steps you think the parent should take to hedge the risk that you have identified.

12. "An equity swap is nothing but a commodity swap!" Do you agree or disagree with this statement? Explain.

13. Consider two interest rate swaps to pay fixed rates and receive floating rates. The two swaps require the same payments each semiannual period, but one swap has a tenor of 5 years, and the second has a tenor of 10 years. Assume that you buy the 10-year swap and sell the 5-year swap. What kind of instrument do these transactions create? Explain.

14. "A swaption is essentially a portfolio of options on futures or options on forwards." Is this statement correct? Explain.

15. Explain how an interest rate swap can be analyzed as a strip of futures.

16. Assume you can borrow at a fixed rate for 10 years for 11 percent or that you can borrow at a floating rate of LIBOR plus 40 basis points for 10 years. Assume also that LIBOR stands at 10.60 percent. Under these circumstances, your financial advisor states: "The all-in cost is the same on both deals – 11 percent.

Therefore, the two are equivalent and one should be indifferent between these two financing alternatives." How would you react? Explain.

SUGGESTED READINGS

Abken, Peter A. "Beyond Plain Vanilla: A Taxonomy of Swaps." Federal Reserve Bank of Atlanta, *Economic Review* (March–April 1991).

Baubonis, Charles, Gary Gastineau, and David Purcell. "The Banker's Guide to Equity-Linked Certificates of Deposit." *The Journal of Derivatives* 1, no. 2 (Winter 1993): 87–95.

Bodurtha, S., and T. Quinn. "Does Patient Program Trading Really Pay?" *Financial Analysts Journal* 46, no. 3 (May–June 1990): 35–42.

Chen, Andrew H., John Kensinger, and Hansong Pu. "An Analysis of PERCS." *The Journal of Financial Engineering* 3, no. 2 (June 1994): 85–108.

Crabbe, Leland E., and Joseph D. Argilagos. "Anatomy of the Structured Note Market." *Journal of Applied Corporate Finance* 7, no. 3 (Fall 1994): 85–98.

Culp, Christopher L., Dean Furbush, and Barbara T. Kavanagh. "Structured Debt and Corporate Risk Management." *The Journal of Applied Corporate Finance* 7, no. 3 (Fall 1994): 73–84.

Kalotay, Andrew, and Bruce Tuckman. "A Tale of Two Bond Swaps." *The Journal of Financial Engineering* 1, no. 3 (December 1992): 235–343.

Kawaller, Ira. "A Note: Debunking the Myth of the Risk-Free Return." *The Journal of Futures Markets* 7, no. 3 (1987): 327–331.

Kolb, Robert W. *Understanding Futures Markets,* 4th ed. Miami: Kolb Publishing Company, 1994.

Kolb, Robert W., and Raymond Chiang. "Improving Hedging Performance Using Interest Rate Futures." *Financial Management* 10, no. 4 (1981): 72–79.

Kolb, Robert W., and Raymond Chiang. "Duration, Immunization, and Hedging with Interest Rate Futures." *Journal of Financial Research* 10, no. 4 (Autumn 1982): 161–170.

Merrick, John Jr. "Early Unwindings and Rollovers of Stock Index Futures Arbitrage Programs: Analysis and Implications for Predicting Expiration Day Effects." *The Journal of Futures Markets* 9, no. 2 (1989): 101–111.

NOTES

1. For a derivation of this relationship and a more extended discussion, see Robert W. Kolb, *Understanding Futures Markets*, 4th ed. (Miami: Kolb Publishing Company, 1994).

2. Strictly speaking, there is no return on a futures contract because a position in a futures contract requires no investment. By the futures return we mean the percentage change in the futures price.

3. For the same period, estimating the CAPM beta by regressing the portfolio's returns against the S&P 500 cash market returns gave $\beta_P = 1.0762$.

4. See R. Kolb and R. Chiang, "Improving Hedging Performance Using Interest Rate Futures," *Financial Management* 10, no. 4 (1981): 72–79; and "Duration, Immunization, and Hedging with Interest Rate Futures," *Journal of Financial Research* 10, no. 4 (Autumn 1982): 161–170.

5. Duration is a key concept utilized in bond portfolio management. In essence, it is a single index number reflecting the sensitivity of the price of a bond to changes in interest rates. It depends most critically on the maturity and the coupon rate of the bond. For more on duration, see Robert W. Kolb, *Investments*, 4th ed. (Miami: Kolb Publishing Company, 1995), particularly Chapters 7 and 8..

6. This example was the focus of a *Business Week* article, "A Real Life Strategy for Making 14 Percent Risk-Free" (April 7, 1986).

7. I. Kawaller, "A Note: Debunking the Myth of the Risk-Free Return," *The Journal of Futures Markets* 7, no. 3 (1987): 327–331, analyzes some of the risk associated with index arbitrage. As the title of the article implies, the process of index arbitrage does not necessarily guarantee a totally risk-free return.

8. Stephen Bodurtha and Thomas Quinn consider a patient program trading strategy designed to minimize execution costs. They conclude that such a strategy can reduce execution costs and provide superior results, see S. Bodurtha and T. Quinn, "Does Patient Program Trading Really Pay?" *Financial Analysts Journal* 46, no. 3 (May–June 1990): 35–42.

9. Kawaller, "A Note: Debunking the Myth of the Risk-Free Return," provides an excellent discussion of these risk elements in index arbitrage. J. Merrick, Jr., "Early Unwindings and Rollovers of Stock Index Futures Arbitrage Programs: Analysis and

Implications for Predicting Expiration Day Effects," *The Journal of Futures Markets* 9, no. 2 (1989): 101–111, studies the possibility of terminating index arbitrage transactions before the contract expires. He finds that early termination can often provide even higher returns than holding the arbitrage position until expiration.

10. This section draws on an article by Peter A. Abken, "Beyond Plain Vanilla: A Taxonomy of Swaps," Federal Reserve Bank of Atlanta, *Economic Review* (March–April 1991), reprinted in R. Kolb, *The Financial Derivatives Reader* (Miami: Kolb Publishing, 1993).

11. See Abken, "Beyond Plain Vanilla: A Taxonomy of Swaps."

12. This account of PERCS relies on Andrew H. Chen, John Kensinger, and Hansong Pu, "An Analysis of PERCS," *The Journal of Financial Engineering* 3, no. 2 (June 1994): 85–108. Merrill Lynch has created a similar security known as mandatory conversion premium dividend preferred stock.

13. This analysis of equity-linked CDs relies on Charles Baubonis, Gary Gastineau, and David Purcell, "The Banker's Guide to Equity-Linked Certificates of Deposit," *The Journal of Derivatives* 1, no. 2 (Winter 1993): 87–95.

14. See Leland E. Crabbe and Joseph D. Argilagos, "Anatomy of the Structured Note Market," *Journal of Applied Corporate Finance* 7, no. 3 (Fall 1994): 85–98.

15. These examples are drawn from Crabbe and Argilagos, "Anatomy of the Structured Note Market."

16. This example is drawn from Andrew Kalotay and Bruce Tuckman, "A Tale of Two Bond Swaps," *The Journal of Financial Engineering* 1, no. 3 (December 1992): 235–343.

17. This example is drawn from Christopher L. Culp, Dean Furbush, and Barbara T. Kavanagh, "Structured Debt and Corporate Risk Management," *The Journal of Applied Corporate Finance* 7, no. 3 (Fall 1994): 73–84.

18. See "Orange on a Banana Skin," *Risk* 8, no. 1 (January 1995): 6.

19. The analysis of this particular inverse floater appeared in Zahid Ullah, "Valuing the Orange County Notes," *Derivatives Strategy* (December 12, 1994): 3.

20. *Derivatives Strategy* 4, no. 1 (January 2, 1995): 1.

21. *Derivatives Strategy*, p. 1.

22. This account relies on "P&G vs. BT," *Derivatives Strategy* 3, no. 17 (October 31, 1994): 1.

APPENDIX

Cumulative Distribution Function
for the Standard Normal Random Variable

	.00	.01	.02	.03	.04	.05	.06	.07	.08	.09
0.0	0.5000	0.5040	0.5080	0.5120	0.5160	0.5199	0.5239	0.5279	0.5319	0.5359
0.1	0.5398	0.5438	0.5478	0.5517	0.5557	0.5596	0.5636	0.5675	0.5714	0.5753
0.2	0.5793	0.5832	0.5871	0.5910	0.5948	0.5987	0.6026	0.6064	0.6103	0.6141
0.3	0.6179	0.6217	0.6255	0.6293	0.6331	0.6368	0.6406	0.6443	0.6480	0.6517
0.4	0.6554	0.6591	0.6628	0.6664	0.6700	0.6736	0.6772	0.6808	0.6844	0.6879
0.5	0.6915	0.6950	0.6985	0.7019	0.7054	0.7088	0.7123	0.7157	0.7190	0.7224
0.6	0.7257	0.7291	0.7324	0.7357	0.7389	0.7422	0.7454	0.7486	0.7517	0.7549
0.7	0.7580	0.7611	0.7642	0.7673	0.7704	0.7734	0.7764	0.7794	0.7823	0.7852
0.8	0.7881	0.7910	0.7939	0.7967	0.7995	0.8023	0.8051	0.8078	0.8106	0.8133
0.9	0.8159	0.8186	0.8212	0.8238	0.8264	0.8289	0.8315	0.8340	0.8365	0.8389
1.0	0.8413	0.8438	0.8461	0.8485	0.8508	0.8531	0.8554	0.8577	0.8599	0.8621
1.1	0.8643	0.8665	0.8686	0.8708	0.8729	0.8749	0.8770	0.8790	0.8810	0.8830
1.2	0.8849	0.8869	0.8888	0.8907	0.8925	0.8944	0.8962	0.8980	0.8997	0.9015
1.3	0.9032	0.9049	0.9066	0.9082	0.9099	0.9115	0.9131	0.9147	0.9162	0.9177
1.4	0.9192	0.9207	0.9222	0.9236	0.9251	0.9265	0.9279	0.9292	0.9306	0.9319
1.5	0.9332	0.9345	0.9357	0.9370	0.9382	0.9394	0.9406	0.9418	0.9429	0.9441
1.6	0.9452	0.9463	0.9474	0.9484	0.9495	0.9505	0.9515	0.9525	0.9535	0.9545
1.7	0.9554	0.9564	0.9573	0.9582	0.9591	0.9599	0.9608	0.9616	0.9625	0.9633
1.8	0.9641	0.9649	0.9656	0.9664	0.9671	0.9678	0.9686	0.9693	0.9699	0.9706
1.9	0.9713	0.9719	0.9726	0.9732	0.9738	0.9744	0.9750	0.9756	0.9761	0.9767
2.0	0.9772	0.9778	0.9783	0.9788	0.9793	0.9798	0.9803	0.9808	0.9812	0.9817
2.1	0.9821	0.9826	0.9830	0.9834	0.9838	0.9842	0.9846	0.9850	0.9854	0.9857
2.2	0.9861	0.9864	0.9868	0.9871	0.9875	0.9878	0.9881	0.9884	0.9887	0.9890
2.3	0.9893	0.9896	0.9898	0.9901	0.9904	0.9906	0.9909	0.9911	0.9913	0.9916
2.4	0.9918	0.9920	0.9922	0.9925	0.9927	0.9929	0.9931	0.9932	0.9934	0.9936
2.5	0.9938	0.9940	0.9941	0.9943	0.9945	0.9946	0.9948	0.9949	0.9951	0.9952
2.6	0.9953	0.9955	0.9956	0.9957	0.9959	0.9960	0.9961	0.9962	0.9963	0.9964
2.7	0.9965	0.9966	0.9967	0.9968	0.9969	0.9970	0.9971	0.9972	0.9973	0.9974
2.8	0.9974	0.9975	0.9976	0.9977	0.9977	0.9978	0.9979	0.9979	0.9980	0.9981
2.9	0.9981	0.9982	0.9982	0.9983	0.9984	0.9984	0.9985	0.9985	0.9986	0.9986
3.0	0.9987	0.9987	0.9987	0.9988	0.9988	0.9989	0.9989	0.9989	0.9990	0.9990
3.1	0.9990	0.9991	0.9991	0.9991	0.9992	0.9992	0.9992	0.9992	0.9993	0.9993
3.2	0.9993	0.9993	0.9994	0.9994	0.9994	0.9994	0.9994	0.9995	0.9995	0.9995
3.3	0.9995	0.9995	0.9995	0.9996	0.9996	0.9996	0.9996	0.9996	0.9996	0.9997
3.4	0.9997	0.9997	0.9997	0.9997	0.9997	0.9997	0.9997	0.9997	0.9997	0.9998

INDEX